Neyland
The Gridiron General

NEYLAND
THE GRIDIRON GENERAL

By Bob Gilbert

Golden Coast Publishing Company
Savannah, Georgia

Neyland: The Gridiron General and other books
by Golden Coast are distributed by
Peachtree Publishers, Ltd., 494 Armour Circle, NE,
Atlanta, Georgia 30324; (800)241-0113

Published by
Golden Coast Publishing Company,
Savannah, Georgia.

Designed and produced by
Lisa Lytton-Smith, Savannah, Georgia.
Edited by Kathleen Durham
and Van Jones Martin.
Type set by Lytton Design.
Cover designed by Lisa Lytton-Smith
and Van Jones Martin.
Printed by Walsworth Press Company, Inc.,
Marceline, Missouri

Library of Congress Card Catalog
Number 90-82899
ISBN 0-932958-10-9
Printed in the United States of America.

The publisher would like to thank the
following people and organizations for their
gracious assistance in locating and reproducing
photographs for *Neyland: The Gridiron General*:
the Neyland family for the extensive scrapbooks
and photographs; Bud Ford and
his staff at the University of Tennessee Sports
Information Department; the University of
Tennessee Photo Center; Hugh and Emily Faust;
A. L. "Bud" Fields, Jr.; the *Knoxville News-Sentinel*; and Molly (Mrs. Bowden)Wyatt.

To Judy,
Who provided inspiration, read every word,
and made welcome improvements.

And to Helen,
Always there in support.

In memory of
Noah L. Gilbert, Jr.,
and Jesse Wadsworth.

No one loved Tennessee football more.

TABLE OF CONTENTS

PART V

PART VI

PART VII

PART VIII

PART IX

ACKNOWLEDGMENTS

I am indebted to publisher Van Martin, who, although painted indelibly with Georgia Tech white and gold, believed the Neyland story should have been told many years ago. Van encouraged and pushed and encouraged some more. Yet, through it all he was patient, understanding, immensely helpful with suggestions, and totally indispensable.

I am grateful to many people who contributed to this book—people who knew General Robert R. Neyland intimately, who played for him and were his assistant coaches, and who wrote about his teams. Many of them shared humorous anecdotes and intriguing stories about the General.

Lindsey Nelson, famous sportscaster and marvelous storyteller, worked for Neyland as a student in the late 1930s and saw a side of the General that perhaps no one else saw. Journalists Ben Byrd and Fred Russell and the late Tom Siler, F. M. Williams, and Ed Harris reported the exploits of Neyland's teams for their newspapers.

Books and monographs from the typewriters of Russ Bebb, Ben Byrd, James Edson, Ed Harris, Lindsey Nelson, Zipp Newman, Edwin Pope, Fred Russell, Tom Siler, John Underwood, and Jack Wilkinson were valuable resources about Neyland and University of Tennessee football.

Dr. Andrew J. Kozar, fullback on Neyland's last three teams and a researcher at the University of Tennessee, previewed the manuscript and made valuable suggestions on documentation. We relied heavily on interviews done by Jack Williams, a UT development officer, during filming in the 1970s for a documentary about the General's career. Gus Manning, long-time Tennessee athletics administrator, shared personal insights from his years of working closely with Neyland.

Reconstruction of General Neyland's military career would have been impossible without the help of Paul D. Gray, assistant director for military records, at the National Personnel Records Center in St. Louis, Missouri. Gray provided copies of Neyland's entire army personnel and medical record.

Also, librarians and historians in various sections of the nation graciously assisted in research about the early years of Neyland's military career. Dr. J. Britt McCarley, the historian at Fort Bliss, Texas, researched Neyland's participation in the military campaign against Mexican rebel Pancho Villa. We also had valuable help from Jeanne Branom and Gail Slater, in the gerontology collections of the library at Greenville, Texas, and from Janet Gehlel of the *Herald-Tribune* library in Sarasota, Florida. Judith Sibley and Marie Capps in the special collections library at the U.S. Military Academy and Colonel F. William Smullen III and Jerri Taylor in the Pentagon helped in our pursuit of the Neyland military record.

Hugh and Emily Faust opened their scrapbooks full of memories of their days associating with Bob and Peggy Neyland. Hugh, of course, played for and coached with Neyland. One of Hugh's assignments most of those years was to scout Alabama. He and Neyland shared pullman staterooms and hotel rooms on football road trips. Hugh fought back the tears as story after story poured from his memory.

Norman Downey provided an insight into the private side of Bob Neyland's life. Downey had been a member of the Tennessee football team in the mid-1930s and idolized General Neyland. They became close friends, almost like brothers, after Neyland returned from World War II. Norman was with the family in Ochsner Hospital in New Orleans when Neyland died.

This book would not have been possible without the Neyland family. The General's sons and their wives—Bob and Anne, and Lewis and Libby—took us into their homes, shared their memories, and gave us access to the General's private papers. Together we searched through boxes containing notebooks, correspondence, and photographs. None of the material was placed off-limits for the book.

Caroline Clapperton, Peg Neyland's cousin now living in Lansing, Michigan, was the sole source of details about the courtship of Bob and Peggy and about the first years of their marriage when he was stationed at West Point.

But most of all, I am indebted to General Robert Reese Neyland for the 30,000-word manuscript he composed about his childhood, his years at West Point, and some of his experiences in China and India during World War II. I learned of its existence when I found a letter Neyland had written to a friend about the possibility of a book. The dust-covered, typed carbon-copy of the original document was located in a box of memorabilia in a basement closet at son Bob's home.

Neyland never got to write his book. I can only hope he would have liked this one.

PROLOGUE

"Sometimes a man's successes in his chosen fields of endeavor shine so brightly that, to the world, his basic attributes are little known. Such a man was Robert R. Neyland, Jr., born an intellectual, disciplined a brilliant scholar, blessed with physical attributes, and trained to be an almost perfect athlete. His accomplishments both as a student and as a soldier will be recorded in the annals of military history."

Thus began Dr. Lenox D. Baker, an orthopedic surgeon at Duke University, in the eulogy he wrote for an alumni publication of the United States Military Academy at West Point, New York, following the March 28, 1962, death of Brigadier General Robert Reese Neyland—a career soldier, a career college football coach.

How Neyland combined those two careers for three decades spanning both world wars is the subject of this book. The project was born in the summer of 1987 when I was asked to review a forthcoming autobiography about retired Georgia Tech football coach and athletics director Robert Lee "Bobby" Dodd, whom I had known for a quarter of a century.

In 1982 I had written a television documentary about the career of Bob Neyland, who had been Dodd's coach at the University of Tennessee from 1927 to 1930. Much has been written about Neyland's brilliant coaching career. Most articles and booklets about Tennessee's football history contain references to Neyland's career as an athlete at West Point and to his coaching years at Tennessee, twice interrupted by military duty. But most of what the public knows about Bob Neyland is limited to his coaching career at Tennessee.

I had known Neyland through my father, the late Noah L. Gilbert, who lived next door to the Neylands for several years in the late 1920s and early 1930s. Neyland had retired from coaching a year and a half before I enrolled as a freshman at the University of Tennessee, but he remained athletics director throughout my college days. His coaching and military careers, and his commanding demeanor, made him an imposing figure to a young college student.

When the publisher of the Dodd autobiography, Van Martin of Golden Coast Publishing Company, asked if I would consider writing the Neyland biography, I jumped at the opportunity—conditional on Neyland's sons, Robert and Lewis, authorizing it as the official biography. They did, and the project was launched.

Much background about the Neyland football career already was available in newspaper files and numerous other publications, but separating fact from fiction about his military career was a mammoth undertaking. Reconstructing the detailed chronology of his military career required the assistance of the United States Department of the Army, the archivists and historians at West Point and at Fort Bliss, Texas, and many hours of searching through newspaper microfilm and Neyland's personal files.

Although we could focus solely on presenting a vivid portrait of Neyland the coach, this book introduces you to a multidimensional personality—a soldier, patriot, educator, engineer, coach, husband and father, a man who loved flowers and music and fishing, a man who was shy and reserved in public, yet dynamic and compelling when leading men in a common cause.

It was the military career of this 1916 West Point graduate—a classmate of General Omar Bradley and General James Van Fleet—which took Neyland in 1925 to Knoxville, Tennessee, where he became legendary as a college football coach. Twice he returned to active duty with the army, but it was his passion for football which both times led him back to Knoxville and the University of Tennessee—each time the prelude to an era of great football teams and the last time to a national championship.

Between graduation from West Point in 1916 and his assignment in 1925 to Knoxville as head of the Reserve Officer Training Program at the University of Tennessee, Neyland served in France during World War I, studied engineering at Massachusetts Institute of Technology, and was aide-de-camp to General Douglas MacArthur when MacArthur was superintendent at West Point.

Neyland's World War II years took him to Norfolk, Virginia, where he supervised construction of defenses for the Chesapeake Bay region, then to China and India,where he played key roles in getting supplies of ammunition, fuel, food, medicine, and clothing to American, British, and Chinese troops fighting the Japanese.

Neyland's football coaching career spanned 32 years, including 21 as head coach at Tennessee. He had the best won-lost percentage of any major college football head coach who coached 20 years or more—ranking him ahead of such Hall of Fame coaches as Paul "Bear" Bryant, Joe Paterno, Bo Schembechler, Ara Parseghian, and Darrell Royal.

In Neyland's first four years as head coach, Tennessee lost only one game. The record for his first seven seasons was 61 wins, five ties, and only two losses. His 1939 team was the last major college team to be unscored on in the regular season. His 1951 team won the national championship. He is in the college football Hall of Fame.

In this book, we shall take you inside Neyland's football mind—utilizing his own hand-written notes from personal journals he kept through the years. The weathered pages of the journals document some of his innermost thoughts about his opponents and players. In a sense, they reconstruct for us the process by which he built powerhouse football teams during three spans of his career—in 1926-32, in 1938-40, and 1950-52. The journals were made available by Neyland's sons and Tennessee coach John Majors, to whom they had entrusted the documents. Neyland's early playbooks reflect his passion for geometrics. The play designs are symmetric, as if drawn for a plane geometry lesson in the classroom. They are a veritable textbook on precision football execution. They reflect Neyland's passion for power football, but Neyland also loved deception, and he practiced it on his adversaries by designing plays that had a "power" look but turned out to be something quite different. The plays in Neyland's journals and playbooks show a Neyland offensive trademark—numerous double-team blocks, always at the point of attack. Several of the actual plays, in Neyland's own handwriting, are reproduced within these covers.

This book would not have been possible without the family diaries and photograph albums, hundreds of newspaper clippings, copies of Neyland's personal wartime correspondence, and many hours of interviews with his former players, assistant coaches, military associates, relatives, and close friends, whom we shall list elsewhere in this book.

We have interviewed coaches who were his most famous and ardent adversaries. One of them, the late Wallace Wade (Alabama and Duke) was unequivocal in his assessment of Neyland the coach: "Bob's the best football coach I ever coached against."

Research for the book uncovered audio tapes of speeches Neyland made to his former players and associates at testimonial dinners following his retirement from coaching. But perhaps most significant among the research documents were several hundred typewritten sheets of paper on which he had dictated to his wife, Peggy, an estimated 30,000 words describing his childhood years in Greenville, Texas, his years at Texas A&M and West Point, and a dramatic segment recalling a nighttime flight over the Himalaya Mountains from Assam, India, to his army base in Kunming, China, in 1944 during the war. Neyland's thoughts contained in those 30,000 words will be recounted in this book as direct quotes, as if we had interviewed him. In a sense, we did.

This is the story of a man of letters, a man of touchdowns, and strikeouts, and bridge construction, and motivation, and strong political convictions, and warm personal emotions. It is the story of a man described in the following words handwritten in pencil on three tiny pieces of paper:

"This is the story of a man. There's nothing unusual about that. Many stories have been written about men—some heroes, some geniuses, some monsters, and some just the average man. Most men have been combinations of various elements. This one was no different, except that he had very little of the monster in him. But he did have most of the requisites of greatness—enduring faith in himself and others, perseverance and determination to a high degree, and integrity in everything he did. Having dispensed with the formalities, I hope to make this a factual account of his life and career. They say . . . that a person's life and character is determined in one's early youth, even before one is born and before one is six years old. However, knowing very little about this and only about his youth by hearsay, my story will start with him when he entered West Point at the age of 20. Perhaps this should be an introduction or prologue. Oh, there's one thing I forgot to mention. I was married to the guy."

Those words were written by Ada Fitch "Peggy" Neyland, the General's widow. She never wrote the story of her husband's life, but much of what she experienced and felt as the wife of a famous soldier-coach is reflected in this book.

So here we go! But as we do, remember how the name Neyland is pronounced. There is no "NAY" in Neyland, although to this day some of his oldest and most ardent admirers still pronounce it that way. Bob Neyland pronounced his own name "Knee'-lund."

The Neyland Legend

PART I

CHAPTER 1

The Neyland Legend

September 20, 1950. The passenger cabin of the chartered flight was quiet except for the drone of engines cutting through the Southern night. The dream of another undefeated season for the University of Tennessee football team had been shattered, 7-0, by Mississippi State a few hours earlier in Starkville.

Suddenly, the silence was broken when the tall man in the gray suit rose from his seat and turned toward his players: "So you think those people back home love you? Well, look around you at your teammates. They're the only friends you have on earth."

Perhaps the speaker, Tennessee coach Bob Neyland, was thinking of the Rudyard Kipling verse which had influenced his life: "If you can meet with triumph and disaster, and treat those two impostors the same . . . you are a man, my son."

Perhaps it was Neyland's way of telling his players to pull themselves together psychologically, to rise from the disappointment of defeat, to rededicate themselves as a team, and to ignore the inevitable criticism of fans.

Neyland's psychology that night obviously worked. After the next season—20 games and 20 victories later—the Tennessee Volunteers were named the 1951 national champions of college football.

Today, a 96,000-seat stadium, a four-lane boulevard, and a $250,000 academic scholarship endowment bear the name of the late Robert Reese Neyland, a member of the college football Hall of Fame and the man who lifted the Tennessee football program from obscurity to national prominence.

Of all head coaches at major colleges 20 or more years, Neyland's won-lost record of 173 victories, 31 losses, and 12 ties (82.9 percent) is the best. The statistics from his coaching career are almost unbelievable by contemporary standards, but, even so, they only reveal a part of his near-legendary stature among his players, his opponents, and journalists.

> "Neyland was the most powerful athletic figure of his time. Other coaches respected him and learned from him."
> Fred Russell, long-time *Nashville Banner* sports editor and protege of sportswriter Grantland Rice
>
> "His greatest rivals always referred to the close personal relationship they shared with him."
> Dr. Lenox Baker
>
> "The outstanding defensive thinker in the game."
> Knute Rockne, Hall of Fame coach at Notre Dame
>
> "Bear Bryant once told me he never became a very good coach until he learned from Neyland how to get along with his players."
> F. M. Williams, *Nashville Tennessean* sportswriter
>
> "General Neyland's defensive theories were magnificent. All of us used them."
> Bobby Dodd, former Neyland player and later Hall of Fame coach at Georgia Tech
>
> "The great defensive master."
> Bud Wilkinson, record-setting Hall of Fame coach at Oklahoma
>
> "The greatest coach I ever competed against. He coaches all phases of the game better than any other coach. We had quite a rivalry and were close personal friends."
> Wallace Wade, Hall of Fame coach at Alabama and Duke

Neyland believed football success was predicated on a few basic principles, the most important of which was "never under-estimate an opponent." He also believed:

- One good blocker is worth three ball carriers.
- The team that makes the fewest mistakes wins.
- The kicking game rules.
- A good blocker is never left off a Tennessee football team.
- No offensive play is used in a game until it has been rehearsed 500 times.
- There are more ways to score on defense than on offense.

Bob Davis, center on Neyland's 1951 national championship team, said Neyland frequently reminded his players before a game: "Resolution and determination. That's what's going to win today."

The famed Tennessee single-wing offense became known as the Neyland system, but the general said it was not his at all. He borrowed from the great coaches of the mid-1920s—Knute Rockne at Notre Dame, Gil Dobie of Cornell, Charlie Daly of Army, and Wallace Wade of Alabama.

"The general told me he really didn't give a damn about offense," said *Knoxville Journal* sports editor Ben Byrd. "He said he would have used another system if it had given him something he didn't already have, mainly power at defensive tackle, which he thought was the most vulnerable point in the defense."

The late Walter Stewart, sports editor of the *Memphis Commercial-Appeal* and one of Neyland's closest media friends, said the Tennessee single-wing was an accurate reflection of Neyland—tough, common-sense, and planned with the skill of a symphony score.

"First of all, General Neyland was a soldier, and when he went to work on an offense, he thought in the pattern of a commander-in-chief plotting a campaign. A graduate of the United States Military Academy, he was well aware of von Clausewitz, the Prussian who reduced military operations to as close an exact science as such things come," Stewart wrote.

Military historians say Karl von Clausewitz, a Prussian general in the early 1800s, wrote the definitive essays on the philosophy, history, and successful conduct of war.

Stewart told how Neyland applied von Clausewitz to football: "Bring major portions of your force into contact with minor forces of the enemy. Operate on the enemy lines of communications without allowing him to operate on yours. Feint at one point and launch your attack against another."

Predicated on blocking and crisp execution, Neyland's offensive scheme was a reflection of the concepts this military man respected: precision, discipline, and strength through teamwork.

"It stressed savage double-teaming—two men [blockers] arriving at the point of contact at the same explosive instant and simply driving a defender from the ball-carrier's path," Stewart wrote. "It was geared to disrupt the defense with a crafty blend of running and passing, but most of all, it was power stuff. Often it went the route in the course of a dozen numbing blows, but each play was designed for the breakaway with brilliant downfield blocking."

Tom Siler, the late *Knoxville News-Sentinel* sports editor, said Neyland believed in a strong perimeter defense.

"You were not going to get outside his ends," Siler said. "He was going to turn the play inside where more players could get to the runner."

John Dottley, an all-Southeastern Conference fullback at the University of Mississippi in 1949-50, said of Neyland's defense: "When Tennessee tackles you, it seems like everybody wants a piece."

Incredibly, in 216 games, Neyland's teams yielded an average of only 5.6 points per game.

Yet Neyland was not just a conservative-thinking defensive coach, he was a great innovator—the first coach in the South to use press box telephones to the field, and the first coach to use: game films for evaluation; light-weight jerseys that would tear away in an opponent's grasp; low-top shoes and light-weight hip pads to enhance speed; and canvas coverings to protect football fields. Insisting that punters and passers release the ball within prescribed time limits, he timed them with a stop-watch during practice and pre-game warmups.

Neyland wanted the attention of his players focused on the opponent the night before a game. So to avoid distractions, he housed the Vols in a motel or tourist court on the edge of town. In some situations, he even rented the entire motel.

Neyland left nothing to chance. He even had his own personal weatherman, a fellow in Memphis who during the season provided an early week forecast, then more precise information as game day approached. If the forecast called for rain during the game, Neyland would have his team practice with a muddy, sometimes soapy, football on a special practice field beside the Tennessee River.

Of course, the press box phone is old stuff today, but *Miami Herald* sports editor Edwin Pope, in his book *Football's Greatest Coaches,* said it was such "top-secret stuff in the beginning that for months after an Associated Press sportswriter named Roy Hutchens wrote a story 'exposing' it, he was barred from Tennessee athletic offices."

Neyland shunned radio interviews and after-dinner speeches. He turned down endorsements.

"I'm hired to teach football, and that's what I do," he said. Notice he said "teach," not "coach." To Bob Neyland, football was just another lesson and the practice field just another classroom. And although he became famous as a football coach and served his country as a career soldier, Neyland was most of all an educator.

"We never talked much when I was playing for him at Tennessee," recalled Jim Haslam, offensive tackle in 1950-52. "The General usually only talked to the tailbacks and captains. But the year I was captain we had some private conversations, and he always talked about being a leader, what it meant to lead, how to lead, and how you must rise above adversity. That's what he talked about mostly—leadership."

1892-1911

PART II

CHAPTER 2

Growing up in Texas

Robert Reese Neyland III was a Texan, something he never forgot or ever let others forget. "I am a Texan by birth, born of native Texans, and cherish the Texas belief that there is no place in the world to equal Texas," he said. Neyland was born in Hunt County, a place rich with heroic progeny even by Texas standards, and it is relevant in several respects to the appreciation of Neyland's origin and character.

Northeast of present-day Dallas, the area that would become Hunt County was once the prairie hunting grounds of the Delaware, Shawnee, Caddo, and Wichita Indians. By the early nineteenth century, however, the region began to have many ties to immigrating "volunteers" from Tennessee—men like Sam Houston and Davy Crockett. In fact, by 1850 the census showed the population of Hunt County was 1,520 and 27.8 per cent of the adults had been born in Tennessee. It is even said that Hunt Countians of the mid-1800s claimed "a Texan was a Tennessean gone west," so there is a certain symmetry in the fact that Neyland, a Hunt Countian "gone east," should achieve his greatest successes hard by the Tennessee River in Knoxville.

In a rich agricultural district noted for the production of cotton, oats, corn, livestock, and poultry, Hunt County also grew heroes. In World War II the county gave the nation Audie Murphy, the most decorated soldier of the war; Lieutenant General Claire Lee Chennault, leader of the famous Flying Tigers; and Lieutenant. Dean E. Hallmark and Second Lieutenant. Nolan A. Herndon, two of the 13 Texans on the historic Doolittle bombing raid over Tokyo

Robert Reese Neyland III was born on February 17, 1892, in Greenville, the governmental seat of Hunt County. Today Greenville has a population of about

23,000, modestly up from a turn-of-the-century total of 7,000. Neyland's father, Robert Reese Neyland, Jr., was a lawyer. His mother, Pauline Lewis Neyland, the youngest of 12 children, was a school teacher. The Neylands were Scotch-Irish, Episcopalian, Democrats. They married in 1888 and had three children—sons Robert Reese III and Mayo and daughter Carroll.

Neyland recalled that his mother "had a warm, generous nature, was very calm and placid, and unquestionably one of the bravest and most resolute personalities I ever knew."

Her father, Neyland's maternal grandfather, Dr. Nicholas Meriweather Lewis of Harrison County, Texas, was a lieutenant colonel in the Confederate Army medical corps during the Civil War.

Neyland's other grandfather, the first Robert Reese Neyland, hailed from Wood County, Texas. He too was a lieutenant colonel in the Confederate Army and was killed in the battle of Shiloh, in Tennessee. He and Emily Wells Neyland had two children—Robert Reese Neyland, Jr., and Mayo Williams Neyland.

"My father [Robert, Jr.] was born in Jasper, Texas, in 1861, was educated in Canada and began the practice of law in Greenville, Texas, about 1885," wrote Neyland in his memoirs. "With jet black hair and moustache, flashing dark eyes and athletic build, he was one of the best-looking men I ever saw. Though one of the keenest legal minds in the nation, he was not a good trial lawyer because of faulty delivery.

"His brother and law partner for 50 years was two years younger, with sandy hair and moustache. A graduate of Royal Military College of Canada, [Mayo] was one of the great all-around athletes of his day. Though not brilliant, he was a plugger and a good speaker, consequently a good teammate for his brilliant but erratic brother."

In Bob Neyland's boyhood days, Hunt County was one of the largest cotton-producing counties in the South. Farmers brought their baled cotton into town on the first Monday in the fall of the year and sold to buyers on the courthouse square. By the end of the day, the square was white with cotton samples pulled out of bales for inspection.

Typical of small-town America, Greenville grew outward from a town square. "In the center of the square was the county courthouse, and it was common in those days to see heavily laden wagons mired down to the hubs in almost impassable mud of the winter," Neyland remembered. "The soil of that region is known in Texas as 'black waxy' which is guaranteed to produce, when dry, the dustiest dust and, when wet, the muddiest mud in the world.

"Our home in Greenville was a large frame structure on Stonewall Street, exactly one-half mile [southward] from the square," Neyland recalled. "Less than one-quarter mile beyond us, the open country began. The plains, the fields, and the woods. So it was relatively simple for us to go hunting and fishing." Swimming was another matter. The boys Neyland's age sneaked into private stock ponds or cavorted in creeks following floods.

Fourteen-foot ceilings and tall windows and doors helped cool the Neyland house during the hot Texas summers. In winter the open coal-burning fireplaces warmed the parlor, sitting room, and bedrooms. The dining room and kitchen had wood-burning stoves.

"We had city water and electric lights, but no inside plumbing and no telephone," Neyland said. Greenville homeowners around 1900 began building the first bathrooms on back porches or in rooms partitioned from the back bedroom. Baths were taken on Saturday in the kitchen in a wash tub with cistern water, heated in a tea kettle on the wood-burning cook stove.

The Neyland property comprised an entire city block. In addition to the house, located on the southwest corner (at Stonewall and Oneal streets), there were two cabins for black servants and a large barn. The Neyland homestead also included a large vegetable garden and a plot for raising feed for the animals.

"We kept from one to three cows, a horse, sometimes some pigs, and a flock of chickens, turkeys, guineas, and pea fowl," Neyland said. "In the feed lot we grew sorghum, corn, sometimes wheat and oats, and various types of farm crops. In the garden we grew every vegetable known to man—and blackberries and strawberries. We also had several different kinds of fruit trees—peaches, pears, cherries, figs, and crabapples."

The Neylands also had a concrete cyclone cellar six feet under ground, with an air vent protruding at the surface. "Whenever a cyclone appeared imminent, the whole family would take to the cellar and remain there for safety until the blow was over," Neyland recalled.

The Neyland homestead, although within the corporate limits of Greenville, was a small farm, and that meant work for Bob and his younger brother, Mayo.

"The stock had to be fed and watered, the barn lot cleaned up, the cows milked, the milk churned for butter, the garden spaded, planted, and weeded, the long grass mowed. In winter time, five fires had to be built and the necessary wood sawed and split, and coal carried into the house. All this was in addition to the normal routine of housekeeping, washing dishes, making beds, sweeping, dusting, washing, and so on.

"We almost always had a cook and maid living in one of the servant houses, sometimes with two or three children to take care of as well. In the other servant house, we usually had a man who took care of the heavy work around the place. However, it must be said that many's the time that we had no man servant available and the necessary chores had to be taken care of by my brother and myself. Since I was four years older, most of the work fell to me. Many's the time that I have climbed out of a warm bed, made five fires, and milked three cows before breakfast, and after school have come home to saw and split wood and carry wood and coal into the house."

It was often dark before Bob finished the last of his chores for the day.

"Most of my friends and all my family cock an incredulous eye at me when I dwell upon this phase of my existence, since during the time they have known me I have never been known to take any kind of a step in relation to any type of chore or handyman or any other kind of work around the house."

But those were the late 1890s and early 1900s. Like most kids of that day in rural, small-town America, doing the chores was part of family life. And there were no movies, radios, or television sets, and there were no automobiles. But there was the King Opera House where the town was treated to the vaudeville act of Eddie Foy, the martial music of John Philip Sousa's band, the *Babes in Toyland* operetta by Victor Herbert, and a 1907 George M. Cohan spectacular featuring his hit songs "You're a Grand Old Flag," "I'm a Yankee Doodle Dandy," and "Give My Regards to Broadway."

Still, for the kids Bob Neyland's age, pleasures were simple. "Fishing and hunting, football and baseball, mainly the latter, and simple games such as hare-and-hounds, one-and-over, taw, kicking the can, and the like were the things we did to amuse ourselves," Bob remembered.

"When you say fishing today, perhaps you visualize a man with a flyrod, casting rod, or a spinning reel, and a tackle box full of lures, a boat with an outboard motor, and perhaps a guide faring forth on some hunt for black bass, trout, or other freshwater fish, or for snook, redfish, tarpon, bonefish, and the like in salt water," he said.

"Not for us. A cane pole, a hook, sinker, cork and line, a can of worms or bucket of minnows, and we were well equipped. What is more, we seldom came home without fish for the pan, something the fancy fishermen seldom duplicate.

"And for hunting, ditto. No shooting quail with a beautifully trained bird dog and no shooting ducks from a smoothly camouflaged blind. Instead, we fared forth with a .22 rifle or single shot shotgun, looking for rabbits or squirrels, or doves or quail, if we could find any. More often still, we went out without a gun at night—with a borrowed possum dog or coon dog or two or three, or in the daytime with a pack of greyhounds chasing rabbits. I doubt if one boy in a thousand of today's crop has ever been on an all-night possum or coon hunt."

Young Bob Neyland and his friends would, as he described it, "borrow or steal or lure away" one or more possum or coon hounds, get a wagon and team of horses,and start out on an all-night hunt, alternately chasing after the baying dogs and trying to find their way back to the wagon. The boys returned home at sunup "tired to death, hungry as a wolf, and sleepy as a sloth."

When young Bob actually tried sampling the results of his nocturnal efforts—"possum and taters"—it was an experience he never forgot.

"I helped myself liberally and started in on this fabled delicacy, noting at the time that neither my father nor my mother appeared to be much interested. Although considerably disheartened by the first bite, I bravely pretended that this delicious food which I had pursued during the hours of the night and lugged home for a feast was really nectar of the gods. About the third bite, however, I got more than a little discouraged. It was greasy, stringy, and tasteless.

"Shortly afterward, I had the opportunity to observe two possums making a meal off of a dead cow in broad daylight, said cow not only being dead but also exceedingly ripe. This experience forever alienated my affection for the storied possum and taters."

Thereafter, most of the time, the Neyland boys gave their possum catches to the other boys. But one night the Neylands decided to keep two possums they had brought home live. Not having a pen in which to house them, the boys turned over an old washtub in the backyard, put a heavy stone on top and put the possums underneath the tub. The boys checked on the possums periodically during the daytime, and mostly the imprisoned animals slept.

"They were apparently making no effort to escape, so we went to bed rather lightheartedly," Bob said. "Next morning early, a neighbor appeared on our porch—an irate neighbor—and demanded to know who the hell had brought those possums in and turned them loose on his chicken house."

The possums waited until dark to dig out from underneath the washtub, tore into the chicken house, killed 27 birds, then went to sleep in the corner.

"Mr. Stinson was a man of little humor," Bob said. "He saw nothing whatever funny about the situation. He not only demanded payment for his chickens, but he demanded satisfaction as well. Now, my brother and I didn't mind my father's paying for the chickens, though we did feel a trifle embarrassed by the situation, but satisfaction was another matter. Apparently, the satisfaction that Mr. Stinson desired and got was to have the whale beaten out of us by our old man. Never again did we bring upon the Neyland premises any more possums, dead or alive."

During Bob Neyland's years in Greenville High School, baseball was the most popular sport in that part of Texas, and he developed a true passion for it. Few area schools even had basketball teams, and although most schools played football, few had coaches.

"Consequently, the players and the team knew little about the techniques of individual and team play," Neyland said of his early experience with football.

"Baseball, however, was quite different since weather conditions in Texas make it possible to play baseball at least l0 months a year. Practically every boy had some skill at the game. Unless they were physically handicapped by some type of crippling injury or unless they had very bad eyesight, practically all the boys in those days could throw and catch the ball and could hit at least average pitching. Most boys were able to play several positions."

So, Bob Neyland grew up on the "black waxy" baseball diamonds of Hunt County, Texas, playing a variety of positions—pitcher, catcher, infielder, and outfielder. He could hit consistently and field well, and he excelled as a pitcher.

The Dallas newspapers gave Neyland a headline the day he hurled a no-hitter for Greenville High against Bonham High. Neyland struck out seven, allowed no walks, and left only two runners on base. No Bonham runner got past second base, and Greenville won 8-0.

In his senior year of high school, young Neyland turned serious attention to his future. In those days, a person could teach in the public schools if he or she passed a battery of certification tests that took about three days to complete.

"Much to Dad's surprise, as well as my own, I passed those examinations with an excellent grade, was awarded a certificate which qualified me to teach in the grade schools of the State of Texas at any time during the next six years. This document was known as a teacher's certificate first grade," Neyland said.

"In the fall of 1909, thinking that I was too young to go away to college, Dad sent me to Burleson Junior which was on the west side of Greenville, about one mile from the square." Bob walked a mile and a half from his house to Burleson each morning and back again in the afternoon.

"Meanwhile, the City School Board of Greenville elected me, at the tender age of 17, a substitute teacher in the public schools, and it was my job to substitute for teachers who became ill or were absent from their classes for any reason for as much as a day or more. This substitute teacher's assignment carried with it the magnificent salary of 75 dollars a month."

Bob taught five grades—third through seventh—even though he was going to Burleson Junior College about half the time that year.

On October 25, 1953, the daily newspaper in Greenville published a commemorative edition about Burleson Junior College. The *Morning Herald* observed that Burleson in the 1909-10 school year had "one outstanding athlete, a young man who was to make his name known throughout the country in the years to come. He was Robert R. 'Bob' Neyland, one of the greatest competitors in football and baseball or any sport he entered. [He] never stopped fighting regardless of the odds or opposition."

When the summer of 1910 arrived, Bob tried out for and made the semi-pro baseball team representing the city of Greenville. The team manager was Ellis "Pop" Hardy, then the baseball coach at Texas Christian University and later manager of the Waco team in the Class-AA Texas League.

The Greenville team had a catcher, a first baseman, a second baseman, and two outfielders from TCU, plus some other players who had professional experience in the Texas League. Only two of the players on the Greenville team were from Greenville—Bob Neyland and Brooks Sorie, a shortstop who that fall enrolled at TCU. The Greenville team beat Wichita Falls in a three-game series for the state semi-pro championship.

"After we had won the deciding game, Ellis Birdsong, who happened to be the assistant cashier of the Greenville National Bank, inquired of the team if they wanted to celebrate. The answer was a thunderous 'yes' and so, after getting dressed, the entire squad toured all the night spots, bars, etc., to be found in Wichita Falls, drinking up a storm," Neyland said.

"At this time, I neither smoked nor drank, and I did like lemonades, so I went around and listened to the celebration and filled up on lemonades. We had a good time, I guess. At least I did until I found out that the celebration was not on club money."

It turned out that the players were going to have to pay for their partying with money the owners of the baseball team owed them.

"Nobody was too unhappy about it until we got back to Greenville and found that the club was broke and that there was not sufficient money in the treasury to pay our last month's salary. My wage that summer [for playing baseball] was a grandiose 50 dollars a month, which was for me quite a bit of money, and to get beat out of 50 dollars made me unhappy, indeed."

On balance, however, Bob considered his baseball experience in the summer of 1910 quite rewarding.

"I learned a great deal about baseball. Pop Hardy was a thorough student of the game. Coaching, experience, and observation all added up to make me a much better baseball player at the end of the summer than I was at the start."

In the fall of 1910, Bob enrolled in the College of Engineering at Texas A&M, 200 miles south of Greenville.

"I spent one year at this institution which was one of the really valuable experiences of my life," he said. It was at Texas A&M, that Bob Neyland came under the influence of Uncle "Charlie" Moran.

CHAPTER 3

Texas A&M

In 1910, U.S. President Theodore Roosevelt returned from his hunting trip to East Africa, the Boy Scouts of America was founded, undefeated heavyweight boxing champion Jim Jeffries returned to the ring after five years of inactivity and lost his title to challenger Jack Johnson, the proper length for women's sweaters was the knee, and young Bob Neyland, at age 18, wanted to become a chemical engineer.

Bob convinced his father that Texas A&M was the place to study engineering. A&M had a reputation for turning out good engineers and, at that time, for producing more army officers than even the U.S. Military Academy at West Point.

"Having once attended Texas A&M, you are never permitted to forget that you once were a student [there]," Neyland said. Thereafter, as a former A&M sports letterman, he annually received a "T" card that entitled him to free admission to all games played on the Texas A&M campus.

"My year at A&M was invaluable from any standpoint, but it was made greatly more worthwhile by the opportunity that I had to play under the coaching of one of the greatest characters college athletics in America has ever produced," Neyland said.

That "greatest character" was Charles Barthell Moran, the football and baseball coach at A&M. Moran was born in Nashville, Tennessee, on February 22, 1878. He attended the University of Tennessee and lettered at halfback on the 1897 Volunteer football team. One of his backfield teammates was Samuel Strang Nicklin, the quarterback. Like Moran, Nicklin was to loom large in the life of Bob Neyland in later years.

Moran was a dynamic personality. Although only five-feet, eight-inches tall, he weighed 180 pounds and had a fiery, competitive disposition. He was multidimensional in sports. In addition to coaching football and baseball at A&M, he was a catcher for the Dallas baseball team in the Texas League during the summer months.

Moran had a brief fling as a major league player with the St. Louis Cardinals. He had a .429 batting average in 1903, but slumped to .175 with the Cardinals in 1908. In between, he played minor league ball and began dabbling in college coaching.

Desiring to learn all he could about coaching football, Moran went to Carlisle Indian Academy in Pennsylvania to be an assistant to Glenn Scobey "Pop" Warner, one of the founding fathers of college football.

Warner built successful football programs at Georgia, Cornell, Carlisle, Pittsburgh, Stanford, and Temple. In 44 seasons, his teams won 313 games, lost 106, and tied 32. More importantly, Warner was a great innovator. He conceived the single-wing and double-wing formations, and among his "firsts" were: the rolling body block, the blocking dummy, fiber padding, and numbered jerseys. So it was in that fertile Pop Warner environment of fundamentals and innovations that Charlie Moran worked and learned in 1907 and 1908.

The Carlisle experience was Moran's springboard to a head coaching job at Texas A&M in 1909 where, in his first year, the Aggies were undefeated. His six-year record (1909-14) was 38-8-4. Following a four-year period when he did not coach, he moved to the bluegrass region of Kentucky where he guided tiny upstart Centre College to surprising success. His Centre teams (1919-23) compiled a 42-6-1 record and, in 1921, beat Eastern power Harvard 6-0 en route to a 10-1 season. The only loss that year was 22-14 to Texas A&M.

"Uncle Charlie" Moran, as he became known, later coached at Bucknell and Catawba College and ended his football coaching career with a record of 122 victories, 33 losses, and 12 ties.

At Texas A&M back in the fall of 1910, Uncle Charlie Moran put out the call for candidates for his second football squad. Bob Neyland was among those who answered, and although most of his memories of Uncle Charlie were played out on the baseball diamond, his most vivid one may have been that first football practice hosted by this most novel mentor.

"I can remember like yesterday the first time he called the squad together," Neyland said.

"I want you fellows to know that I can out-run, out-jump, and whip every man on this squad," Moran said. "Anybody that thinks different, speak up now."

"Then he challenged any of us to stand off 10 yards, get a running start, and butt heads with him," Neyland recalled years later at Tennessee. "There were no takers. But I've never exactly cared to include that kind of skull practice in my system."

As Neyland remembered, Moran was stocky and strongly built.

"His hands were large, and his fingers were gnarled and broken, the result of catching too many wild tips with his bare hands while catching in professional baseball," Neyland recalled.

"His eyes were little and mean, his chin and jaw heavy and prominent, his mouth compressed to a tiny slit drooling brown tobacco juice out of one corner. After one quick look at him, I believed that he could do exactly what he said he could do. I was tall and skinny, weighing about 150 pounds, and he was a lot bigger than I was, and I was sure that he was a whole hell of a lot meaner, so I begged to be excused."

In baseball, Moran's style was no less confrontational, as Neyland learned in the spring of 1911. Although he had played most baseball positions, Neyland regarded himself as a natural catcher and decided that would be his position. Moran had other ideas. He already had a good catcher, Dutch Holmes, and assigned Neyland to play first base.

In his first game as an Aggie, Neyland made errors on two ground balls hit toward him. After the game, a dejected Neyland sat on a locker room bench and looked at the floor. One of the players, by now showered and dressed, wanted to know what was bothering Neyland.

"I replied in a voice louder than necessary, louder because I knew that Charlie Moran was dressing on the other side of a thin plank wall and hoping that he could hear what I had to say." Neyland said.

"I never have played first base in my life until I came to Texas A&M," Neyland said loudly for Moran's benefit. "It's the one place on the baseball team that I never have played and can't play. I can't play first base and don't want to play first base."

There was a loud crash in the coaches' room. Moran threw a baseball shoe as hard as he could against the wall. Then he stalked into the locker room and stopped directly in front of Neyland. Moran was braced, his legs spread wide apart.

"As I was sitting down on the bench at the time and looking upward, he looked twice as big and twice as mean as he had the previous fall in his first speech to the football team," Neyland said. "There was a dead silence in the dressing room. Nobody moved a foot, a hand, or a muscle, and I doubt if any of them moved an eyelid. Charlie stared at me for a full minute, compressing his lips and looking meaner every second."

Finally, Moran spoke.

"All I've got to say to you, Neyland, is for Pete's sake get some guts—repeat—guts!" Moran shouted.

Moran waited there for a few more moments, still staring at Neyland, then whirled and walked back into the coaches' dressing room.

"The next day I went out and played first base like I liked it," Neyland said. "I went out and played as if I loved that position more and better than any position I had ever played. I put my whole heart into it. And furthermore, though I shouldn't say so myself, I was a danged good first baseman."

The moral to that incident, which Neyland used many times with his football players, was: "If you can't play wingback, play blockingback. If you can't play tail-back and they want to move you to guard, move to guard," Neyland said. "One of the best football players we ever had . . . thought he was an end and resisted every effort of ours to move him to a more favorable position. Finally, during spring practice of his senior year, I took the bull by the horns and moved him to guard. He played guard all spring with a sullen, resentful fury. When fall came we started through our schedule, he was one of the very best men we had on the entire football team, no matter what position. He made all-Southern guard in his one and only year at that position.

"The moral of this story can be expressed in another way. There are many instruments in the band. Not everybody can play the first violin or the first anything. If you are a clarinet player and you can't play first clarinet, for goodness' sake grab the second clarinet and start tooting. You never know. Sometimes the thing that looks the worst for you turns out to be the best.

In the early part of the 1911 baseball season, catcher Dutch Holmes became ill with the mumps and Neyland took over at his position on the team.

"I was so enthused over the chance to catch again that I literally went wild when we went to Fort Worth to play Texas Christian University a two-game series. I was lucky enough to get five or six hits, two of them over the fence. I threw out at least a half-dozen men trying to steal second, and made several rather difficult catches of foul balls."

The following week, in a game with Baylor University in Waco, Neyland was injured at first base trying to flag down a wide throw from third. The batter, future major leaguer Dave Danforth, collided with Neyland's extended glove hand and the ball popped out. Danforth advanced to third base. Neyland recalled the play: "When I saw the throw was wild and toward home plate, I hooked first base with my right foot, took a long lunge with my left foot and extended my arm in a driving lunge to try to make a one-handed catch. Meanwhile, 200 pounds of Dave Danforth were steaming down the base path." Actually, Danforth weighed only 167 pounds, but the damage was done.

"I pulled off my glove and looked at my hand," Neyland said. "It was tingling and hurting as if every bone in it was broken. However, I put my glove back on and finished the inning."

During warmups before the next inning, the infielders' return throws to first base felt to Neyland as if his hand was being "struck by lightning." Neyland played two more innings before convincing Moran the hand was injured so badly that it was a handicap.

"When I got back to A&M after the road trip, my hand was swollen up as big as a first baseman's mitt," Neyland said. "When the doctor examined it, he said that my fingers were sprained at the first, second, and third knuckles and also at the wrist, and he put a bandage of lead and opium on it." The injury produced a knot where the index finger joins the palm, a knot Neyland carried with him the rest of his life.

The hand injury ended Neyland's baseball season for A&M, but in early June he received an offer to try out with the Bonham, Texas, team in the Class-D Texas-Oklahoma League. The rules applying to Texas colleges in those days permitted athletes to receive money for playing summer baseball, provided the league was no higher than Class-D.

"Due to my long layoff with my injured hand, I had a great deal of difficulty in getting into playing condition," Neyland recalled. "All the other players were ahead of me in physical shape, and they had their batting eyes all sharpened up." Neyland had been idle for six weeks, and the idleness took its toll.

So the Bonham manager, Dewey Humphries, released Neyland and kept another first baseman. Neyland packed his bags and moved on to the tiny south Texas town of Taylor, where he played for an independent semi-pro team.

"Unhappily, however, the team got into financial difficulties and ended up going broke, owing me a month's pay," Neyland said. "I had to wire my father for funds to get back to Greenville."

Intent on playing baseball until the end of the summer, the nomadic Neyland finished the season with a team in the town of Windom, 25 miles north of Greenville. The Windom team played three or four games a week, met its payroll, and enabled Neyland to earn a little money and gain more game experience.

"We had a very good team [at Windom]," Neyland said. "Among our players was one 'Reb' Russell, who was one of the greatest kids I have ever seen come up from the sticks and go into semi-pro and then professional baseball. I enjoyed catching him because he had everything that a pitcher needs—good control, a very fast, fast ball, and a very quick-breaking curve."

That summer Neyland shared the rough Texas diamonds with two future major leaguers, Danforth and Russell. Coincidentally, both later played on the infamous 1919 Chicago White Sox team that will forever be known as the "Black Sox," although neither was implicated in the allegations of throwing the World Series.

In the fall of 1911, Neyland returned to Texas A&M ready to sell newspapers, haul laundry, and do other odd jobs to supplement the money his father provided for school. However, fate intervened. Two or three days after reporting back to the A&M campus, Neyland got a telegram from his father. Their congressman, C. B. Randell, was giving competitive examinations to select nominees for the U.S. Military Academy at West Point.

Neyland went to Charlie Moran with the news.

"Bob," Moran said, "you can finish here and go into the regular army from Texas A&M, as many officers have done, and do just as well as though you had graduated from the Point."

But Neyland could not be dissuaded.

"I have always wanted to go to West Point," he told Moran. "It has always been an ambition of mine. And the next three years are going to be quite a struggle for me here [at A&M] financially. I know that if I go to West Point, I won't be a burden to my family as far as education is concerned."

Moran replied that he hated to lose Neyland but that he respected his ambition and would help him at any time. In parting, Moran added, "Don't ever gaze backward."

Nine young men, including Bob Neyland, took the West Point competitive exams at Sherman, Texas, on December 15, 1911. Exactly one month later, Neyland was notified he had been selected to take the entrance exam at Fort Sam Houston on March 15, 1912.

So, Neyland studied diligently during the winter. "I prepared very strenuously to take these examinations," Neyland said. "I think there were 18 subjects in all, [taken] over a two-day period.

"On May 15, I received word that I had passed the examinations and that I was to report on June 1 for entrance to the Military Academy," Neyland said.

There were, of course, no airplanes and few good roads in 1912. And even if there had been better roads, traveling from Greenville, Texas, to West Point, New York, by automobile was not practical. There was only the railroad, and it took the better part of three days to make the trip.

"All of a sudden, my father, who had been quite eager for me to take the examinations, decided that he didn't want me to go to West Point," Neyland recalled."I have a good law practice here in Greenville," his father said. "It's going to be better, and I wish you would change your mind and go to the University of Texas, take the law course there and come back here and go into partnership with me."

It was an important moment for young Bob Neyland—one of those crossroads in a man's life.

"Dad," he replied, "I don't know what I am getting into, but I have made up my mind that I would plow this furrow if it killed me. I've got hand to the plow handle, and I am going to proceed on down the road as far as I can go. And I'll do the best I can not to disgrace you."

1912-1925

PART III

CHAPTER 4

West Point 1912-13

Duty!"
"Honor!"
"Country!"
The motto of the United States Military Academy.

As time and experiences honed Robert Reese Neyland III into a man whose attributes seem best described with mottos and aphorisms, it was entirely appropriate he should end up at West Point. From its humble beginnings in 1802, the United States Military Academy has been a great molder of character. In all aspects of its program West Point has stressed integrity, discipline, motivation, physical stamina, agility, courage, and the ability to coordinate. In other words, it suited Bob Neyland to a "T."

1912-13

Even so, for a young man from the relative frontier of Greenville, Texas, that first summer of 1912 was an eye-opener.

"It is difficult, if not impossible, to chronicle with accuracy the kaleidoscopic impressions acquired by a 1912 plebe during his first day at West Point," Neyland recalled. "A mid-summer dive into a tank of icy water could hardly be more breath-taking."

Neyland was met at the barracks sally port (ground-level passage through the building) by two upperclassmen whom he described as "sourpussed." Suddenly, one of the cadets bellowed contemptuously and insultingly: "Wipe that smile off your face! Put that suitcase down! Get your heels together! Take off that tie; put it in your pocket! Turn up your coat collar! Turn down the cuffs on those trousers!"

That was just the beginning.

"Now, stand up!" shouted the upperclassman. "Get your shoulders back! Pull in your chin!"

"Don't look at me! I don't want to know you, Mister Dumbguard! Pick up that suitcase! Forward, double-time, march!"

Neyland and the other plebes marched from sally port to headquarters, to a fourth-floor room in a barracks building, and to the "cadet store" to be issued uniforms, bedding, and other required equipment. They marched to meals and were harangued and insulted every step of the way.

"Almost ready to stop and fight the tormenters a dozen or more times, by bedtime I was thoroughly shaken, bewildered, and cowed," Neyland said.

The bugler at West Point sounded reveille at 6:00 a.m., and cadets' rooms had to be ready for inspection 20 minutes later.

It was a physical impossibility for Bob Neyland to strip his bed, sweep, dust, and place all articles of clothing in the prescribed places, and to shave, bathe, and dress in complete uniform within the allotted time. Therefore, he set an alarm clock for 5:15 a.m., 45 minutes ahead of reveille.

"My roommate was Jack Nygaard, from Wisconsin, and he was almost as inefficient a housekeeper as I was," Neyland said. "After a month of this arduous 'boot' training, called Beast Barracks, we were moved over to summer camp and dispersed, according to height, in the six companies then comprising the Corps of Cadets."

After the experience of Beast Barracks, plebe camp was a welcome relief to Neyland and his fellow plebes. But the monotonous, humiliating hazing continued. In ranks, when at guard or parade, when marching to meals, seated in the mess hall, and after supper at night, the hazing was endless.

Under the academy code of conduct, upperclassmen were not allowed to question a plebe's courage or to abuse him physically. But the upperclassmen were skilled in the art of insult and humiliation, and the traditional ordeal rained on the plebe during his 12 months of trial.

"It was 'Mr. Dumbjohn this' and 'Mr. Dumbknee that.' Pull those shoulders back! Tuck that chin in! Suck up that gut!'" Neyland recalled.

"Plebes, of course, could not address an upperclassman without 'May I ask a question, Sir?' or 'May I make a statement, Sir?' We were not permitted to speak to each other in the presence of an upperclassman," Neyland said.

"At tables, plebes were required to sit like trussed-up dummies with an exaggerated brace and their eyes firmly fixed on the table. One of the worst sins a plebe could commit was to gaze around the messhall."

Many times a day, the plebes were hit with the same question: "What is your PCS?" PCS was an abbreviation for "previous condition of servitude," which meant: "If you had a job [prior to West Point], what was it?"

"This question got me into a little trouble since the only monthly salaries I had ever earned were in the capacity of school teacher or as a baseball player,"

Neyland said. "Of these two alternatives, I chose baseball for my answer, and the next question was 'what position?'"

Neyland gave a multiple answer: "Catcher, pitcher, or first base." And that, he said, prompted such reactions as: "What the hell do you think you are, Mister, a whole damned baseball team?"

About the first of August, Army baseball coach Sammy Strang scheduled preliminary tryouts for all plebes. Neyland reported with 30 other hopefuls and said he was a first baseman.

"You look like a pitcher to me," Strang told Neyland.

"I found out later that coach Strang thought I had a build and a facial resemblance to Bob Hyatt, who had graduated the previous June after pitching and winning four straight games against Navy," Neyland said.

"Strang was one of the most remarkable of several extraordinary personalities with whom I had the good luck to be associated during the next four years. His real name was Sam Strang Nicklin, and he was a scion of an old Chattanooga family who objected strenuously to his participation in baseball. He had a glorious tenor voice, with operatic range and volume, and had for several years studied voice in Paris under one of the great teachers."

Because of his family's opposition to baseball, Sammy Strang Nicklin dropped "Nicklin" from his name. Actually, Sammy Strang Nicklin used a combination of names during his life. As "Sammy Strang," he played baseball at the University of Tennessee and afterward spent a number of years with the New York Giants under the management of John McGraw. As "Strang Nicklin," he lettered in 1896-97 as a football player at Tennessee and was captain of the 1896 team, which incidentally was undefeated in four games.

Neyland remembered thinking to himself, during his days at West Point, that Sammy Strang must be the best baseball coach who ever lived.

"His Army teams won the annual Navy game nine consecutive times. This is much too remarkable a record over too long a time to be attributed to luck or any factor other than superlative coaching," Neyland said years later.

"He was the first to visualize the preponderant importance in college baseball of hitting, base running, and pitching as opposed to fielding. Because of his vision in this regard, we spent practically all of our extremely limited practice time in batting and running bases. Sammy was practically alone in debunking the pet shibboleth of batting coaches who maintain that the bat should be swung in a level plane. How such an atrocious theory could persist is incomprehensible, since a moment's reflection should force the conclusion that, in order to hit a knee-high strike with a level swing, it would first be necessary for the batter to assume a batting stance on both knees! How he would go about hitting a letter-high strike from a kneeling position with a level swing is yet another problem!"

Neyland said Strang coached his players to "golf" the low pitch and "club" the high one.

"Sammy was an authentic genius with a brilliant mind, unfailing judgment of men, and a great gift of getting the most out of his boys. Off the field, he was a happy-go-lucky guy, witty and immensely popular around the Officers' Club."

If Sammy Strang was a character as a coach, Neyland said, so was Louis Merillat as a cadet.

"I expect Louie was the most popular cadet in the Corps. As a plebe, he made both the Army football team and the baseball team. He was a 10-second man, a great pass receiver, a wonderful blocker, punt coverer, and defensive end in football. In baseball, he was an outstanding hitter, outfielder, and base runner. He was a merry hail-fellow-well-met type of individual whom everybody loved and admired."

In a practice game during the August plebe workouts, Merillat was playing centerfield for one team and Neyland was pitching for the other. Neyland picked up the story:

"The first time he came up to bat, I threw him two curve balls and had a count of two strikes and no balls on him. I had been taught in Texas to throw a high fast ball close to the batter's chin in this situation to drive him away from the plate before coming back with the curve. Being anxious to strike the famous Merillat out, I rared back and fired a fast ball as hard I could possibly throw it.

"Instead of going where I intended for it to go, the ball went directly at Louie and struck him on the breast directly over the heart. He threw his arms up with a choked cry and fell face forward across the plate. I ran in, scared to death. Thought I had killed him. My composure wasn't helped by Strang who also ran up, glared at me and snarled, 'You dumb plebe, you've killed the best ball player we've got!'

"An ambulance came and took Louie to the hospital. The rest of us showered, went to parade, then to supper, then to bed. But no one took the time or trouble to let me know whether Merillat was living or dead.

"Next day, to my infinite relief, Louie walked up to my tent, grinning, and thrust out his hand."

"Bob," Merillat said. "I'm glad to know you."

"Later, I had the good fortune to play left end while Merillat was making all-American at right end. And I had even better fortune to have his batting and fielding strength behind me during the baseball seasons of 1913, '14 and '15," Neyland said.

At the end of August 1912, the Corps of Cadets was moved back to the barracks, and the Second Class (juniors) returned from furlough. Academic classes began September 1.

"West Point teaching methods of those days were based on the assignment of cadets to small sections, approximately 10 to each section," Neyland recalled. "At the close of each day's recitation, assignments were made for study in preparation for the next meeting in that class. Each cadet was required to recite each day and a grade [was] given him, based on 3.0 for a perfect recitation."

The daily grades were posted on the bulletin boards each Saturday, displaying each cadet's total for the week. The best students comprised the first section, and the lower grades were relegated to the second, third, and fourth sections. Every two weeks, transfers were made upward and downward as cadets' grades improved or regressed.

Class sections were formed in the South Barracks area and they marched to and from the appropriate classrooms in the academics buildings. The section "marcher," the number one student academically in that section, would march his group into the classroom and report to the instructor: "All present, Sir!"

As soon as the class was seated, the instructor would say, "Draw cards." There were just enough cards for each member of the class. Each card represented a different topic for the assignment that day. Drawn randomly, the cards dictated each cadet's recitation of what he had learned from that assignment.

Entrance exam grades were the criteria by which plebes were assigned initially to the numbered sections—the better the grade, the lower the section number. Upperclassmen looked forward to the published lists with considerable curiosity. Because they had observed the plebes all summer, upperclassmen had formed definite opinions about the mental capacity and alertness of each plebe.

"What math section are you in, Mister?" That was the stock question asked of plebes. In those days, more plebes were victimized by West Point math than any other subject. The importance of math was emphasized by the fact that it was scheduled for one hour and twenty minutes per day, six days a week, from September 1 to June 1 for two straight years."

Neyland recalled that he was in the 16th of 18 math sections.

"I told you that plebe was a Dumbjohn," the upperclassmen said that first week of classes when Neyland answered their "what math section" questions. "You won't be here after Christmas, Mister!" they told him.

"But I gained a slight revenge on Saturday [of the first week] when the weekly marks were posted," Neyland said. The maximum grade was 18.

"What was your grade, Mister Dumbjohn?" the upperclassmen demanded of Neyland.

"Seventeen-point-one, Sir," Neyland responded. That was equivalent to 95 percent.

"Wow! What are you, Mister, a math shark?" one of the upperclassmen asked.

"I didn't confide in them that the work assigned was, for me, a review of the first quarter math at Texas A&M," Neyland said. "At any rate, when the general transfer [from one section to another] took place three weeks later, I went up to the first section and thereafter vibrated between the first and second sections for the next three years."

English was the next most important subject at West Point. "However, I consider it first," Neyland said. "English came easy for me because of a little native talent and an excellent background of early training. Pure memory courses such as history, economics, drill regulations, and the like were much more difficult."

On September 1, 1912, Army's head football coach, Captain Ernest "Pot" Graves, issued the call for candidates to report for practice. A week later, he divided the plebes into two groups—some joining the varsity squad, others assigned to a freshman team. Neyland went to the varsity.

One of Army's starting halfbacks was a fellow named Dwight David Eisenhower. Eisenhower and Neyland developed a friendship that would last through two world wars and Eisenhower's eventual ascendance to the presidency of the United States.

Coach Graves's staff of seven assistants included two lieutenants—Dan Sultan and Joe Stilwell—who would play major roles in Neyland's life years later in faraway places called Kunming and Calcutta.

"Pot Graves was a brilliant man," Neyland said. "[He] had graduated third in his class, was widely recognized as an engineer officer, and was considered an authority on [football] line play." Graves later had a distinguished career as resident engineer for the United States Board of Engineers for Rivers and Harbors. But he was not successful as Army's head football coach. His 1912 team lost important games to Yale, Carlisle, and Navy.

Carlisle, an Indian school in Pennsylvania, easily defeated Army, 27-6. The star of the Carlisle team was Jim Thorpe, who a few months earlier had won gold medals in both the decathlon and the pentathlon in the 1912 Olympic Games at Stockholm, Sweden.

"Thorpe ran our team crazy," Neyland recalled of the 1912 game. "In retrospect, I do not recall ever seeing one individual so dominate an entire game by the sheer brilliance of his personal exploits." Thorpe that day ran for 238 net yards and scored two touchdowns.

At any rate, Neyland got into only two games, and only after Army had built an overwhelming lead. By his own evaluation, Neyland was "a very low-ranking member" of the Army varsity.

"We had nine pairs of ends on the varsity, and my classmate [Bill] Britton and I were the last pair on the totem pole. Whenever the cry went up for Neyland and Britton, there was murder to be done because we were expendables," Neyland said. "After that Carlisle game, Pot came to me and said, 'Neyland, how good is your spirit?' My heart sank, but I muttered, 'Good enough, I hope.'"

Coach Pot Graves looked Neyland eyeball to eyeball: "I mean how much physical punishment can you take or will you take for the good of the team?" Neyland said again he would do his best.

"Pot took me to the center of the field, directly on the 50-yard line and yelled for [Lelund] 'Bigun' Devore, our captain and all-American tackle the previous year. Devore was six-foot six-inches tall and weighed about 240 pounds. [He] had played a poor game against the Indians."

Carlisle had effectively blocked Devore most of the game. With Neyland standing there on the practice field, coach Graves ridiculed Devore. Neyland is going to "block your all-American behind all over the lot," Graves shouted at Devore. "I want blood—blood out of his nose, mouth, and ears."

"Naturally, Devore was blind with rage," Neyland said, "and I believe this blindness saved me. I could tell, from the way Devore set himself, which hand he would hit me with. And a little boxing training I had undergone the previous summer stood me in good stead. When Pot snapped the ball, I charged Devore—not all out, but warily—watching for his hand blow. When it came, I ducked or rolled my head to take it, not in the face but on the headgear. Or I simply blocked it with a forearm."

After about 10 plays, Neyland said it was a stalemate.

"True, I hadn't accomplished much in the way of blocking him out of the play," Neyland said. "But by the same token, he had not as yet drawn a single drop of blood. In exasperation, Pot screamed, 'Get out of there, Devore!"

Then, coach Graves lined up in front of Neyland. "Now charge me," he shouted at Neyland.

"Charging a captain in the U.S. Army was a little rich for my blood, and I moved to the attack with some reluctance," Neyland recalled. "Pot looked fat, but he belied his looks. Never before or since have I been hit that hard. Sky and Earth whirled as I felt myself gingerly for internal injury."

"Now get back in there and get me some blood," Graves shouted.

The two cadets, Neyland and Devore, lined up facing each other, and coach Graves resumed snapping the ball. "For the next fifteen or twenty minutes, Devore and I tussled inconclusively—me trying mostly to save my life," Neyland said.

Then, coach Graves wanted to demonstrate against Neyland again, and all hell broke loose.

"In a red haze, I broke through his arms, got my shoulder sunk deep in his protuberant belly, lifted him off his feet with a surge and carried him 10 yards straight down the field," Neyland said. "There I dumped him unceremoniously flat on his back and stood there glaring at him. Had I followed the momentary impulse, I would have kicked him a couple of times for good measure."

Neyland said the practice field incident involving Devore and Graves taught him a valuable lesson that served him well years later when he was coaching at Tennessee: "It is folly for a coach who has been out of active competition for several years to pit himself physically against young athletes in top condition."

Army's 1912 season ended with a 6-0 loss to Navy. The game taught Neyland another lesson—the value of a kicking game. "Offensively, the two teams were evenly matched," he said. "Navy's victory came by reason of some extraordinary punting. The kicks didn't look too good, but in an uncanny fashion they were placed to the side of our safetyman and just out of his reach. It seemed that they bounced on down the field for incredible distances. Each time the two teams traded punts, which was often, Navy gained yards on the exchange. The two field goals which provided the winning margin came as a result of such gains."

The 1912 Army football record was five victories and three defeats.

That December, after his freshman football season, Neyland became a candidate for the basketball team but realized, after two weeks, that he could contribute little to the squad and dropped off the team.

"While I had played basketball in high school, I had never had any coaching, and in truth not much aptitude for the game," he confessed. "I did some fooling around with gymnastics, the horizontal bar, the parallel bars, swinging rings and trapeze, and some boxing, but mostly I devoted time to studies and waiting for the spring and baseball season."

Neyland studied intensely that winter and raised his grades high enough to qualify for the first section in each of his subjects.

"However, after watching Joe Grant, Stan Rhinehart, Jeff Baldwin, and 'Hearse Horse' Henderson stand up and recite verbatim words, periods, and commas, visibly turning the pages mentally as they did so, I concluded that the air was too rarified for such as me and slid back into the third section where I belonged," he said.

Truthfulness on the part of all West Point cadets was assumed. Upperclassmen did not accuse a fellow cadet of lying without proof. The penalty for lying was dismissal from the academy. Neyland remembered the day an upperclassman challenged his veracity.

"At supper one day I was the 'gunner,' whose job it is to see that the waiter keeps all food platters adequately supplied and to divide desserts, such as pies, equally among the cadets present at the table," Neyland said. Before dividing a pie, he said, it was customary to inquire, "Does anyone wish to 'fall out' on pie, Sir?" To "fall out" on pie meant to decline accepting a piece.

At the table that evening was an upperclassman named Taylor, "who had been particularly nasty to me on many occasions, and I naturally disliked him with a passion," Neyland said. "To my question about the pie, his answer was a low mutter, and I misunderstood what he said. Tediously, I divided the pie into nine approximately equal parts and passed the portions to all except Mister Taylor.

Where's my pie?" Taylor asked gruffly.

"Sir, I understood you to say you were falling out on pie," Neyland replied.

"You did no such thing!" Taylor said sternly.

Neyland suddenly leaned across the table and, without the required "Sir," said to upperclassman Taylor: "Yes, by God, I did!"

Every cadet at the table became silent, and every eye turned toward Taylor.

"I didn't mean to doubt your word, Mister," Taylor said to Neyland after a momentary hesitation.

"Then watch your language hereafter!" Neyland said.

With that, the upperclassman stiffened. "I want to see you in your room after supper, Mister," he said to Neyland.

"I will be there," Neyland replied.

The cadets at the table resumed eating, and the conversation continued as if nothing unusual had just happened.

"After supper, I raced up to my fourth floor room, took off my blouse, moved the study tables and chairs back into the alcove and, when Taylor walked in, I was standing in the middle of a large cleared room," Neyland said. "He hesitated for a moment and then stepped forward.

"I would like to shake hands with you," Taylor said to Neyland.

"I accepted his hand, and we both grinned," Neyland said. "He looked around the room and chuckled."

"You were expecting to fight, weren't you?" Taylor said.

"I sure was," Neyland answered.

"Well," said Taylor, "let's get the tables and chairs back in here and chat a while."

Neyland and Taylor straightened the room, had their chat, and became good friends.

Winter mellowed into spring, and coach Sammy Strang assembled his players for the 1913 Army baseball season. Neyland began the season at first base, but a disabling injury to Louie Merillat, who had become the star pitcher, forced Strang to turn to the plebe from Greenville, Texas.

The previous August, when Neyland and the other plebe baseball candidates had reported for tryouts, Strang had seemed intrigued by the young Texan's appearance. He had said then that Neyland looked like a pitcher. Now, seven months later, Neyland indeed was about to be Army's pitcher.

Neyland's first game on the mound for the Cadets was against New York University. "NYU was not a very good team, and we won, 11-1," Neyland said. "I gave up four hits, walked one man, and struck out 12. Even though I knew they weren't very good, this helped my confidence quite a bit."

Strang knew a winner when he saw one, and young Bob Neyland was a winner.

"Sammy pitched me in the next six games. This was too strenuous for a young pitcher," Neyland said. "When we played a good Penn State team after three weeks of constant pitching, the inevitable happened. Their batters hit the ball all over the lot and we lost, 13-3. I guess Sammy realized he had been crowding me because he used Sandy Patch in the next game and alternated other pitchers so as to afford my arm a little more time to recover. Meanwhile, I played first base, second base, and centerfield."

As the season progressed, Neyland pitched a 2-0 victory over Notre Dame, then lost by the same score to Fordham. The Fordham game marked the last time Neyland would suffer a loss until two years later. After the Fordham defeat, Neyland began what turned out to be a 20-game winning streak.

"Deserving perhaps more than passing mention was the Army-Navy baseball game of 1913," Neyland said. "We played at West Point, and the game drew 15,000 spectators."

Two dignitaries showed up for the game—Lindley M. Garrison, the United States Secretary of War, and Josephus Daniels, Secretary of the Navy. They saw Neyland limit Navy to four hits and help his own cause by leading off the eighth inning with a single and scoring the tying run a few minutes later. Army scored again in the ninth to win, 2-1.

The Army-Navy game was played June 1, at the beginning of "hell week" when the groveling of the plebes reached a crescendo and was climaxed with the graduate parade.

Then, according to custom, the upperclassmen shake hands with all the plebes and say, "Glad to know you," as if they had been total strangers for the past 12 months.

At any rate, toward the end of hell week 1913, Colonel Clarence P. Townsley, the academy superintendent, gave a reception for Secretary Garrison. West Point officers, their wives, and many upperclassmen were invited to the reception.

"When an orderly arrived at my room in Cadet Barracks with the message that the 'Supe' desired my attendance at the reception, I went into a blue funk," Neyland confessed. Neyland assumed he was invited because he had been the winning pitcher in the Army-Navy game that Secretary Garrison had seen. Garrison did indeed want to congratulate Neyland personally.

"To proceed all by myself, an extremely bashful plebe from far away Greenville, Texas, up the long walk to the Supe's front door and into and through the receiving line was one of the worst ordeals I ever had to face," Neyland said. "Although the superintendent's two lovely daughters tried their best to tide me over, I was in an agony of embarrassment until I could manage to escape."

The 1912-13 academic year was history. The juniors the next year, the class of 1915, went on the ten-week furlough allowed at the end of two years at the academy. So the classes of 1914 (the seniors-to-be) and 1916 (the sophomores-to-be) and the incoming plebes, the class of 1917, comprised the summer camp cadre.

"The first year's hazing was difficult to take as well as interminable, yet, I endeavored to accept its inevitability and wait for the day of deliverance," Neyland said in reflection. "When plebe year finally ended, I counted up my blessings and found no reason for disappointment. I had managed to sweat out the constant nagging of the upperclassmen. I had made the football squad, had stood in the first ten in academics, had made the first team in baseball, pitched against the Navy, won my 'A,' and, in military, had been appointed senior corporal of my company."

CHAPTER 5

West Point 1913-14

Bob Neyland emerged from his first year at West Point ranked seventh academically in the plebe class and was appointed senior corporal in Company F. Senior corporal was the highest military rank a second-year cadet could achieve. So he was off to a good start in summer camp—but not for long.

"Since I wasn't interested at that time in dates, dances, and the like," Neyland said, "I stayed around the company area after duty hours and tried to look after the F Company plebes. This turned out to be my undoing."

One evening after the corps had marched back to camp from the mess hall, Neyland was in his tent changing from dress uniform into less formal attire normally worn at night by upperclassmen. There was a knock on his tent pole.

"Who is it?" Neyland asked.

"Mister Cecil, Sir," came the reply.

"Who are you?" Neyland asked.

"Sir, I'm from Company E. Mister Hudnutt told me to report to you." Cadet Dean Hudnutt was one of Neyland's classmates.

Neyland did not know why Cecil had been ordered to report to his tent, and he did not have the immediate inclination to find out why. Nature called.

"Okay," Neyland ordered Cecil, "pull your shoulders back and your chin in, and stay there till I return." Neyland then left the tent hurriedly, bound for the latrine.

When he returned from the latrine, Neyland encountered a commotion—a group of upperclassmen verbally chastising Cecil, who was then kept standing at attention for two hours. It was severe punishment, but Neyland did not interfere, because he, as an upperclassman, was expected to support the disciplinary actions imposed on plebes by other upperclassmen.

In August, toward the end of summer camp, a board of officers held an inquiry about the Cecil incident, and Neyland was among those questioned. Neyland and eight other upperclassmen were cited for "harassing" a plebe.

"I submitted a two-page explanation and justification stating definitely that I had harassed no one, that I had merely done my duty as I saw it—as had been done to me scores of times by cadet officers and non-coms," Neyland said.

"I heard nothing in reply. Meanwhile, football practice had begun on September 1. A new coach had been designated—Charles Dudley Daly, twice all-American at Harvard and West Point, one of the greatest coaches of all time, and certainly the finest gentleman of all." Daly would have instant success. The 1913 team won eight games, including 22-9 over Navy, and lost only to Notre Dame, 35-13, in what turned out to be a landmark game in the history of college football. On that historic afternoon, Notre Dame stunned the nation by attempting 17 passes and completing 13 for 243 yards. The forward pass, as a principal weapon, had arrived in college football.

Neyland had gained 20 pounds, weighing close to 180, and was the first team left end. But on September 10, without warning, the cadet adjutant announced: "For harassing a fourth classman in violation of Section 5, Paragraph 152, Regulations of the United States Military Academy, the following named cadets are reduced to the grade of privates, confined to barracks, the area of the barracks, and the gymnasium until April 10, 1914, and will serve punishment tours at the usually prescribed hours." The name of Cadet Corporal Robert R. Neyland was on the list.

To do a punishment tour, called a "slug," a cadet marched back and forth in the barracks quadrangle—in full uniform, with rifle, and always in rigid posture. For seven months, the young Texan marched on what West Pointers called the "bull ring," an area behind the barracks. "I had to walk up and down the space in front of our barracks on Wednesday and Saturday afternoons—which are our only afternoons off—from September 10 [1913] to April 10 [1914]," Neyland said.

"I missed the whole [1913] football season, three weeks of the [1914] baseball season, and walked over 500 miles for this alleged offense," Neyland said.

"This harsh and, to my mind, completely unjust punishment—for doing what I thought was my duty and which had been done to me innumerable times when I was a plebe—was never comprehensible to me," Neyland said. "More than 40 years later, I still hold a deep and abiding resentment." In fact, Neyland described his feeling toward the academy superintendent, the head of the hazing board, and the commandant of cadets as "bitter contempt."

In addition to Neyland, each of the other cadets "convicted" of harassing Cecil was given seven months confinement and approximately 500 miles in the bull ring—a combined total of five years and three months, plus 4,500 miles.

"Mister Cecil was found deficient in math and was discharged from the academy January 1, 1914. Nine upperclass cadets were still serving punishment long after his departure," Neyland said. "My classmate of Company E, Dean Hudnutt, who had sent Mister Cecil to my tent, escaped scot free—since he had taken no part in the 'harassment.'"

Despite his bitterness at what he considered a gross injustice, Neyland said the results of the experience were beneficial.

"I am sure that the 500-mile walk did not harm me physically, even though it ruined walking for me forever as a pleasant exercise. Moreover, when I was later in positions of command and had to discipline military personnel, I remembered how I felt as a recipient of arbitrary and unjust punishment, and [I] tended to lean backward when carrying out such responsibilities. Finally, since I was permitted to use the gym during the winter afternoons, I took the opportunity to turn out for boxing. This brought me into immediate close contact with another remarkable personality, the boxing and wrestling coach, Tom Jenkins."

Until then, Neyland had never worn a pair of boxing gloves. Classmates made fun of his first pugilistic efforts, but he promised them: "I'll win the heavyweight championship before I leave here."

Tom Jenkins was a Welshman who had helped train heavyweight boxing champions Jim Corbett, Bob Fitzsimmons, and Jim Jeffries. He was about 5-foot-10, and, although he weighed about 280 pounds, was in good physical condition. Jenkins could manhandle three cadets in the ring at one time and frequently sparred with cadet boxers.

"He knew as much about boxing and wrestling as any man alive," Neyland said. "Also, he was honest, sincere, and took a deep personal interest in any cadet who appreciated his coaching. I thought the world of him. He was, in fact, one of the four men who most vitally affected my life in my cadet days—the other three being Charlie Daly, Sammy Strang, and Tom Hammond, [football ends coach]."

Neyland asked Jenkins to teach him the art of boxing.

"That I will, son, and you'll do well as long as you know you're ignorant," Jenkins replied in his heavy Welsh accent. "Now," he said, beginning Neyland's first lesson, "any fool can hit with his right hand. You learn the left."

"For several months he raised merry hell with me every time I even looked like I wanted to hit him with a right," Neyland said. "Hour upon hour I practiced the left jab, left hook, left swing, left feint, all with the left arm almost fully extended. In my room at night I used a four-pound dumbbell to build up strength in my left hand and arm. At the end of four months I was amazed to find that I had increased the circumference of my left forearm by one inch and my biceps by an inch and one-half."

The West Point boxing championship tournament of 1914 was held in March. Bob Neyland advanced to the championship finals and won a decision over Freddy Boyer for the heavyweight title. He successfully defended the West Point heavyweight championship in 1915 and 1916.

"Being a sort of 'hit and run' boxer, I had never hit anybody as hard as I could. Late in the spring of 1916, Coach Jenkins came into the boxing room, and I asked him to spar a few rounds," Neyland said. "The first opportunity I had, I threw a left hook at Tom's jaw with all the power I could summon. The timing was perfect and [the] blow landed on the jaw angle with a force that numbed my arm, from knuckles to shoulder. I waited for Tom to drop, but as far as I could tell it didn't faze him at all."

Neyland and Jenkins sparred a few more minutes, then the coach excused himself and left the room.

"I was trying to flex the numbed muscles of my arm and wondering what in the world would prevail against a man who could take your best Sunday punch without blinking an eye," Neyland said.

About then, someone ran into the boxing room and asked what had happened to Jenkins.

"I laid a left hook on his chin, but as far as I could tell he never felt it," Neyland replied.

"Well," said the cadet, "I saw him in the shower and he was feeling his jaw and moving it from side to side, muttering, 'That damn Neyland damn near broke my jaw.'" Neyland had hurt his coach, but the old Welshman was not about to admit it.

Years later, reflecting on that incident and his entire West Point boxing career, Neyland expressed mixed emotions about the sport.

"I know that it did a lot for me—sharpened my reflexes, gave me greatly increased confidence, and helped me in other ways. But, as I [have] said before, I was a 'hit-and-get-away' type. I disliked the idea of taking a punch in order to give one. On the contrary, most of the collegiate boxing I had occasion to observe since World War I was in the nature of a slug fest—a 'take-it and dish-it-out' carnival. In such contests, there is grave danger that one or both contestants may receive lasting brain damage. Actually, I have observed several boys who became punch-drunk as a result. Finally, I came to the conclusion that the bad aspects [of boxing] outweighed the good and recommended to the athletic board at Tennessee, where I was then serving as director of athletics, that boxing be dropped from our intercollegiate sport program."

Although still doing a punishment tour for the hazing incident the previous summer, Neyland was released from barracks confinement on April 10 and pitched his first game of the season the next day against Colgate. It was a no-hitter.

Neyland faced only 30 Colgate batters. He struck out 11 and walked only two. He retired the side, 1-2-3, in the first, third, fifth, sixth, eighth, and ninth innings. Remarkably, the following day he hurled another no-hitter against Colgate and won his remaining three games of the season. New York newspapers headlined the achievement. The *Tribune* said: "Neyland Pitches a No-Hit, No-Run Game." The *Times* declared: "Easter Eggs for Colgate."

Army, with Neyland on the mound, concluded its 1914 baseball campaign against Navy at Annapolis. Neyland allowed Navy only three hits and struck out eight. The *Washington Post*, referring to Neyland, said the "big Army lad, the Walter Johnson of service baseball, had the midshipmen at his mercy." Through eight innings, Navy had only one hit. Army won, 8-2, and Neyland extended the winning streak he started in 1913 to 11—his won-lost record for the year was eight wins and no losses.

But Neyland's second year at West Point had tested his patience, his durability, and his maturity. He had been knocked off the football team because of the hazing incident and subsequent punishment tour. He also had missed part of the baseball season and had dropped from seventh to 24th in academic standing in his class.

"On the other side of the ledger," he said, "I won the heavyweight boxing championship and won all the baseball games I pitched, including the Navy game at Annapolis. Perhaps this record was not [one] to be ashamed of, but I nursed a deep sense of injustice as our class departed on furlough."

CHAPTER 6

West Point 1914-15

Before the summer of 1914 ended, Germany would be at war with France, Russia, Japan, and Great Britain, and the newly completed Panama Canal would be opened to shipping.

When he had first reported to West Point in June 1912, Bob Neyland had traveled by railroad from Greenville to Texarkana to St. Louis to New York City, then up the Hudson to West Point. But now, for his return trip to Texas—on his 1914 summer furlough—Neyland decided to take an ocean steamer from New York to New Orleans, and then by rail to Greenville.

"I must admit that this six-day trip was not an unalloyed pleasure," he said. "I got seasick before we were well out of New York Harbor and didn't get cured until the ship had turned the tip of Florida and entered the Gulf of Mexico."

During the previous winter, Neyland had received a letter from his father. It seems Cadet Neyland's brother, Mayo, four years younger, had put on weight and height, had been taking boxing lessons, and intended to repay his older brother for some earlier childhood lickings.

"I carefully refrained from reporting any participation in boxing at West Point," Bob said. "Of course, Dad couldn't wait to get the boxing gloves on us and staged the bout in our back yard. Mayo, who was two inches taller and 15 pounds heavier, possessed at most a very rudimentary knowledge of the pugilistic science, and it was ludicrously easy for me to avoid his punches."

By using a crisp jab and fancy footwork in the large backyard area they had roped off for a ring, the West Point heavyweight champ kept his younger brother off balance and swinging wildly.

"Dad laughed till his sides split," Neyland recalled. "After we decided to call it a day, I took my heavyweight championship gold medal out of my pocket and showed it to them."

Apparently unimpressed and convinced he could handle his older brother in a smaller "ring," Mayo challenged Bob to another bout in a vacant upstairs bedroom.

"The first thing I did was to step into a clinch and lock Mayo's arms," Bob said. "I just walked him around in a narrow circle, cuffing him with both hands on the face and body, and holding, blocking, and moving inside every punch he tried. Dad laughed 'till the tears came, then sat on the floor hugging his knees and rocking with mirth."

"I declare, Mayo," the father said to the younger brother, "if you could get Robert into that little clothes closet there, I believe you'd beat him to death."

Neyland had been home on furlough only a short time when he started receiving long-distance phone calls from small-town, pitcher-hungry, baseball teams all over northeast Texas.

"Since I had rather play than eat, I took as many engagements as I felt like filling, charging in each case what the traffic would bear. My stipend varied from $5 and expenses up to $50 and expenses, averaging about $25 per game. This meant I could earn about $250 during the summer, which always came in handy in our family."

The manager of the team at Forney, a little town on the eastern outskirts of Dallas, invited Neyland to play. When Bob got to the game site, he saw a baseball diamond marked off in an oat field. The distances between the bases and between home plate and the pitcher's mound had been laid out "by guess and by gosh," Neyland said.

When Neyland asked about the spot from which he was to pitch, he was told to "step it off and mark the spot." So he did—and got a little greedy. Instead of stepping off the regular 60 feet, six inches from home plate, Neyland stopped after 54 feet. And when the game started, he fired nothing but fast balls which, at that close range, seemed to the opposing batters like bullets whizzing past. Finally, the suspicious umpire marked a new distance to the mound.

"I pitched the rest of the game from what I estimated as approximately 70 feet, and never before or since have I worked so hard for so little. The final score was 9-8 in our favor, but I have always believed that I severely strained my pitching arm. It's certain that I never again seemed to get as much on the ball."

When his ten-week furlough ended Bob Neyland returned to New York for his third year at West Point.

The 1914 football season was Charles Daly's second as head coach. His assistants were former head coach Pot Graves, Dan Sultan, Joe Stilwell, Tom Hammond, and Dan Pullen.

"Plenty of brains and ability there, but tops in every respect was the head man himself, Charles Dudley Daly," Neyland said. "Smart, energetic, and dynamic, he had the knack of organizing practice, making best use of his assistants, and inspiring his players who respected, admired, and loved him. I know of only one other man, Douglas MacArthur, who so profoundly influenced my thoughts and actions."

When Neyland reported for practice in September 1914, he found himself facing an immediate handicap. Although 20 pounds heavier and stronger and faster than when he had been a plebe two years earlier, Neyland had not played in 1913 and was unfamiliar with the offensive and defensive systems Daly had installed that year.

"It was almost mid-season before I caught up, but I did earn a starting berth then and played practically all of each of the games from then on," he said. "We had a very good team that year—beating Notre Dame and Navy."

Even though unfamiliar with the offense, Neyland caught two touchdown passes in the opening game, a 49-0 victory over Stevens Institute. But Neyland, plagued by some nagging injuries, missed the next four games—victories over Rutgers, 13-0, Colgate, 21-7, Holy Cross, 14-0, and Villanova, 41-0.

Then came the big game with Notre Dame, boasting a 4-1 record, its only loss against powerful Yale. Neyland played well against Notre Dame, offensively and defensively. Army won, 20-7.

Army victories over Maine, 28-0, and Springfield, 14-7, set the stage for the season finale against rival Navy at Philadelphia. Against Springfield, Neyland took a pass from Vernon Prichard for a 70-yard play down to the five-yard line, setting up an Army touchdown.

In the Navy game, with the Army leading only 2-0 in the second quarter, Neyland recovered a Navy fumble at the Midshipman 20-yard line. Prichard passed to Merillat for the first touchdown of the game. Army scored again in the second quarter and capped the scoring with a touchdown in the fourth quarter. Final: Army 20, Navy 0.

Three starters in that Navy game were Neyland and Bill Britton at ends, Paul Parker at tackle. The three were classmates, and a decade after graduation from West Point they would be reunited on the football coaching staff at the University of Tennessee.

Army's 1914 won-lost record was 9-0, and the Cadets were named the Helms Athletic Foundation collegiate national champions. By the time Neyland again tasted the sweetness of a national title—37 years later—he had gone overseas in two world wars, had risen to the rank of brigadier general, and had built a college football dynasty.

During the cold winter months of 1915, Neyland devoted himself to his studies and to boxing. He again won the heavyweight boxing title at the academy. He had become a champion in a sport he learned only by an accident of circumstance.

Jack Johnson, a powerfully built black man, was the world heavyweight champion in 1915. He had won the title with a 15th-round knockout of Jim Jeffries in Reno, Nevada. Until Johnson, the heavyweight title had been held by white boxers—and white boxing fans yearned for a "white hope" to take the championship from Johnson.

Asked by a reporter if he had any thought about becoming a "white hope," Neyland quickly replied: "I must confess that I never had any thoughts along those lines, and merely took up the sport because I like it as a means of exercise." Besides, in sports, his first love still was baseball. And he was eager for the 1915 season to begin.

Neyland won his first seven games of 1915 without giving up an earned run. In the eighth game, against Georgetown on May 1, Neyland helped his own cause with a run-producing triple. Bill Britton chipped in a three-run homer, and Omar Bradley helped out with a double. Neyland struck out eight and walked only three. Army won, 11-4. It was Neyland's 19th consecutive victory.

One week later, Neyland made West Point history against visiting Washington and Lee University. Neyland recorded his 20th consecutive pitching victory. New York sportswriters began comparing him to Rube Marquard, the future Hall of Fame pitcher who in 1912 had won 19 straight en route to a 26-win season. "Neyland breaks Marquard record," they said.

W&L batters discovered what so many other teams had learned (and what his later gridiron opponents would expect)—Neyland would not allow his own mistakes to hurt his chance for a victory. Neyland's control was his strength. He could move the fast ball up or down, inside or out, and he could break the curve exactly where he wanted it. W&L that day scattered nine hits and scored five runs, but Neyland struck out 12 and walked only one. Meanwhile, Army's heavy-hitting lineup got 16 hits and scored nine runs, enough for the team's 12th straight win and Neyland's 20th. The 1915 Army team was developing into one of the best in college baseball.

"Don't give me too much credit for whipping these boys into shape," Army coach Sammy Strang told the *New York Evening World*. "They are the easiest men to train that I ever saw in my life. A coach can get more results out of a squad of Army men in ten days than he could get out of ordinary young fellows in two months."

Many modern coaches dislike dealing with sportswriters, but Strang took them in stride and in fact enjoyed an occasional encounter.

"We haven't been beaten this year yet, and Neyland hasn't lost a game since 1913, but just as soon as you fellows come around looking for interviews, it means that defeat is on its way," Strang told a group of reporters.

About that time, Neyland came toward them from the barracks, and Strang shouted: "Throw out your chest, Bob. You're going to get your name in the papers again."

"Is Neyland a really great pitcher?" a reporter asked Strang.

"You bet he is," the coach replied. "That boy would make good in any company. He has what we call the ballplayer's instinct—knows just when to extend his arm and when to let it rest. He is a wonderful young fellow."

Indeed, Neyland's mounting reputation as an all-around great athlete brought a growing stream of reporters to West Point, 40 miles up the Hudson River from New York City.

"In Cadet Robert R. Neyland, West Point possesses the most remarkable athlete that ever represented a college," a story in the *New York Evening World* said. "The record achieved by Neyland in the pitcher's box is the greatest ever made." Another New York newspaper said: "Neyland could command almost any salary he might desire to sign a contract with one of the big league clubs." A *Houston Post* headline proclaimed: "Neyland, Army Star, May Go to the Big League."

John McGraw, manager of the New York Giants, kept a sharp eye on Neyland's progress. McGraw reportedly offered Neyland the astronomical sum of $5,000 to sign with the Giants. The Boston Red Sox, who had a young pitcher named George Herman "Babe" Ruth, expressed interest in Neyland, as did the Detroit Tigers and the Philadelphia Phillies. But Neyland was dedicated to a military career. And despite the seven-month punishment tour for the hazing of plebe Cecil, Neyland genuinely liked life at the academy.

Late in the 1915 season, a reporter for the *New York Evening World* newspaper asked Neyland if he would consider professional baseball.

"I might if the offer were sufficient," Neyland replied. "It would take a lot of money to tempt me to leave the army—as much as I like baseball."

Because of his desire for a military career, Neyland regarded baseball as an extreme gamble.

"I might go out tomorrow and sign up with the big leagues for a year," he told the reporter. "In the very first game, I might break or strain my arm, and then where would I be? I couldn't go back to the army and my goose would be cooked as far as the diamond is concerned. No sir! They can't get me unless it is on a [long-] term contract, and even then they can't ensnare me until I graduate from West Point next year."

There was more. Bob Neyland was doing well in school. In the spring of 1915, he estimated he was ranked academically about 15th in his class of 125.

"I have fond hopes of landing in the Engineering Corps and then remaining in the army working for Uncle Sam the rest of my life," Neyland told a New York reporter.

Neyland's 20-game winning streak ended abruptly against Fordham.

"I lost in grand style," Neyland said. "Fordham gave us a lacing I'll never forget. As I recall, I gave up 18 hits, struck out nine, walked seven, and hit three batters. They just pounded everything I threw all over the lot and beat us, 16-3."

But a few days later at West Point, Neyland redeemed himself when Army climaxed its 19-2 season with a 6-5 victory over Navy. Neyland said Army won because the fleet-footed Louie Merillat made "one of the greatest plays I have ever seen in baseball." With the bases loaded and no outs, Merillat made a spectacular running catch of a long drive, then turned and threw a strike to third base to catch the runner trying to advance. Only one run scored on the play and Neyland held on for the narrow victory.

By June 1915, the end of his third year, Neyland had helped the football team go undefeated in nine games. He had beaten Navy in baseball for a third straight time, had been voted (in a *Vanity Fair* magazine poll) the number one pitcher in college baseball, and had dropped to 34th academically in a class of 125. "Surely not impressive," he said, "but still creditable by some standards."

CHAPTER 7

West Point 1915-16

Since becoming Army's head football coach in 1913, Charlie Daly's teams had compiled a 17-1 record. The 1915 season began with Neyland at quarterback against Holy Cross, but he was injured and had to leave the game with it tied, 14-14, ultimately the final score. Because of the injury, Neyland missed the second game, a 22-0 win over Pittsburgh, but returned in time to feel the sting of a 13-0 loss to Colgate.

Neyland was moved back to end for the Georgetown game, a near-brawl from which three players were ejected. It was so rough, in fact, that it was never completed. With only a minute or two left and Army leading 10-0, Army reserves entered the game. Among them was a cadet who immediately squared off against a Georgetown player, triggering a free-for-all. The referees blew the whistle and declared the game history.

The Cadets then went on a two-game skid, something that had not happened to an Army team since 1906. The losses were to Villanova, 16-13, and Notre Dame, 7-0. Neyland was injured again in the Notre Dame game and was held out of the victories over Maine, 24-0, and Springfield, 17-7, the next two weeks. A heavy fog shrouded the Polo Grounds on the afternoon of November 27, and a crowd estimated at 40,000 braved a light drizzle to see the annual Army-Navy game. The series was even— nine victories each and one tie. Army had won the two previous years. The box seats became a "who's who" of Washington and New York societies.

President Woodrow Wilson and his fiancee were there with Secretary of State Robert T. Lansing, Treasury Secretary William G. McAdoo, and other cabinet members and their wives. The entourage also included members of the United States Senate and House and ranking army and navy brass. President Wilson—in top hat, cutaway coat, and gray trousers—sat on Navy's side the first half and Army's after intermission.

Neyland made the first big play of the game—tackling a Navy punt returner and causing a fumble that Army recovered at the Midshipmen five-yard line.

"The Navy's safetyman raised his arms over his head to catch the ball," Neyland recalled. "Coming from about 30 yards away, I could see that I had a chance to tackle [him] just as the ball touched his hands. I crowded on all the speed I could summon and shifted my aim from his thighs to his solar plexus," Neyland said. "I struck him a terrific blow on the soft part of his body, just above the belt, and drove him clear over the goal line. The ball popped out of his hands, and our [William] Redfield recovered on the five." Four plays later, Elmer Oliphant scored the first touchdown and kicked the extra point. Late in the second quarter, Neyland caught a long pass from Oliphant, but Navy intercepted Army's next aerial. Neyland threw a Navy back for a five-yard loss, and the first half ended seconds later. While President Wilson and the other dignitaries endured the dampness and cold of the Polo Grounds, the two teams warmed themselves in the dressing rooms and changed into clean, dry uniforms.

Oliphant scored Army's second touchdown and extra point early in the third quarter, and Navy received the kickoff.

"Covering from the left, I thought I saw another chance to knock the runner loose from the ball," Neyland said. "I must have miscalculated, because I got knocked unconscious and finished the game on the sidelines. This was my last play in Army football."

A New York paper reported it the next morning: "While his ten teammates and the Army mule . . . were guests of 2,000 football enthusiasts at a dinner in the Hotel Astor last night, Bobby Neyland, the end who was knocked out of the game in the third quarter, twisted and turned in his bed five floors above, suffering from a slight fracture of the skull."

"Would you mind telling me what year this is?" the newspaper said Neyland asked after waking up. "When do we play the Navy?"

"You played the Navy this afternoon and beat them, 14-0," a doctor told him.

"Oh! And I wanted to play in that game," Neyland said.

Neyland's condition was not serious, but doctors kept him in bed for observation that night, just to be certain. Meanwhile, his cadet teammates took a walking tour of the glittering lights of Broadway.

At West Point, in the winter of 1916, Neyland won the heavyweight boxing championship at the academy for the third consecutive year, kept battling the books, and, like other cadets, kept an eye on the daily news reports on the mounting war in Europe and the insurrection in Mexico.

His teammates elected Bob Neyland captain of the 1916 baseball team. He missed two weeks during mid-season when a horse kicked him on the right leg during a cavalry drill, but nothing could keep him from pitching his fourth and final game against Navy on May 27 at Annapolis.

"In our half of the first inning, [Navy's pitcher] hit me squarely behind the ear with a terrific fast ball, knocking me colder than the proverbial cucumber," Neyland said. The team trainer and physician carried Neyland behind the grandstands to revive him and determine whether he could continue in the game.

There was a considerable delay. Some Navy fans demanded that the game continue without Neyland. Some claim Army's coach refused to resume play until Neyland's condition was determined. Finally, Neyland reappeared and took the mound to pitch the bottom half of the first inning.

"I could not see the batter or catcher, other than as blurs, and I could not see my catcher's signals," Neyland said. "I could see one finger [fast ball], but couldn't see two fingers [curve ball]. Consequently, twice during that half of the first, two shoulder-high fast balls sailed over the surprised catcher's glove and back against the wire screen."

After that, Neyland and the catcher met halfway between home and the pitcher's mound on every pitch until Neyland's vision cleared in the sixth inning. After a somewhat shaky start, he settled down and pitched a five-hit, ten-strikeout game, and Army won, 13-3.

"The victory was the triumph of Neyland's career as an athlete at West Point," said a Washington newspaper. Neyland's four wins over Navy equaled the record by Robert Hyatt, West Point class of 1912. Sammy Strang used only two pitchers in eight consecutive games against Navy and won all of them.

A week later, in a letter to the West Point commandant of cadets, Secretary of War Newton D. Baker praised Neyland's performance against Navy: "Would you kindly express to the pitcher on the Academy baseball team my admiration for his courage and determination. I saw the game at Annapolis and was much pleased by his pluck."

At the close of his fourth year at West Point, Neyland found himself beset by regrets despite his athletic accomplishments. "True, I had again made the first team in football, again participated in a [football] victory over Navy, again repeated in boxing, and pitched in a fourth straight win over Navy. Meanwhile, the Army Athletic Council had seen fit to split the award for the best athlete in the graduating class between W. H. Britton and me. But again I slipped a few files in class [academic] standing and felt certain it was hopeless to expect to make the Engineers."

Assuming his academic record would keep him from being assigned to the Corps of Engineers, Neyland ordered all of his officer uniforms in the red stripes of the Field Artillery. But, unknown to him, the army had decided to assign to the Corps of Engineers an unusually large number of 1916 graduates—and Bob Neyland was one of them.

"I was one of the few cadets who thoroughly enjoyed West Point," Neyland said. "There was then, and probably is now, a cult which flagellated themselves with gloomy epithets on cadet life and a 'sourball' attitude concerning all its phases.

"While I won't pretend that I especially liked close-order drill in the hot sun or standing at 'Parade Arms' with the sweat running off my rump and knees, to me these things were necessary evils to be taken in stride. On the other hand, the close association with classmates and friends, the high and effervescent spirit of the corps, and the continual excitement of athletic competition more than counter-balanced the adverse aspects met in our daily routine.

"Then, too, there was always a certain pride and sentiment attached to being a part of that elite corps with its everlasting traditions of patriotic service. There was never a single time the band played the 'Star Spangled Banner' that cold chills didn't chase up and down my spine. And when, at graduation parade, our class stood and saluted as the remainder of the corps passed in review, there were very real tears in my eyes."

Beneath Bob Neyland's picture in the 1916 West Point yearbook, the *Howitzer,* is a prediction: "If this man ever directs his energies toward a military career, he will be a great general."

But first, he had to be a second lieutenant.

CHAPTER 8

Travels of a Young Army Officer

1916-21

World War I, which had begun in Europe in August 1914, continued into 1916—the Central Powers (Germany, Austria-Hungary, Turkey, and Bulgaria) against the Allies (Great Britain, France, Russia, Belgium, Serbia, Montenegro, Japan, and Italy). Although the United States officially remained neutral in 1916, popular sentiment began shifting gradually against the Central Powers after the sinking of the Lusitania and the German introduction of poison gas.

By July 1, soon after graduation from West Point, Bob Neyland was promoted to first lieutenant. Then, after a few weeks at home with his family in Greenville, he received his marching orders—first to Brownsville, Texas, and eight months with the First Engineers, Company A, then to Washington, D.C., where the First Engineers spent four months getting additional unit training, anticipating that the United States would enter into the war.

Two events in March 1917 stunned the world—the revolution in Russia and the sinking of three American ships by the Germans. Saying the world "must be made safe for democracy," President Woodrow Wilson asked Congress for and got a declaration of war. The first American division was sent to France in June, and General John J. Pershing was made commander of the American Expeditionary Forces fighting alongside the Allies in France. Units of the Army Corps of Engineers were among the first American army units in France. By now a captain, Bob Neyland was among the first engineers there. They constructed docks for unloading supply and troop ships, built depots and warehouses for assembling and storing supplies, and laid railroad tracks on which trains could move the war material to the front line.

Neyland was an engineering company commander at Gondrecourt le Chateau, at the southern tip of the Argonne Forest, only 55 miles south of Verdun and within earshot of artillery shells exploding behind the front lines. A few months later he was transferred as an instructor to the First Corps Engineering School at Langres, and there he was given a temporary promotion to the rank of major. The school at Langres was one of several where troops just arriving in France were acquainted with special combat problems they would encounter, such as trench warfare, bad sanitation, and distribution of supplies to the front.

As each new assignment came his way, Neyland received "excellent" or "superior" grades on his efficiency reports. But it rankled Neyland a bit that he had been only on the fringes of a combat zone, not actually in the front lines. In Neyland's mind, soldiering meant combat, and he had not really been in the midst of the fighting.

By the summer of 1918, the tide of battle had turned against the Central Powers, and the two sides began negotiating an end to the fighting. On September 1, prior to the November armistice, Neyland received orders to sail for home. His next assignment: Fort Bliss, just outside El Paso, Texas, on the Rio Grande.

In 1913, Pancho Villa, an ex-cattle rustler and Mexican revolutionary leader, mobilized a well-fed, well-equipped army of small ranchers, unemployed workers, and cowboys to take de facto control of northern Mexico. The government in power at the time was headed by General Victoriano Huerta, but he was challenged by Emiliano Zapata, the leader of landless peasants in the south; by Venustiano Carranza, a wealthy landowner from a northern province bordering Texas; and by Villa.

By mid-1914, Huerta had resigned, and the forces that had overthrown him gathered to discuss a possible coalition government. But elitist Carranza, suspicious of the agrarian origins of the Zapata and Villa forces, withdrew from the negotiations and established his own government. Carranza's army decisively defeated Villa in 1915, and Villa, no longer a national threat, retreated to the northern state of Chihuahua—from time to time crossing the border into New Mexico and Texas, looting and killing in retaliation for U.S. recognition of the Carranza government.

Villa raided the border town of Columbus, New Mexico, 70 miles due west of El Paso, and killed 17 persons. The United States sent General Pershing with 15,000 troops into Mexico in pursuit of Villa, and President Wilson called out 150,000 militia and stationed them along the border. Pershing overtook Villa on April 12, but Villa escaped during the battle. After 11 months of fruitless search for the outlaw, Pershing's army returned to the United States.

Major Neyland reported to Camp Courchesne, part of the Fort Bliss complex, on October 4, 1918, and a few months later took command of the Eighth Engineers (Mounted). Except for 210-mile training marches to Deming and Cloudcroft, New Mexico, the work of his unit until mid-1919 was routine—building bridges and roads and maintaining the international bridges spanning the Rio Grande.

But on Saturday, June 14, Villa sent a message to the Associated Press office in El Paso, urging Carranza officials and military units in Juarez to surrender and receive amnesty or to face attack. A few hours later, Villa broke camp and led his column of mounted troops to the mesa overlooking the green valley of Juarez.

At 12:10 a.m., Sunday, the "Villista" forces attacked the city. Within three hours, Villa troops were charging down the main street. Residents of the city—men, women, and children—hurried with armloads of belongings across the international bridge into El Paso.

Meanwhile, Neyland's Eighth Engineers and the Ninth Engineers from Camp Courchesne were thrown into action in advance of the 24th Infantry and regiments of the Fifth and Seventh Cavalries and a battalion of the 82nd Artillery. The Seventh crossed the Rio Grande on a pontoon bridge built by Neyland's Eighth Engineers who then followed the cavalry in an attack on Villa's camp west of the city. The Ninth Engineers built other temporary bridges over which other units crossed the border. The operation was so effective that approximately 3,600 American troops were on Mexican soil within 10 minutes after receiving orders from Brigadier General James G. Erwin to cross the river.

Erwin quickly issued a dispatch saying he had sent his forces across the border to prevent indiscriminate firing into El Paso by rebel soldiers, endangering the lives of Americans. "As soon as the Villistas have been dispersed and the safety of the citizens of El Paso has been assured, the troops of my command will be withdrawn to the American side of the border."

The Villista casualties numbered an estimated 50 dead. Remarkably, fewer than a dozen civilians were killed or wounded during the battle. The American military units suffered only two casualties, two enlisted men wounded by gunfire.

The balance of Villa's army fled—some in small bands and one 200-man mounted column that rode into the hills southwest of Juarez. American cavalry troops pursued, but Villa escaped. By Tuesday morning, 24 hours after crossing the pontoon bridges into Mexico, the American forces were back on the Texas side of the border.

About four months after the Juarez battle, American consular agent William O. Jenkins was kidnapped and jailed in the city of Puebla, 50 miles east of Mexico City. When the U.S. government demanded his release, the Carranza government balked and tensions flared on both sides. Talk of war began to circulate.

U.S. companies operating in Mexico told their representatives to be prepared to return home on short notice. The Texas governor ordered the Texas Rangers to stand ready along the border. Last, but not least, Major General Joseph T. Dickman moved 12 regiments—two cavalry, two artillery, two engineers, and six infantry—into position along the border. The force of American regulars ready to engage in combat with the Mexicans totaled 60,000 men.

The November 30 issue of the *New York Times* carried an eight-column story about the various units deployed by General Dickman.

"One of West Point's famous athletes is the commanding officer of the 8th Engineers," the *Times* said. "He is Major Robert R. Neyland, a Texan, who from 1912 to 1916 was the star of the West Point football and baseball teams. Neyland is only 27 years of age, and yet he is the senior engineer commander now on the border."

The *Times* noted that Neyland and Major Layson E. Atkins, commander of the Ninth Engineers at El Paso, "are the two youngest regimental commanders in the United States Army."

In the face of threatened military action, the Carranza government released Jenkins on December 4, but the violence against Americans in Mexico continued until General Alvaro Abregon overthrew Carranza and stabilized the country.

Also in December 1919, Neyland received notification that his commanding officer had recommended his demotion to captain from the temporary rank of major. Neyland responded with a memorandum to officers up the chain of command.

He said his immediate superior, a Colonel Erwin, "stated that he had not a criticism to make of me other than that I was too young to be a major. He did not recommend that I be relieved from command of the Eighth Engineers, nor did he express himself as dissatisfied with my work, but merely recommended my demotion and left me to perform the same duties as before, but with decreased rank and prestige of the lower grade. This action is thought to be inconsistent and unjust."

But Neyland's appeal did not change the decision, and he found himself once more a captain. Demotion in those days was not unusual for young officers who had received "temporary" battlefield promotions during the war in Europe. Neyland was reduced to a company commander and, for the first time in his army career, he received an unfavorable fitness report. The man who had succeeded him as regimental commander of the Eighth Engineers, Lieutenant Colonel A. E. Waldron, gave Neyland a "below average" rating for leadership, tact, and handling men.

"This officer's manner in speaking to others, especially enlisted men, is overbearing and irritating," Waldron's report said. "Neither officers nor enlisted men seem to like him. It is for this reason that I would prefer not to have him in the organization."

Within days, Neyland was reassigned to the Massachusetts Institute of Technology in Boston and told to further his education there for one year. So he returned to the classroom as a post-graduate student at MIT and in June 1921 received a bachelor of science degree in civil engineering.

CHAPTER 9

Duty, Honor, Marriage

1921-25

The year at MIT had been a cool-down period for Bob Neyland. In a little less than five years, he had gone from the United States Military Academy at West Point to posts at Brownsville, Texas; Washington, D.C.; Gondrecourt and Langres, France; El Paso, Texas; and Boston, Massachusetts. He had seen war in Europe and near-war along the Texas-Mexico border.

Then, unexpectedly, in the summer of 1921 he received orders to report to West Point. He was excited. He had loved his four years at West Point. He was going back, going home—this time with a fresh promotion from captain to major, and this time as assistant adjutant and aide-de-camp to the superintendent of the academy, Brigadier General Douglas MacArthur, the Rainbow Division hero of World War I.

The academy was in disarray in 1919 when MacArthur was asked by Army Chief of Staff Peyton C. March to become superintendent. MacArthur, who had been promoted to brigadier general in France during World War I, at first declined, saying he was a soldier, not an educator. In the MacArthur biography, *American Caesar*, author William Manchester described March's method of persuading MacArthur to become superintendent.

"If he [MacArthur] agreed to do it," Manchester wrote, "he would be confirmed as a brigadier general in the regular army; if he refused, he would revert to his pre-war rank of major. He accepted."

One of March's chief concerns about West Point was the tradition of hazing. He wanted it stopped. A plebe who had been subjected to severe hazing had shot himself on New Year's Day. Congress demanded reforms at the academy. March also wanted the curriculum updated and the military instruction modernized. In MacArthur, he saw an officer with charisma, one with a comprehension of world affairs, a man who could implement drastic changes.

So in June 1919, MacArthur set about to change the Military Academy. He curtailed hazing. He endorsed an "honor system" in which the corps is answerable for the honesty of its member cadets. He permitted first classmen to fraternize with officers. He allowed each cadet five dollars a month for spending money. He permitted six-hour weekend passes and two-day summer leaves. And he stopped censorship of cadets' mail. All of this was new to the academy. Conservative West Point alumni criticized the changes, saying MacArthur's "permissiveness" would ruin the academy.

But MacArthur stood firm. He believed in the dignity of cadets. He instituted those changes which he thought would inspire cadets to greater achievement at West Point. Two of the cadets during his tenure were future Army chiefs of staff—Maxwell Taylor and Lyman Lemnitzer—and two would become Air Force chiefs of staff—Hoyt Vandenberg and Thomas D. White.

MacArthur believed strongly in the value of athletics and physical conditioning. Accordingly, he made intramural athletics compulsory for the entire corps. He urged congressmen to appoint gifted athletes to West Point. He turned the West Point athletics program over to Captain Matthew B. Ridgeway, who incidentally would succeed him as commander of United Nations forces three decades later during the war in Korea.

To Neyland, the time spent serving on MacArthur's staff at West Point was perhaps the highlight of his military career. Neyland revered MacArthur. Years later, when Neyland held a command in the China-Burma-India Theater, and in that decade of retirement and reflection after he quit coaching, he often quoted MacArthur: "Upon the field of friendly strife are sown the seeds that, upon other fields, on other days, will bear the fruits of victory."

So when Neyland arrived at West Point in August 1921, he responded affirmatively to any request made of him by MacArthur. In addition to serving as MacArthur's aide-de-camp and assistant adjutant, Neyland also served as the West Point recreation officer, as commanding officer of the band, as prison officer, and as assistant football and baseball coach.

Charlie Daly was still the Army head coach, and being Daly's assistant gave Neyland an insight into the finer points of strategic planning. Daly was a master at getting a team ready to play a strong opponent. Neyland coached the ends.

"In 1921 and 1922, football was changing rapidly," Daly said. "Bob Neyland became a student of the possibilities of the new game. We had an unbeaten team in 1922 because of Bob's insistence on the careful preparation of certain critical plays he had worked up. The Navy game that year was won on just such a play."

"The play was a reverse forward pass, which was completed three times out of three attempts," *Nashville Banner* sports editor Fred Russell related later in a 1939 *Saturday Evening Post* article. "Each completion put the Army in position to score. Under Neyland's direction, this one play was rehearsed more than 100 times." Army went undefeated in 1922, and Daly retired.

Meanwhile, the new Army Chief of Staff, General John J. Pershing, was taking a hard look at the changes MacArthur had instituted at West Point. Pershing did not like them. In fact, Pershing liked hazing, and he did not approve of cadets receiving spending money or getting six-hour leaves to visit New York. On January 30, 1922, Pershing announced the transfer of MacArthur to the Philippines, a transfer which in future decades would affect the course of world history. But before leaving West Point in late June, MacArthur filled out one final fitness report on his aide-de-camp, Major Neyland.

"A most excellent young officer in every respect," MacArthur wrote in longhand. "An extraordinary athlete." MacArthur rated Neyland's performance at West Point "superior." Then, the general responded to two questions on the fitness report form:

"How long have you known him [Neyland]?" and "How well do you know him?" "Many years," MacArthur replied, and "Very well."

With that, Brigadier General Douglas MacArthur signed his name—and left for the Philippines.

Life for a staff officer at West Point in 1922 was enjoyable, especially for Bob Neyland. He liked the picturesque setting—the gray stone buildings, "the plain" where cadets drill, the surrounding mountains, the bluffs overlooking the Hudson River. It was beautiful, and Neyland appreciated the beauty. Also, the love between Neyland and football was growing. And then, there was that spring night in 1922 when a young editorial assistant from a New York publishing company caught his eye at a West Point dance.

Ada "Peggy" Fitch, the 25-year-old daughter of Michigan lawyer Charles Lewis Fitch and Mary Searles Fitch, was dating a cadet and had driven up from New York for the dance. The Fitches lived in Grand Rapids and, although not rich, they were financially comfortable.

Peggy was an extremely attractive brunette, a good dancer, obviously intellectual, and an articulate conversationalist.

"Young girls in Grand Rapids in those days took dancing and studied French, and she was a singer with a beautiful soprano voice," recalled her younger cousin Caroline Clapperton of Lansing, Michigan. "Peggy also was feisty. Her close friends called her 'Fitch bitch.'"

Peggy had been married in her early 20s to Morris Nelson, an engineering student whom she had met while they were attending the University of Michigan. "Peggy's parents, who were quite elderly, worried about Peggy being left alone after their deaths, and they talked her into marrying Nelson," Caroline said. Peggy and Morris had a baby—a boy—who died in infancy, and that tragedy shattered them. Peggy divorced Morris, left Grand Rapids, and went to New York to start over."

Neyland was fascinated the moment his eye caught Peggy for the first time at the West Point dance. Late that evening, Neyland mustered the courage to "cut in," introduce himself, and dance with Peggy Fitch. "I believe Peg sang while they danced. That may have put him over the precipice," Caroline said, recalling her many conversations with Peggy about the courtship with the handsome army major.

"It was instant romance, and the romance flourished. They saw each other as often as possible from that night on." And, after a few months, on one of Peggy's now-frequent visits to West Point, Neyland proposed.

By then, however, he was no longer Major Neyland. For the second time in his career, he had been demoted—this time to captain on the recommendation of the man who had succeeded MacArthur as superintendent, Brigadier General Fred W. Sladen, even though Sladen continued to give Neyland "superior" and "excellent" fitness grades. Temporary promotions simply were the rule, rather than exception, in the U.S. Army of the 1920s. And the latest demotion did not seem to bother Neyland, as had the one three years earlier in El Paso. He was preoccupied with a growing interest in football and in the dazzling young lady from Michigan.

"Peg and Bob set a wedding date for early June [1923], but Bob made them delay it because of a boil on his nose. It stayed swollen and red for weeks," cousin Caroline said. Once his nose had healed, Neyland gave the Fitches the green light to proceed with the wedding plans.

The nuptials took place at the Fitches' summer home on the lake in Grand Haven, Michigan, on July 16, 1923—Peggy in a bright dress, Captain Neyland in his uniform. It was a small wedding, limited mainly to family members and very close friends. Caroline was there. As soon as they exchanged vows, were pronounced husband and wife, and dashed through the shower of rice, Peggy and Bob left for a honeymoon in Canada.

The newlyweds set up house in staff quarters for married officers on the post at West Point. "They ate all of their meals at the Officer's Club next door," Caroline recalled.

"I visited them in 1925. Bob was in charge of the social arrangements for a reception for General Pershing, and I got to meet the general. But I was more interested in the young cadets than I was in meeting a general. Those were prohibition days, and Bob took us to a road house on Bear Mountain across the river from West Point. They served beer, liquor, and pretzels. We also attended band concerts on the post, and Bob took us to Yonkers on June 21 to see the tennis match between [Bill] Tilden and [Vincent] Richards."

Peggy not only was getting acclimated to life as the wife of a military officer, but she also was learning football. Bob remained on the Army staff when his former West Point teammate, John J. McEwan, succeeded Daly after the 1922 season.

In 1923, Army opened its season at West Point against the Tennessee Volunteers. Army won 41-0, and that score would figure prominently in a decision Neyland would make a year and a half later.

Army's only loss in 1924 was to Notre Dame, coached by Knute Rockne and starring the fabled "Four Horsemen" backfield—Harry Stuhldreher, Jim Crowley, Don Miller, and Elmer Layden.

Before the game, McEwan met Rockne at mid-field. "How about playing four 12-minute periods today?" Rockne proposed to McEwan.

"Nothing doing, Rock," McEwan replied. "We get 60 minutes of instruction from Notre Dame every year, and you're not going to cheat us out of 12 minutes of it." With that, the Irish beat Army, 13-7, finished the regular season with a 9-0 record, were acclaimed national champions, and beat Stanford, 27-10, in the Rose Bowl.

"It was at West Point that he [Neyland] became convinced that football could be perfected mathematically . . . that defense was the key to football success," wrote Ed Harris of the *Knoxville Journal.*

"If two teams are evenly matched," Neyland said, "it is impossible for either to advance the football 40 yards in a drive—unless a crucial mistake is made. Winners don't win. Losers lose. The team that makes the fewest mistakes will be the winner."

Neyland began to feel the urge to try his ideas elsewhere. He wrote to several universities, asking if they were interested in an assistant coach and an ROTC instructor. Tennessee and Iowa needed an instructor for their Reserve Officers Training Corps programs, so they contacted Neyland. He chose Tennessee.

"There was an opening at Iowa and one at Tennessee," Neyland said. "I studied the Tennessee record. It didn't look good. We [Army] beat them, 41-0, in 1923, and in 1924 they lost the last five games in a row, scoring only 15 points. I knew there was hardly a chance of doing worse."

So, the War Department cut the orders reassigning Neyland to the University of Tennessee as an ROTC instructor. He and Peggy packed their bags, drove into Canada for a brief vacation, then headed south. Bob Neyland was soon to write new and glorious chapters in the history of college football.

1925-1934

PART IV

CHAPTER 10

Opportunity Knoxville

1925

The Roaring Twenties had America kicking up its heels—clapping its hands and slapping its knees to the "Charleston." Alcoholic beverages were outlawed, but the nation said "to hell with the Constitution" and drank booze to its heart's content in behind-the-peep-hole speakeasies. Babe Ruth was hitting home runs like crazy for the New York Yankees. Madison Square Garden opened. F. Scott Fitzgerald wrote *The Great Gatsby*, and a storm sweeping through Missouri, Illinois, and Indiana killed 830 people. Hit songs flowed like fine wine from the pens of composers Buddy DeSylva, Irving Berlin, George Gershwin, and a couple of youngsters who had not yet met—Richard Rodgers and Oscar Hammerstein.

In 1925, in the tiny Tennessee town of Dayton, young school teacher John T. Scopes was convicted and fined $100 for teaching Charles Darwin's theory of evolution. The trial attracted national attention and brought head-to-head in the Dayton courtroom two famous lawyers—Clarence Darrow (defending Scopes) and William Jennings Bryan (a special prosecutor). Army Colonel William "Billy" Mitchell, a strong advocate of air power who believed the next war would be decided by airplanes, was suspended for five years without pay after accusing superiors of "almost treasonable administration of national defense" for failing to see the growing military importance of airplanes.

An elusive halfback named Harold "Red" Grange flashed across the college football landscape in 1924, and sportswriters nicknamed him the "Galloping Ghost." As the 1925 season approached, Alabama was preparing for what would become an undefeated season and a trip to the Rose Bowl. And a young army captain formerly stationed at West Point, Robert R. Neyland III, showed up in Knoxville, Tennessee, to teach military science and, on the side, coach football.

The University of Tennessee played its first football game in 1891. It was a loss, perhaps a portent of things to come, because the school suffered losing records in 10 of its first 20 football seasons. But undefeated seasons in 1914 and 1916 whetted the appetite of Tennessee fans. The "Volunteers," as Tennessee teams were known, enjoyed three consecutive winning seasons under coach M. Beal Banks from 1921 to 1923. In 1924—after opening with three victories over soft-touches Emory and Henry, Maryville, and Carson-Newman—Tennessee lost in successive weeks to Mississippi A&M, Georgia, Centre, Tulane, and Kentucky.

Dr. Nathan W. Dougherty—Tennessee's dean of engineering, chairman of the school athletic council, and captain of its 1909 football team—decided Banks needed an assistant coach who could breathe some new life into the program. And because the university also needed a senior instructor in its military department, Dougherty wrote to Army head coach John J. McEwan, who had been a starting center for Army in 1915, Bob Neyland's senior year. McEwan answered Dougherty's inquiry: "Captain Neyland is an excellent prospect as a coach. He is a maker of ends."

Dougherty also queried the head coach at Bucknell, Uncle Charlie Moran, who had coached Neyland at Texas A&M and who had kept an admiring eye on the young army officer's career—first as a player and then as an assistant coach at West Point. Moran also endorsed Neyland for the Tennessee job.

That was all Dougherty needed. He corresponded with the appropriate army officials about getting Neyland assigned to the University of Tennessee. Neyland visited Knoxville in the spring of 1925 and liked what he saw and heard. Then came his orders from the War Department, signed by Major General J. L. Hines, army chief of staff: "Captain Robert R. Neyland III, Corps of Engineers, is relieved from his present assignment and duties at the United States Military Academy, West Point, New York, effective June 30, 1925, and is then detailed, by direction of the President, at the University of Tennessee, Knoxville, Tennessee."

So Peggy and Bob Neyland packed and moved to the valley of east Tennessee.

"I remember him as Captain Neyland," recalled Dr. Lenox D. Baker, Neyland's first team trainer at Tennessee and later a famed orthopedic surgeon at Duke University. "They were paying me $500 a year, and Bob got $750 a year for coaching the ends."

Neyland knew he had stepped into the big leagues. College football in the South was blooming. The North had coaches Knute Rockne (Notre Dame), Percy Haughton (Columbia), Fielding Yost (Michigan), and Gil Dobie (Cornell). But the South had Dan McGugin (Vanderbilt), Wallace Wade (Alabama), Bill Alexander (Georgia Tech), and Clark Shaughnessy (Tulane).

McGugin, who had played for Yost at Michigan, had coached a powerhouse at Vanderbilt for 20 years and was showing no signs of slowing down when Neyland arrived in Knoxville in 1925. Vanderbilt was a painful thorn in Tennessee's side. Tennessee had beaten Vanderbilt only twice in the 19 times they had played and had lost to Vandy, 51-7, in their last meeting in 1923.

With only 10 lettermen returning, Banks and Neyland faced an uphill climb.

Moreover, Banks knew he was in a "win or else" situation. One of the criticisms of Banks was that he would change his offensive scheme three or four times during a season. Neyland, however, convinced Banks to stick with one offense and to refine it with practice repetition.

Relying on seven sophomores in the starting lineup—tackles Dave McArthur and Frank Elliott, guard John Barnhill, center Elvin Butcher, and backs Charles Rice, Ed Young, and Dick Dodson—Tennessee easily beat Emory and Henry, 51-0, and Maryville, 13-0. Next, however, Vanderbilt smashed Tennessee, 34-7, and the following week Louisiana State tied the Volunteers.

Heavily favored Georgia, which had beaten Vanderbilt, 26-7, was Tennessee's next opponent. A few days before the game, Banks became ill. Neyland and another assistant coach, Bunny Oakes, took charge of the team's preparation for the game.

To annoy and distract Georgia, Neyland told sportswriters that the Bulldogs were using an illegal shift, and that he would prove it by taking still photographs during the game. The Volunteers won 12-7, and newspapers proclaimed it the biggest upset of the year in the South. The Tennessee season ended with a loss to Kentucky and a 5-2-1 record. Banks resigned on December 17 and became head coach at Knoxville Central High School, where he would build great teams in later years.

There were rumors in Knoxville that Tennessee would try to hire coach Wallace Wade away from Alabama, which in 1925 was undefeated in ten games, including a 20-19 victory over Washington in the Rose Bowl. But Dougherty had his mind set on the young army captain, Bob Neyland.

CHAPTER 11

A Football Dynasty is Born

1926-27

Before they left West Point and scattered to their respective assignments as second lieutenants in June 1916, classmates Robert R. Neyland, William H. Britton, and Paul B. Parker had made a pact. The first one to get a football head coaching job would summon the other two.

Britton, an engineer, was assigned to the Hawaiian Islands until 1917, when he was transferred to Camp Humphreys, Virginia. In 1923, after resigning his commission, Britton moved to Florida and entered the real estate business.

After graduation from West Point, Parker had been assigned to the infantry. He served in France during World War I, then was assigned to the Military Academy as a professor of tactics and football line coach. He remained at West Point until resigning his commission in early 1926. He then moved to Florida also.

The very first notations in the upper lefthand corner of the inside cover of Neyland's personal Tennessee football notebook were the Florida addresses of Britton and Parker:

"Britton, 156 NE First St., Miami, Florida."

"Parker, Box No. 3970, Tampa, Florida."

When Neyland called in the summer of 1926, Parker and Britton came running. Neyland also asked Lenox Baker, the 1925 team trainer, to continue in that capacity. And he recruited Charles Lindsay, a member of the 1919-1921 Tennessee teams, to coach the Volunteer freshman team.

Two others who would contribute much to Tennessee football in the years ahead joined the staff in 1926. One was John Hoskins—a bearded, tobacco-chewing handyman in overalls. They called him "Dean." His job was to maintain the football stadium and the playing field. The other newcomer was J. M. Forgey—a mute, easy-going black man who served as the team's masseur. They called him "Dummy," but it was a nickname of affection, for Dummy was the biggest Volunteer fan of all. And he was convinced that the rabbit's foot kept in his pocket contributed far more to Tennessee's football success than did the coaching of the young squirts from West Point.

Neyland clearly defined the responsibilities of each member of the coaching staff:

—Parker was to coach the line, supervise the kickoff drills, and take charge of defensive preparations. Parker also was in charge of scouting opponents, keeping team records, and seeing that the playing and practice fields were in good condition.

—Britton was charged with coaching the ends and supervising the dropkick and placekick phases of the game. Britton also made arrangements for team trips.

—Baker supervised the trainers and managed the dressing room and the training table where the players ate their meals.

—Lindsay coached the freshmen.

—Neyland took responsibility for coaching the backs, punters, and passers and for buying and maintaining football equipment.

At 8 a.m., Monday, September 6, 1926—appropriately, Labor Day—the new head football coach of the University of Tennessee Volunteers greeted his squad of 32 players:

"Men, we will practice two and one-half hours each day. That's all. Each practice will be organized. We will know what we want to accomplish each day, and we will work full speed. Any questions?"

There were none.

"Then, let's go," he commanded, and the Neyland dynasty was born.

Physical conditioning was to become a trademark of Neyland-coached teams, and he devoted the first practice mostly to calisthenics and a lecture in which he discussed "training, morale, spirit, brains, and destiny." The temperature that day was 79 degrees, and it got hotter each succeeding day—86 on Tuesday, 91 on Wednesday.

Three days later, Tennessee's practices were closed to the public for the first time, and Knoxville sportswriters realized it was a new day for them. Captain Neyland in the days and years ahead gave them very little information about his football team—and never any information which, in his opinion, could offer aid and comfort to the enemy.

Jimmy Elmore, Neyland's first starting tailback and future mayor of Knoxville, said the Tennessee players had learned quickly to appreciate and respect Neyland's football knowledge when he was an assistant to Banks. And that respect was magnified when Neyland became head coach a year later.

Neyland was an organizer," Elmore said. "We always started [practice] with a warmup period of some 15 to 20 minutes, and then we would have group work. But Neyland would call us together before we went to group drills, and he'd tell us what his objective was for the next game—and what we were going to have to do to win it."

Elmore said Neyland encouraged players to visit his office and talk football.

And he would tell them about his experiences at West Point and in France during World War I.

"He had a dignified air about him, but I don't think he realized it," Elmore said. "I think the fact that he was a military man caused some people to sort of keep their distance. But I always felt close to General Neyland. You just recognized him for the man he was, and you didn't try to get by with anything."

Laying the groundwork for the 1926 season, Neyland studied offensive plays designed by coaches Charlie Daly at Army, Knute Rockne at Notre Dame, Gil Dobie at Cornell, and Glenn "Pop" Warner at Stanford. Neyland entered notes to himself in his personal ledger—what would work, what would not. "Don't think much of this," he wrote, referring to a play used by Stanford in 1924. "Scouting will nullify it, I believe." Halfway down the same page, Neyland reminded himself that a play works because of every offensive player being involved—the linemen and backs executing their blocks with precision and the ball carrier arriving quickly at the point of attack.

On an adjacent page containing notes about things to accomplish in practice, Neyland reminded himself: "See that blockers . . . get credit [for big gains]."

In that same sequence of notes, Neyland translated his football theories and principles into "maxims," defined by Webster's dictionary as "a general truth or rule of conduct." Neyland thought of his maxims as a football corollary to the Ten Commandments—only there were more than ten Neyland commandments. There were 38. And in his own handwriting, he listed them:

1. Thou shalt charge and block.
2. Thou shalt charge and fight.
3. A good interferer [blocker] never looks back.
4. One good interferer is worth three ball-carrying stars.
5. A team that won't be beat can't be beat.
6. The team that makes the fewest mistakes wins.
7. Never stop till the referee's whistle blows.
8. Press the kicking game.
9. Make and play for the breaks. When one comes your way, score!
10. If the game or a break goes against you, don't lie down; put on some steam.
11. Don't save yourself. Go the limit. There are good men on the sidelines when you are exhausted.
12. Football is a battle. Go out to fight and keep it up all afternoon.
13. A man's value to his team varies inversely as his distance from the ball.
14. If the line goes forward, the team wins; if it comes backward, the team loses.
15. Never lose the ball on downs.
16. You can't fight like a man with less than 100 percent loyalty and college spirit.
17. You can't do yourself justice without getting and staying in condition.
18. At least three men make every tackle. Gang tackling.
19. Let none escape.

20. First rush [from scrimmage] equals 6 yards.
21. Eleven men in every play.
22. Use your head; 75 percent of football is above the neck.
23. One increasing purpose.
24. A quitter never wins, and a winner never quits.
25. Keep everlastingly on the job.
26. Be the first to line up.
27. Never stop fighting.
28. No good blocker and tackler was ever left off a football team.
29. Use your eyes, your hands, your legs, and your head.
30. Be aggressive; you can't win the game on your side of the scrimmage line.
31. If the game is going against you, keep your head up, set your jaw and dig in. This is what tests the stuff you are made of.
32. (Neyland's handwriting faded and illegible.)
33. 'Turf' their defense! Get them down!
34. A winning team quickens its play as it nears the goal line!
35. Get the jump on your teammates on the charge.
36. Follow the ball!
37. Play your own position well—first.
38. Line—Charge with the ball!

On September 20, 1926—six days before his first game as a college head coach—Captain Neyland received a communique from the adjutant general at the War Department: "The President has promoted you to the grade of Major in the Corps of Engineers." Captain Neyland was now Major Neyland.

By the opening game against Carson-Newman on September 26, the seating capacity at Tennessee's football stadium, known as Shields-Watkins Field, had been enlarged from 3,200 to 6,800 by adding 17 rows of concrete stands on the east side of the field. After only three more seasons, in which the Volunteers lost only one game, 32 additional rows were added to the east side, boosting the capacity to 17,860.

The Carson-Newman game, Neyland's first as head coach, was not the "breather" he had hoped it would be. He had written in his ledger prior to the game: "If comfortably ahead, use kicking game and practice pass defense. Lots of substitutes." But entering the fourth period, the Volunteers led only 7-0 on a touchdown by Allyn McKeen. *Knoxville Journal* sportswriter Russ Bebb, in his book on the history of Tennessee football, The Big Orange, described how Jimmy Elmore put the game out of reach in the final period.

"Carson-Newman had tried several field goals on drop kicks, and I kept noticing that their linemen didn't go downfield to cover," Elmore said. "They just dropped to their knees and watched the ball. Well, when that one came I decided to try it. I knew that I could get back at least 25 or 30 yards before they could get me. I started up the east sidelines and cut back at a right angle. I must have run 150 yards, but not one of the Carson-Newman players laid a hand on me. [Vol guard] John Barnhill was with me all the way."

The next day Neyland and Elmore met on campus. "It's hard to question success," the coach told the pupil. "You've had your instructions so from now on you carry them out."

"He [Neyland] didn't seem the least bit mad at me," Elmore said, "but he let me know that you didn't field kicks inside your own 20."

Neyland's first starting lineup at Tennessee for that Carson-Newman game included McKeen and Sam Jones at ends, L. B. "Farmer" Johnson and Howard Johnson at tackles, Arthur Tripp and John Barnhill at guards, Elvin Butcher at center, Charlie Rice at wingback, Billy Harkness at quarterback, Dick Dodson at fullback, and Elmore at tailback.

After beating Carson-Newman, the Volunteers defeated North Carolina, 34-0, LSU, 14-7, Maryville, 6-0, Centre, 30-7, Mississippi State, 33-0, and Sewanee, 12-0. Dougherty had told Neyland that one of the expectations was that the Volunteers begin collecting some victories over Vanderbilt. It did not happen in Neyland's first year as head coach—the Volunteers lost 20-3, but they would not lose again to Vandy until 1935. And Neyland's career record against Vanderbilt would be 16 wins, three losses, and two ties.

"There is no need to conceal the fact that the loss to Vanderbilt was a bitter blow," Neyland told *Atlanta Journal* columnist Morgan Blake. "I felt mighty bad about it. I remember when I was walking into the Vanderbilt clubhouse after the game to congratulate [coach] Dan McGugin and his men, I thought to myself that I would much prefer engaging Dan in physical combat. I was that sick over it."

Blake told Neyland that he was impressed by the sportsmanlike statement Neyland issued after the loss to Vandy.

"That just shows that we are all more or less hypocrites," Neyland replied. "No coach, who has just lost a game to his main rival, ever feels in the humor to make a sportsmanlike statement."

Tennessee responded to the loss to Vandy by defeating Kentucky, 6-0, the following week, touching off a string of 33 games without a loss.

"Spring" practice for Neyland's Volunteers began in early February and was divided into three segments. The punters reported first, and Neyland personally drilled them for three weeks. Next came the freshmen the last week of February. Finally, the returning players practiced for a week in early March.

Perpetually writing memos to himself, then acting on them and evaluating the results, Neyland spent many hours during the winter and spring months at his desk—analyzing Tennessee's personnel, studying the strategies used by upcoming opponents in previous years, developing practice and game plans for the next season.

Each summer, in his first few years at Tennessee, Neyland was assigned to an ROTC training unit at Fort Bragg, North Carolina. He clearly would have preferred being in Knoxville, getting ready for the upcoming season, but he dutifully pulled his annual summer tour at Fort Bragg.

A few weeks before Tennessee's September 24, 1927, opener against Carson-Newman, Atlanta sportswriter Ed Danforth visited Knoxville and filed a pre-season story on Neyland, Britton, and Parker, whom reporters had labeled "the Three Musketeers."

"No need to enlarge on this triumvirate," Danforth wrote. "Their 1926 record speaks eloquently of what three men, working in harmony on sound football principles, can do. The Three Musketeers rule the gridiron at Knoxville with a sort of benevolent Prussianism. Military order is observable from dressing room to field and back."

Danforth found a gloomy atmosphere as the Volunteers prepared for the opener. Halfback Ed Young, on whom Neyland had counted heavily for punting, suffered a wrenched knee that kept him out for the entire season. And ten players, on whom Neyland had counted as reserves, quit the team for personal, academic, or financial reasons during the off-season and did not return.

"We lost only two regulars from last year's team," Neyland said, "but unless our reserves and our sophomore recruits show more stuff than [they have] to date, I am afraid our substitutes won't be up to the mark of other conference teams; and in a football campaign, a team's success depends largely upon its first string substitutes."

Hugh Faust—a Tennessee tailback from 1927 to 1930, a member of Neyland's coaching staff for two decades, and the man who scouted Alabama and Vanderbilt many years afterward for Vol coaches Harvey Robinson and Bowden Wyatt—remembers Neyland's passionate concern about quality depth on the roster.

"Neyland had what you would call a first team during his first few years at Tennessee, but later on he used complete 11-man units interchangeably," Faust said. "He believed in people working together in units, and he believed in having a fresh unit ready to play." In 1938-40, when Tennessee had undefeated regular seasons, Neyland used three units almost equally.

A final blow was dealt the Volunteers just a week before the 1927 opener. Charley Rice, the starting wingback, was declared ineligible by the Southern Conference because he had played one year at Union College in Jackson, Tennessee, before enrolling at Tennessee. Everett Derryberry, who years later would be president of Tennessee Technological University, took Rice's place in the starting lineup.

The Volunteers, or "Vols" as more and more fans began to call them, mowed down Carson-Newman, 33-0, North Carolina, 26-0, a strong Maryville College team, 7-0, Mississippi, 21-7, Transylvania, 57-0, and Virginia, 42-0.

After outscoring their first six opponents 186-7, the Vols felt confident as they got ready for the next foe, Sewanee, which at the turn of the century had been a football power in the South.

The 1927 Sewanee team, however, was only a shadow of its predecessors and its record was only 1-4 going into the Tennessee game. The Vols, on the other hand, were riddled with injuries. Two regulars, tailback Jimmy Elmore and quarterback Roy Witt, watched the first half from the bench. Elmore, hobbled by a sprained instep, was in civilian clothes. Witt had a painful shoulder injury, but trainer Lenox Baker heavily bandaged the shoulder and Neyland sent Witt into the game.

After Sewanee shocked the Vols and took a 12-7 lead before halftime, Neyland turned to Elmore: "Jimmy, get dressed!" Baker rushed Elmore to the dressing room, braced and bandaged the bruised foot, and together they returned to the field just as the first half ended. In the dressing room, as always, Neyland spent time correcting mistakes, reminding the Vols they were better prepared and would win. In the second half, Elmore's appearance built a fire under the Vols, and they scored four more touchdowns—beating Sewanee, 32-12.

In a dispatch from New York, Associated Press sports editor Alan J. Gould wrote about Princeton, Georgia, and Tennessee being the only undefeated, untied teams in major college football after the first week in November. But down in Knoxville, nobody was thinking about national rankings. Tennessee's next foe was Vanderbilt, coached by Dan McGugin and sporting a 5-1-1 record. The Vols had not beaten a McGugin team since 1916.

McGugin had cried the blues earlier in the year, complaining about Vandy being inexperienced because of the loss of many seniors from the previous year.

Neyland, recognizing the classic coaching poor-mouth ploy remarked: "Dan McGugin is one of the greatest figures in American football, and one of the finest characters that ever lived, but he is smart enough to know how to spread on the banana oil where it will do the most good. They don't make 'em any slicker than Dan."

A crowd estimated at 13,000 watched the Vol-Vandy game in Knoxville, scoreless in the first half. Vandy went ahead 7-0 in the third quarter when Bill Spears threw a touchdown pass to Kitty Creson. Tennessee fans began to sense another loss to the cross-state rival, but the Vols had other ideas. In the fourth quarter, Elmore's running and Witt's passing advanced the ball to Vanderbilt's 18. From there, fullback Dick Dodson rambled for a touchdown, and Witt's extra point salvaged a 7-7 tie.

"Tennessee's team shows the effect of good coaching," Vandy's Spears said.

Meanwhile, on that same day in Nashville, Tennessee's freshman team smashed Vandy's freshmen, 26-14. A young man named Joseph Sandy "Buddy" Hackman, who had been a prep star in Nashville, scored four touchdowns for Tennessee that day.

While the varsity Vols had been cruising along undefeated in 1927, few Tennessee fans had realized what the Vol freshmen, known as the "Rats," were accomplishing. Coached by Neyland's 1926 captain, Billy Harkness, the 1927 Vol freshmen had gone undefeated in five games. In addition to Hackman, the group included Gene McEver, Bobby Dodd, Paul Hug, Harry "Hobo" Thayer, Fritz Brandt, Phil Beane, Charles "Dutch" Reineke, Hugh Faust, Ed Corbett, Ben Fuller, and Herb Brown.

In the last game of the season, the varsity Vols scored two quick touchdowns in the first quarter and one more in the fourth to beat Kentucky, 20-0. Tennessee's final won-lost record for 1927 was 8-0-1.

Following the season, Neyland pulled out his ledger and made notes to himself on the 1927 team. Among them:

"Marked by team morale, ability to keep feet on ground, better physical condition, fourth-quarter tradition, team determination, smartness. . . . Showed wonderful improvement in the kicking game, especially in returning punts."

Then, in his notes, Neyland focused on the injury problem. "Of the 15 injured men [during the season], only Tripp and Witt were injured in games," Neyland wrote.

"Conclusions:

— "On a veteran team, eliminate scrimmage. Time plays in spring, or use second team to time them. Better not have new plays if necessary to scrimmage them [in the fall].

— "Cut scrimmages to the irreducible minimum. Hold those [scrimmages] that are absolutely necessary [only] in September.

— "Never scrimmage any good man who knows his stuff.

— "Better to have all in good condition and morale than the extra knowledge to be gained by scrimmage.

— "Witt's injury came after we were three touchdowns in the lead. Lesson—take your key men out just as soon as you have a safe lead."

And so, Bob Neyland committed to his journal the lessons he had learned from the undefeated 1927 season.

Meanwhile, he had to give one of the deans at the university a little lecture. Neyland had been called on the carpet because no student in his military law class had scored lower than a "B" grade. Neyland related the incident to Wirt Gammon of the *Chattanooga Times.*

"In our system of grading, the outstanding students get A's, the good ones B's, the average ones C's, and those below [get] D's and F's," the dean said.

"Now you listen, dean," Neyland replied sternly. "I'm teaching military law. I know military law. My father was a Texas lawyer, and my grandfather was a Texas judge. I was brought up on law. Furthermore, I have a good class, and I'll tell you why I have a good class. In my first lecture, I told this class that it would learn military law, that I would teach it to them."

Neyland had told the class he would not tolerate students who did not study. "If there is anyone here that I find isn't studying," he told his students, "that man and I will then retire behind this building to settle a question of disobedience, man to man."

The surprised dean tried changing the subject by asking about the next season, but Neyland, still upset at the challenge to his teaching integrity, simply used the football team for more emphasis.

"I'm paid big money, and I get big headlines," Neyland continued. "I'm worth it because I'm the best teacher at Tennessee. My students have a public exam every Saturday. If they flunk, I lose my job."

His 1928 team was about to make all A's.

CHAPTER 12

The Flaming Sophomores

1928

It was 1928. Singer Al Jolson was making "talky" motion pictures. Amelia Earhart became the first woman to cross the Atlantic Ocean in an airplane. Herbert Hoover was elected president of the United States. Walt Disney produced his first movie cartoon. Heavyweight boxing champion Gene Tunney retired. And the University of Tennessee's "Flaming Sophomores" burst onto the college football scene.

In spring practice, Neyland was impressed with the group who would be sophomores in the fall. And, although such stars as John Barnhill, Elvin Butcher, Dave McArthur, and Allyn McKeen were gone, Neyland privately was enthused about the 1928 outlook.

"We'll have a fast team and should make the most of it," he wrote in his ledger. "Marked by individual improvement. McEver shows great promise."

It did not take Neyland long to realize the wisdom of his prophecy. Gene McEver, whom the newspapers called the "Bristol Blizzard" and the "Wild Bull," scored three touchdowns in each of the first two games as Tennessee whipped Maryville, 41-0, and Centre, 41-7. Next, the Vols beat Mississippi, 13-12, when Hackman deflected an extra point pass attempt in the final minute.

Now 3-0 in mid-October of 1928, the Vols had lost only one game in Neyland's first two seasons as head coach, but it was the game played in Tuscaloosa, Alabama, on the afternoon of October 20, 1928, that first focused the full glare of the national football spotlight on Bob Neyland and the University of Tennessee.

The Alabama Crimson Tide, coached by Wallace Wade, was the scourge of Dixie. The 1925 Alabama team had beaten Washington, 20-19, in the Rose Bowl to finish the season with a 10-0 record. In 1926, 'Bama was 9-0 in the regular season and tied Stanford in the Rose Bowl. Alabama had come to be regarded as the best team in the South.

The Rose Bowl was special to Wallace Wade—not just because it was the only bowl game in the 1920s, but also because Wade had played in it once and lost. A native of Trenton, Tennessee, Wade attended college at Brown University and played right guard on the Brown team that lost to Washington, 14-0, in the 1916 Rose Bowl.

Wade told his 1925 Alabama team that a trip to the Rose Bowl meant three weeks of hard work. "I want you to realize that to the fullest," he said. "But remember this, too. Southern football is not recognized as being anywhere near what it is in the East, West, and Midwest. So here's your chance."

Tim Cohane, sports editor of *Look* magazine for more than two decades, said the "general regard for Alabama's chances [in the 1925 Rose Bowl] was epitomized by Will Rogers, the rope-twirling cowboy-philosopher from Oklahoma, who called 'Bama a 'team from Tuska-loser.'" Alabama, led by quarterback Pooley Hubert and tailback Johnny Mack Brown, defeated Washington, 20-19.

Tennessee and Alabama had not played each other in 1925, 1926, or 1927, Neyland's three years at Tennessee; therefore he and Wade had never met until that October 1928 weekend.

"Alabama, in Tuscaloosa, that's big stuff," Vol quarterback Bobby Dodd said in his autobiography, *Dodd's Luck*. "That was our first big game. Everybody tells us Alabama is going back to the Rose Bowl again. Alabama had a great team. The betting odds said 500 dollars even-money Tennessee wouldn't even score."

The Vols traveled to Tuscaloosa by train. En route, Neyland called each player into his private compartment.

"He talked to us about our preparation, about our assignments, about what it meant to win a big football game," tailback Gene McEver said. "But I guess the most important thing he said was that we were better, man for man, than the Alabama players."

The night before the game, Dodd and McEver had roomed together. "If they kick that ball to ol' Gene, to ol' Ephrem, he's gonna run it back for a touchdown," McEver told Dodd. "Gene called himself Ephrem, but I never knew why."

Neyland—always the psychologist, always the strategist—assembled his players in the locker room before the game and reminded them they were better prepared than the bigger Alabama team. Then McEver addressed his teammates: "If I get that ball on the kickoff, everybody try to cut down a man. If you can't cut down a man, just move over and let me through."

Neyland also warned his players against looking at Alabama when the Crimson Tide ran onto the field. "They were wearing white jerseys that made 'em look like elephants," Buddy Hackman said. "Neyland had thought that would put the fear of the Lord in us, like you were in a prize fight and nobody told you how big the other guy was. But we weren't scared of anybody, even if we were about 20 pounds lighter a man."

Alabama had opened the 1928 season by defeating Mississippi, 27-0, and Mississippi State, 46-0. And despite Tennessee's 3-0 start, Neyland, hoping to lull the opponent into a false sense of security, suggested to Wade that the second half be shortened to prevent an Alabama rout.

"Bob wanted me to cut the third and fourth quarters short," Wade recalled. "And I told him I would if the game was getting out of hand, but I knew he had a good team. After all, they'd only lost one game in his two years as head coach. Of course, Bob always had his team prepared for any eventuality, and he was always looking for that little extra edge that could mean the difference in winning and losing. One of the things that made Bob such a great coach was his attention to detail, the smallest little detail."

Ellis "Dumpy" Hagler, a guard on the Alabama team, remembered Wade's warning that Tennessee would be a tough opponent. "We knew Tennessee would be good, but we thought we'd win," Hagler said.

The two teams lined up for the opening kickoff. The Vols were dressed in new orange jerseys and new lightweight silk pants. Dodd and McEver had a pre-kickoff routine, a special handshake. They grasped hands, then McEver retreated to the goal line.

Alabama kicked off.

McEver, a shifty, 185-pound runner drifted under the ball, cradled it in his hands and started upfield. Tennessee blockers began to mow down the attacking Alabama wall. Vol players on the right side of the field crossed to the left; those on the left crossed to the right. It was a classic Neyland concept—geometric angles of attack. Cross-blocking on kickoffs would become a Neyland trademark.

The Vols "started cutting down the Crimsons like a reaper in a field of grain, wrote the late *Knoxville Journal* sports editor Ed Harris.

"The blocking was so efficient that McEver ran the last 20 yards looking back over his shoulder to see if there was any pursuit. There was none."

The late *Knoxville News-Sentinel* sports editor Tom Siler, in his book *Through the Years with the Volunteers,* described McEver's kickoff return as an "electric display of his elusiveness, power, and speed."

"I was looking for every one of the officials to see if any was about to call any kind of foul," Neyland said. "It was by far the most tense moment I spent as a coach."

Dodd kicked the extra point, and the Vols led powerful Alabama, 7-0. Fans and players alike, Tennessee's included, were stunned at the sudden turn of events.

"I made Bob Neyland that day," said Frank Howard, long-time Clemson University coach. "I was the last man between McEver and the goal line, and he broke my tackle." But Dumpy Hagler says Howard, one of the most entertaining after-dinner speakers in college football history, injected himself into the scenario merely to add spice to the story. "Frank didn't even play in that game," Hagler said. Howard lettered in 1928, but the lineups of that game with Tennessee do not list him as playing.

Now, with only a few ticks gone off the game clock, the Vols led Alabama, 7-0, but Alabama answered with a touchdown in three plays. Billy Hicks returned Dodd's kickoff 25 yards. John Henry Suther, a 'Bama sophomore, gained six yards at right end, then broke through tackle and ran 45 yards to a touchdown. A missed extra point left Tennessee ahead 7-6.

Alabama was threatening again with a drive to Tennessee's 20 when Bernard "Tony" Holm, Alabama's star fullback, fumbled. The left end for the Vols, Paul Hug, scooped up the ball and ran 26 yards to the Tennessee 48. Tennessee failed to gain a first down, and Dodd punted out of bounds at the Alabama three. Tennessee guard Harry "Hobo" Thayer jolted Suther on a snap from center, and Vol guard L. B. "Farmer" Johnson recovered in the end zone. Under rules of that day, the recovery was a safety, giving the Vols a 9-6 lead.

In the second quarter, Tennessee put together another touchdown drive. McEver ran for 22, and Buddy Hackman passed to Hug for 15 more and a first down at the Alabama 10. On fourth down at the Alabama four, McEver scored to give Tennessee a 15-6 lead.

Alabama quickly retaliated. Davis Brasfield returned the kickoff 57 yards to Tennessee's 15. Neyland rushed two fresh ends, Fritz Brandt and Houston Herndon, into the game to strengthen the defense, but Alabama could not be stopped. Holm scored three plays later, and the conversion made it Tennessee 15, Alabama 13.

On the final play of the first half, Alabama punted. Neyland had given strict orders to fair catch all punts, but Dodd was prone to do things his own way when the opportunity for success looked good to him.

"I tried to run when I should've made a fair catch," Dodd said in his book. "But we didn't know how much time was left, and I was trying to make something happen before the half."

In those days, there was no clock on the scoreboard. The official time was kept by a referee on the field. Just as he fielded the ball, Dodd was hammered by a couple of 220-pound Alabama players—sophomore Fred Sington, who would become an all-American the next year, and guard Molton Smith. The blow severely bruised Dodd's kidney. He was carried from the field on a stretcher and did not return to the game. It was the only time in his career at Tennessee that Dodd was injured.

Dutch Reineke, a 155-pound quarterback, took Dodd's place in the second half and punted sensationally.

"All of the scoring in that Alabama game was in the first half," recalled reserve tailback-quarterback Hugh Faust, later a long-time assistant coach on Neyland's staff. "It was a defensive game after that. Alabama moved the ball a lot in the second half but couldn't score on us."

Alabama opened the second half with a 53-yard drive, which ended when the Vols recovered a fumble at their own nine. Tennessee drove to the 50 but lost the ball on a pass interception. The game settled into a punting duel. Late in the game, another Alabama penetration to the Tennessee 25 ended with the Vols recovering a fumble. Field position quickly changed. Reineke punted out of danger, then intercepted an Alabama pass two plays later. Reineke then punted out of bounds at the

'Bama 25. The game ended before Alabama could get to midfield again.

Associated Press sportswriter Horace Renegar's story of the game began with the following paragraph: "An inspired Tennessee football team, led by two great sophomore halfbacks, McEver and Hackman, Saturday scored the greatest triumph in Volunteer gridiron history by defeating Alabama's Crimson Tide, 15-13.

"Frank Godwin of the *Knoxville Journal* wrote: "If you want to know the names of all other Vols who starred, just gaze over the lineup. To the last man, the Vols came through like all-Americans."

"I know we won," a nearly delirious Neyland said after the game, "but what was the score?" Someone told him. "Our boys played far better than we dreamed they could," Neyland said. "They made up for their lack of experience by their unquenchable fight. I'm so proud of them that I'd kiss every one of them if I wasn't afraid they would all take a poke at me when I did."

"I take off my hat to McEver and Hackman," Alabama coach Wallace Wade said. "In McEver and Hackman, Bob Neyland has two of the finest sophomore backs I've ever seen. If they continue to improve with age, there's no telling what great fame may really be in store for them. My hat's off to the entire Tennessee team. They justly won a great battle."

Neyland praised both teams, and singled out the sportsmanship exhibited by Alabama players. The only penalties in the game were for offsides.

Harry "Hobo" Thayer, a sophomore Tennessee guard, said years later that the 1928 Alabama game was physically the most punishing game he played as a Volunteer. "I had two teeth kicked out, both eyes were beat shut, and I was generally horse-tromped by Fred Sington, Foots Clements, and Tony Holm," Thayer said.

On Sunday, when the Tennessee train pulled into the station in Knoxville, a cheering crowd of hundreds met the triumphant Tennessee team. Standing on a fire engine, students unfurled a banner proclaiming: "In Dodd We Trust." But Dodd missed seeing the honor.

Herndon said Dodd had spent the night on the train in great pain. As the train slowed and pulled into the station, Dodd asked Herndon for assistance in getting to the bathroom.

"He put his arm around my shoulder, and I maneuvered him into the tiny toilet," Herndon recalled. "He was relieving himself when he passed out, flat cold. So there I was, holding him up and he was wetting all over the trousers of my new cream-colored suit. So I held him. But the way I looked, I couldn't go out and enjoy the cheers of that wild crowd."

And how the fans did cheer—loud and long. There were station platform speeches. It was a happening. It was, up to that time, the biggest day in Tennessee football history.

"I don't know that it was the greatest game we played," McEver said. "But it was the one that put Tennessee on the map."

Seven sophomores eventually were starters on Neyland's 1928 team, nicknamed the "Flaming Sophomores" by newspaper reporters. "Coach Neyland has made a remarkable showing in bringing along a green team so fast," wrote Horace Renegar of The Associated Press.

"Neyland has made good at Tennessee, and it wouldn't be a surprise to see his alma mater, West Point, recall him to coach the Cadets," said Zipp Newman of the *Birmingham News*. "No one expected Tennessee's sophomore team to overthrow the Crimson Tide," wrote Morgan Blake in the *Atlanta Journal*, "and the victory was a wonderful tribute to the fighting spirit of the team and the coaching ability of Bob Neyland."

By the time the Tennessee-Vanderbilt game rolled around in mid-November, the Vols were 7-0 and growing more confident. Just before the Vols took the field for the kickoff, Neyland told them: "We'll meet a crying bunch out there at the kickoff. While the tears are in their eyes, let's throw a few passes." Roy Witt's 15-yard touchdown pass to Paul Hug was all the Vols needed to beat Vandy in a defensive struggle. "I'm extremely proud of my fellows," Neyland said. "They played a great game and defeated a great Vanderbilt team."

The final two games of the season were struggles, a scoreless tie with Kentucky and a 13-12 victory over previously unbeaten Florida, which had outscored its foes 324-31. Neyland, confined to bed with influenza that week, got out of bed Saturday morning and joined his players for the game. As soon as the game ended, Neyland returned to his home and bed.

"The best Eastern teams this year probably were New York University, Penn, Navy, and Princeton," wrote W. B. Hanna of the *New York Herald-Tribune* after watching Tennessee beat Florida. "Tennessee might have beaten any of them, just as it beat Florida, Alabama, and Vanderbilt."

Shortly after the 1928 season ended, Lenox Baker, Tennessee's team trainer the past four years, talked to Neyland about entering medical school at Duke. "I wanted to study medicine, and Bob went to bat for me with the people at Duke University," Baker remembers.

"Neyland not only urged him to go, but in 1930 when Wallace Wade made known that he was moving from Alabama to Duke as head football coach, Neyland urged Wade to get Baker as his team's trainer," Fred Russell recalled.

"I'd love to keep you, Lenox," Neyland said, "but you're going to be a great physician, and you need to get on with it."

So Lenox Baker left Bob Neyland at Tennessee, enrolled in the new School of Medicine at Duke, and later joined forces with Wallace Wade. But Baker and Neyland remained close, even as Baker was forming a new bond of friendship with Wade. "Mrs. Bob Neyland [Peggy] once told me that Doc Baker had been her husband's closest friend when both were at UT," Russell said. "And Doc certainly became one of Wallace Wade's closest friends."

After graduating from Duke, Baker interned at the medical center at Johns Hopkins University, then returned to Duke where he taught future orthopedic surgeons and eventually served as director of the Lenox Baker Cerebral Palsy and Crippled Children's Hospital in Durham.

Meanwhile, in 1928, Vol fans had acquired a taste of Neyland football—25 victories, two ties, and only one loss in three years. And suddenly, they feared that Tennessee's newfound football success might not last, that the army might take Major Neyland from them. It was a valid concern.

"Neyland . . . already has been at Tennessee a year longer than the usual allotment for an officer at one place, and he is certain to receive a notice of transfer somewhere else about next April," wrote Bob Wilson of the *Knoxville News-Sentinel.* "It has become known that Neyland has been approached by several eastern universities desiring to obtain his services as coach. In order to remain at Tennessee and coach, or accept any of the offers he now has, it would be necessary for him to resign from the army."

University officials were not about to let the army take Neyland from them—not if they could help it. Dr. Harcourt A. Morgan, the president of the university, formally requested that the army reappoint Neyland to his Tennessee post.

On the morning of Sunday, January 20, 1929, Morgan received an official communique from the War Department. The dispatch informed Morgan that Neyland had been granted a one-year extension as professor of military science and tactics and ROTC commandant at Tennessee. "Needless to say, we are greatly pleased," Morgan said.

Supposedly the extension would keep Neyland at Tennessee through September 1, 1930, but *Knoxville Journal* writer Frank Godwin speculated that Neyland would coach the Vols through the 1930 season by taking the three months of annual leave which he, Neyland, had accumulated over the past three years. The army had other plans. Within a year Neyland would be transferred to another city, setting in motion a controversy that altered his military career and his life.

CHAPTER 13

The Greatest Team

1929

As the autumn of 1929 approached, the world economy grew steadily more volatile and uncertain. Steel and automobile production in the United States declined. Farmers became desperate for relief from unstable prices. The entire national economy showed signs of weakening. Yet, prices on the New York stock market continued to rise until late September.

On October 29, the infamous "Black Tuesday," the stock market collapsed as 16 million shares were sold at rapidly declining prices. Within two weeks, $30 billion of listed stocks in the New York Stock Exchange had been wiped out. The Great Depression had arrived. The hard times ahead would be a little more endurable for football fans in the valley of east Tennessee because of the exploits of Major Bob Neyland's team.

The Flaming Sophomores of 1928 were a year older, and the Vols had strung together three consecutive undefeated seasons. Neyland promised a "wide-open" offense. Fans anxiously waited.

"Tennessee will have a light and fast team this year, with its material generally considered better than that of 1928," said a United Press wire story from Atlanta.

"Forward passes—yea, oodles of them—lateral passes and sweeping end runs will again be in vogue," wrote Bob Wilson of the . "But Major Neyland has something else up his sleeve. He is sold on 'spin plays,' and the Vol backs will be equipped with a varied assortment of plays featuring this attack."

But as the 1929 opener approached, public concern about Tennessee's football future mounted. Neyland's tour of duty as the university ROTC commandant was to end in the mid-1930s. And even though it was possible for him to coach through the 1930 football season by taking accumulated vacation leave, fans and university officials alike feared he might resign from the army and accept one of his many offers from schools up East.

Knowing he would be directly affected by the changes in Neyland's career, Vol assistant coach Bill Britton wrote to Secretary of War James A. Good.

"When I signed a two-year contract last year, Major Neyland, the head football coach, and members of the Athletic Council intimated that when Major Neyland was relieved [and transferred from Knoxville], I would be the logical choice as his successor," Britton wrote. "I had had an offer as head coach from another institution, but refused it because I liked Knoxville and believed that I would get this position when Major Neyland was relieved. Major Neyland and I are classmates and have been very close friends for years. Whenever we talked the matter over, he lead [sic] me to believe that he would not resign from the army to accept a long contract as head coach."

Britton's letter continued: "Considerable pressure has been brought upon him [Neyland] recently by the business men of Knoxville to resign from the army and I think that if they make the salary satisfactory, he will do so."

At that point in the letter, Britton told Secretary Good that Neyland knew Britton was writing the letter.

"The University is paying him [Neyland] about $7,500 a year and giving him a house to live in, since he is professor of military science in addition to his other army duties. In order to save paying him the salary they would have to pay him for resigning from the army, they have suggested that he get a three months leave and come back here [to Knoxville] during September, October, and November 1930. Then they would decide about meeting his salary demand. Major Neyland would be relieved in June 1930 and this leave would give him another [football] season.

"Major Neyland wants to decide the whole thing now because he realizes that he will be making enemies in the army if he asks for three months leave to come back here. If this leave is not granted, then the matter will be decided in the near future. This will give me time to make other connections if Major Neyland does resign from the army."

Good replied to Britton by letter, saying he could not state with certainty whether Neyland would be granted a three-month leave of absence for the fall of 1930. So, while the fans waited anxiously to learn of Neyland's future, his trusted assistant, Bill Britton, waited also. Meanwhile, excitement about the 1929 Tennessee football season overshadowed concern that Neyland might leave.

The varsity squad had only 39 players. The line averaged 183 pounds per man. Gene McEver, the "Wild Bull" from Bristol, had been permitted to report late for opening practice because he was helping an amateur baseball team in his hometown win some late season games.

"Mack and Hack . . . two of the most versatile backs that ever trod Southern sod . . . will step high, wide, and handsome this year," wrote Ed Danforth, sports editor of the *Atlanta Constitution*. "They still have lanky Bobby Dodd, a canny mountaineer, to call their signals and throw them passes. And they have Ty Disney, a tow-head fullback, to run interference and crash the line."

Even with Dodd, McEver, and Hackman returning, plus fullbacks Disney and Quinn Decker and a healthy line, Neyland publicly was apprehensive about the season. "I'll not be surprised if we lose three conference games," he told Fuzzy Woodruff, columnist for the *Atlanta Journal.* "Too much schedule to go through undefeated." The opponents that could beat Tennessee, Neyland said, were Ole Miss, Alabama, Vanderbilt, Kentucky, and Florida.

"We beat Alabama last year in the most thrilling game I ever saw," he said. "You can depend on it that Wallace Wade is going to have his team ready for us this year. He didn't have them peaked last year. He was looking for something easy. A coach of Wade's caliber doesn't make that mistake two years running."

Tennessee began the 1929 season as every coach dreams of launching a campaign. McEver returned the opening kickoff 90 yards for a touchdown, and the Vols beat Carson-Newman, 40-6. By the time the Vols had rolled over Chattanooga, 20-0, and "tough" Ole Miss, 52-7, McEver had scored nine touchdowns and was on his way to 130 points, the Tennessee record through 1989. He scored three TDs in the first quarter against Ole Miss.

Tennessee's 6-0 victory over Alabama in a classic defensive struggle, the kind Neyland loved, had sportswriters reaching for dramatic descriptions. *Knoxville Journal* sports editor Bob Murphy wrote of "an unconquerable Tennessee team" plunging the "mighty Crimson Tide into a bottomless pit of oblivion." One wrote of the "battle of speed versus power," another of "a tale of heroism and desperate encounter."

The only touchdown came in the second quarter after Tennessee tackle Jake Johnston penetrated the Alabama line and blocked Tony Holm's punt. Harry Thayer recovered for the Vols at the 'Bama 39, and from there Dodd, Hack, and Mack went to work, alternately advancing the ball to the two. McEver then scored.

The gallant Vols turned back three Alabama scoring threats, one of them late in the game at the Tennessee one. Dodd took precious seconds off the clock by eluding tacklers in the end zone before intentionally throwing incomplete passes on first and second downs. Frustrated Alabama players threw their helmets to the ground. "I probably should have taken a safety," Dodd said, but instead he caught Alabama napping and quick-kicked to the 'Bama 45. The game ended two plays later.

"We had a better team than Tennessee, but Dodd just beat us himself," Alabama tackle Fred Sington said years later. "He had us so mad at him, we couldn't play football."

Between handshakes of congratulations from fans crowded near the victors' dressing room door, Neyland told reporters: "I can't single out an individual performance during the game. The team did better than I had expected them to do. In winning, our boys did themselves proud and defeated a gallant foe."

Nashville Tennessean sports editor Blinkey Horn labeled Dodd "the greatest quarterback in Dixie."

Dodd was a "bold gambler on the field and a relaxed nonconformist off the field, and how he thrived under strict, ultra-conservative Bob Neyland is, to me, one of the modern sports miracles," wrote *Nashville Banner* sports editor Fred Russell in his book, *Bury Me in an Old Press Box.* Dodd, indeed, had his own way of doing things.

"It was more genius than brains," Neyland said of Dodd. "I do not believe that Dodd arrived at his decisions by any deductive process, but unerringly played his hunches." That Neyland, disciplined and analytical, was able to effectively utilize Dodd's free-style "genius" is one of the clearest examples of Neyland's coaching abilities. These were two extraordinary men. Obviously, they appreciated each other more than either ever let on.

Taking a cue from the 6-0 win over Alabama, the Vols held their next four opponents scoreless. Neyland did not even play his first team against Carson-Newman; the final was 73-0, setting the stage for games with Vanderbilt and Kentucky. Vandy had lost only once, but Commodore coach Dan McGugin spoke of unbeaten Tennessee's superiority. "That sob stuff about Vanderbilt is old McGugin stuff," Neyland said.

Neyland, the football conservative, surprised his players when he unveiled a hidden-ball play in the game plan for Vanderbilt, and the man for whom he designed it was the master nonconformist, Bobby Dodd. Dodd said he took the snap from center at the Vandy 16, turned his back to the line, faked a handoff to McEver, then walked backward across the line of scrimmage. "I almost tripped over a Vanderbilt guy," he said. "He didn't know I had the ball, and I didn't see him." Once clear of the line, Dodd turned and ran toward the end zone and was tackled just as he crossed the goal. "After the game, Neyland said nothing about the success of the trick play. He just winked at me," Dodd said. The Vols won 13-0.

"Words cannot express my admiration for those boys," Neyland said of this team. "They won such a glorious victory over a team that fought throughout and exhibited the clean, hard fight which always has characterized Vanderbilt teams."

McGugin, in turn, praised Tennessee, especially the work of Hack and Mack and Dodd. "There is probably not a greater back than McEver on the American field. He has abundant weight, unusual strength, wonderful speed, is as elusive as a fly buzzing around a honey jar, and a durned sight more tantalizing," McGugin said. National sportswriters, he added, "would do well to consider Tennessee along with the two or three best teams in the country."

As the Vols prepared for the Kentucky game on Thanksgiving Day, stunning news came from Washington, D.C. In a dispatch from the nation's capital, correspondent C. J. Lilley of the *Knoxville News-Sentinel* reported: "The University of Tennessee can celebrate a big Thanksgiving holiday this year because of an official announcement made today by Major General Lytle Brown, chief of the Army Engineers, that an arrangement has been worked out in the War Department that will keep Major Robert Neyland at the school during football seasons."

Brown explained that Neyland would remain in the army on another assignment but would be permitted to continue coaching the Tennessee football team.

"Major Neyland will wind up his connection with the University of Tennessee with the expiration of his present detail," Brown said. "He has served five years there and for him to serve any longer [at Tennessee] would not be in harmony with the policy of the department. . . .

"Major Neyland will be detailed as assistant to the district engineer at Chattanooga where he will be situated close to the University [110 miles away], and whatever he wants to do for the University on his own time will be agreeable to the Office of Chief Engineer."

Brown said Neyland would receive furloughs to coach the Tennessee Vols. "The assignment will be for four years, or as long as I am chief engineer."

Coupled with news that Neyland would be Tennessee's coach at least through 1933 was growing speculation that the Vols would be invited to play in the Rose Bowl—still the only bowl game in those days—if they beat Kentucky.

Snow had started falling the night before the game in Lexington, and the wind-swept storm continued on game day. The temperature was in the low 30s, and swirling snow covered the yard-stripes as the game progressed.

Tennessee was trailing 6-0 late in the fourth quarter when Hackman told Dodd: "Throw me that damn ball, and I'll catch it." The ball in those days was more oval. Only one ball was used during a game, and the one that day became heavy with water and ice. Dodd heaved the wet, heavy ball as far as he could, and Hackman, who had broken clear down the sideline, made the catch.

"The referees thought Hackman had crossed the goal and signaled a touchdown, and Neyland sent our placekicker, Charlie Kohlhase, into the game," Hugh Faust recalled. "But when the officials were spotting the ball for the extra point, they scraped away the snow and discovered Hackman had gone out of bounds at the 6. Neyland wanted to be certain we scored the tying touchdown, so he sent Paul Heydrick in for Kohlhase. Hackman scored two plays later from the 4. But under the rules of that day, Kohlhase could not re-enter in the same quarter he left the game."

So Heydrick attempted the extra point and it sailed through the goalposts, but just under the crossbar. "If it had been two feet higher, we would have gone to the Rose Bowl," Faust lamented. "But it was a tie, and someone else [Pittsburgh] went to the bowl."

Eddie Brietz of the Associated Press summarized the game this way: "Across the snow-covered Bluegrass country tonight, the sharp, shrill scream of the Kentucky Wildcats sang a funeral dirge for blasted Tennessee championship dreams." The following Saturday South Carolina paid the price for Tennessee's disappointment. McEver scored five touchdowns and Buddy Hackman three as the Vols won 54-0.

McEver was a consensus all-American, Tennessee's first, and led the nation with 130 points. Dodd and ends Paul Hug and Fritz Brandt were named to all-Southern teams. The Vols held their opponents to a season-long total of 13 points. Neyland was selected to coach one of two Southern all-star teams that played a game to raise money for the Scottish Rite Children's Hospital. Neyland's team won

21-12 as Hackman scored the three touchdowns, and Dodd kicked the extra points. McEver played, too, but this time it was Hackman's show.

Meanwhile, the Associated Press compiled a list of the "winningest" teams for the previous five seasons (1925-29), and Tennessee was first (39 wins, three losses, four ties) at 92.9 percent. Pittsburgh was second (87.8 percent) and Southern Cal third (86.5). Vanderbilt was 13th, Alabama 17th.

Events shaping Neyland's life were moving rapidly during the winter and spring of 1930. On February 11, Peggy gave birth to their first child, Robert Reese IV. The April 27 Sunday front page of the *Knoxville News-Sentinel* featured a two-column picture of infant Bobby, wearing a helmet and a sweater with a big orange "T" on the front. The headgear came from Frank Callaway at the Athletic House; former Vol line coach Bunny Oakes, then at Nebraska, sent the sweater. And Lenox Baker tossed in a pair of tiny football shoes from Duke.

As promised, General Brown on March 17, 1930, pushed through the orders reassigning Neyland to assistant district engineer in Chattanooga, commanded by Lieutenant Colonel Lewis H. Watkins. Neyland reported for duty in Chattanooga the following June 16.

Neyland's twin career, the army and football, was moving forward. He had the best of both worlds. And, as he looked ahead to 1930, he saw Hack and Mack and Dodd returning for their senior seasons.

CHAPTER 14

Football and Engineering

1930

In the summer of 1930, life suddenly became very complicated for Major Bob Neyland and Peggy. He was still head coach of the University of Tennessee football team. But now he was also assistant district engineer in the Army Corps of Engineers' Chattanooga office, which was responsible for navigation control of the Tennessee River. The Tennessee River begins at the confluence of the Holston and French Broad rivers a few miles above downtown Knoxville and flows 650 miles through Tennessee, Alabama, and Kentucky to the Ohio River near Paducah, Kentucky. The Tennessee had been a wild and unpredictable river, flooding the valleys when it was swollen with the runoff from melting snow and stopping boat traffic when the water was low. The Chattanooga district engineer's office was responsible for that section of the river from Knoxville to Riverton, Alabama, near the point where the states of Tennessee, Alabama, and Mississippi meet.

The district engineer's first assignment for Neyland, conveniently beginning August 25, 1930, was temporary duty at Knoxville to supervise dredging the upper reaches of the Tennessee River. That reporting date coincided closely with the Labor Day start of Tennessee's pre-season football practice. Neyland and Peggy kept their residence in Knoxville.

Two mid-summer incidents and the loss of six players to academic ineligibility or inadequate finances drastically altered Neyland's plans for the 1930 season. Hackman, his splendid wingback, injured a knee while playing tennis. The next day McEver, Tennessee's all-American tailback, tore knee ligaments during a baseball game.

"I was running across first base and turned for second, and then the knee just busted. The ligament was gone," McEver said. "They sent me to the Campbell Clinic in Memphis for an operation. I got to see the team play Alabama and went straight to the hospital. I was in there until Thanksgiving."

With McEver apparently lost for the season, Neyland wanted to move Hackman to tailback. He had Decker at fullback and could move fullback Disney or tailback Faust to wingback in a backfield quarterbacked by Bobby Dodd. Not a bad lineup. But first, he held Hackman out of the opener with Maryville, buying more time for the knee to mend. Paul Hug, Charlie Kohlhase, Hugh Faust, Ty Disney, and Harvey Robinson took care of Maryville, 54-0.

Neyland "leaked" the story that Hack and Mack would return to the lineup for the second game, against Centre. Hackman did. McEver did not. But the Centre game, which the Vols won 18-0, was costly. Tennessee's two all-Southern ends, Hug and Fritz Brandt, went down with knee injuries.

The third game, against Ole Miss, was barely under way when Dodd passed to Hackman for a touchdown. Early in the second half, Hackman reciprocated with a TD pass to Dodd. The Vols won 27-0 with a makeshift backfield of Dodd, Hackman, Faust, and Decker.

Injuries continued to plague Tennessee as the Vols prepared for the Alabama game at Tuscaloosa. McEver was gone for the season. The ends, Hug and Brandt, were on crutches, and their top substitute, Merton Derryberry, was sidelined also. And Faust was hobbling.

Alabama coach Wallace Wade, who would move to Duke after the 1930 season, started his second team against the Vols. On Tennessee's second possession Dodd advanced the Vols to 'Bama's 13, and Wade hurriedly inserted his first team. Alabama held, led 12-0 at halftime, and ultimately won 18-6. It was Tennessee's first loss in 33 games and the only one the Vols would suffer in 61 games—seven fat years from November 1926 to October 1933.

"That's when I had to abandon my one and only superstition—wearing the same underwear throughout a winning streak," Neyland said.

Victories the next three weeks over North Carolina, Clemson, and Carson-Newman set the stage for the game against Vanderbilt in Nashville. Neyland anticipated that his respected rival, Dan McGugin, would direct his offensive attack against Tennessee's injury-riddled flanks. To meet that threat, Neyland designed a new defense—a seven-man line, two linebackers (Kohlhase and Hackman) between the ends and tackles, and two defensive backs. It worked; the linebackers provided the needed support to stop the end sweeps. The Vols held Vandy scoreless, and Dodd threw a couple of touchdown passes to Hackman for a 13-0 win.

Neyland admired Hackman's graceful stride and the effortless way he caught passes. "Old Buddy used to float down the field like a ghost, pull the ball down and continue his long strides," the major said. "He never made a pass catch look difficult. He just floated down the field, pulled the ball down, nestled it in his arms, and kept traveling."

Occasionally, Neyland would get to the practice field early, just to throw passes to Hackman. "I used to throw them as far as I could, but there would be Hackman floating along. If I threw one five yards farther or five yards shorter, Hackman was there to receive. If I managed to get one over his head, he would just look up and let it go. He simply refused to make a mad dash and make it look hard. But most of the time he was at the right spot and caught them."

After the Vols beat Kentucky, Hackman's athletic abilities were showcased in the season-ending win over Florida. Team captain "Hobo" Thayer remembered the scene: "We were playing Florida at Jacksonville, and each team had a touchdown. Buddy Hackman intercepted a forward pass and ran for the apparent winning points. The officials ruled that he had stepped out of bounds at midfield. We accepted the tough break, but I called the team together and told them this was the last time we'd ever play together as a team." Hackman promptly intercepted again and, escorted by a wall of Vol blockers, returned 48 yards for the game-winning touchdown.

Three weeks later, while talking with reporters on the train en route to the Rose Bowl (where Alabama would beat Washington State and finish the season 10-0), Wallace Wade paid a glowing tribute to Neyland. "Bob Neyland has done the best job of coaching during the past four years of any coach in the South. Especially was this so this year." Wade compared the tasks faced by his and Neyland's staffs during the 1930 season.

"We had, for instance, about 22 mighty fine football players. We had no weaknesses in talent or manpower. On the other hand, Bob had about three or four artists, and the rest of his team was not outstanding," Wade said. "Bob had to manipulate and maneuver those artists around in such a way as to make them win ball games. I think his job of winning all but one game—after losing McEver, Hug, and Brandt—was as brilliant an exhibition of coaching as I have ever seen."

"We won because we knew we were better prepared than our opponents," Hackman said. "Coach Neyland gave us the edge."

The 1928 Flaming Sophomores were now graduated, but 1931 brought new hope and new opportunities for Major Bob Neyland and the Tennessee Vols. A promotion had made him the Chattanooga district engineer, and Gene McEver was coming back for a final season of eligibility.

CHAPTER 15

Neyland Feathers a New Nest

1931

Spring practice was a time for evaluating the new sophomores—among them tailback Beattie Feathers of Bristol, Virginia; fullback Herman "Breezy" Wynn of Dublin, Georgia; and lineman Gordon Smith of Paris, Tennessee.

"There wasn't anybody left but me from the old bunch," Gene McEver said. "I came in there with the first group that Neyland recruited in 1927. So all those guys left after 1930. That left me kinda by my lonesome. And they had a pretty good freshman team the year before that. That was Beattie's bunch."

Knoxville Journal columnist Russ Bebb, in his book *The Big Orange,* quotes McEver as saying the knee injury cost him whatever it is that makes a natural runner.

"A fellow's born to run; nobody can teach him," McEver said. "I had a heavy steel brace on my knee, and that thing would get heavy."

So, in spring practice of 1931, Neyland moved McEver to fullback, and sophomore Beattie Feathers won the starting tailback job. Meanwhile, 159-pound Gordon Smith was trying to win a place on the team. In practice one afternoon, Smith stopped a play for a five-yard loss, but his right shoe broke at the instep, his toes hit the ground, and the shoe flopped on top of his foot. Smith headed for Neyland.

"If you want me to play any more of your damned football, you can buy me a pair of new shoes that fit," Smith bellowed, fully expecting to be kicked off the team for his outburst of temper. Instead, Neyland laughed heartily and yelled to line coach Paul Parker: "Paul, order this man three new pairs of shoes."

"I was in a state of shock," Smith recalled. "I learned later, when on the [Tennessee] coaching staff, that Neyland was always on the lookout for new talent and, when he observed someone who might make the team, he would put them under all the heat and pressure possible to see if they would give up and quit or fight back under pressure. This was the day I passed his first test."

During the summer of 1931, Neyland was temporarily assigned to the Fourth Corps Area, headquartered at Fort McPherson, Georgia, as an engineering instructor—a duty he would perform each of the next three summers as well.

On September 15, Neyland gave a preview of his 1931 team at the noon luncheon of the Knoxville Rotary Club in the Farragut Hotel: "We have the largest squad we ever had. The men are heavier. The spirit is better than ever before. We lost some good men, but if the sophomores come through this season, we should have as good a team as in previous years." It was not just talk among friends. Neyland knew that *Nashville Banner* sports editor Fred Russell and Atlanta writers Ralph McGill and Ed Danforth were seated in the back of the room.

"I'm not going to count heavily on McEver and then be disappointed," Neyland said. "Of course, he may be able to play. He says he feels no sensation in the knee, but you never can tell how a fellow's gonna' be after a year's layoff. One hard lick on that knee might ruin him for the season, and he's sure to get plenty of them."

McEver was hobbled by "a heavy and unwieldy brace," wrote Tom Siler of the *Knoxville News-Sentinel*. "He was converted into a plunger, passer, and father-confessor to the sophomore clan. Mac played fullback, left half, and right half, anywhere needed."

As his single-wing offense evolved during his early years at Tennessee, Neyland increasingly saw the need for "triple-threat" tailbacks—players who could run, pass, and punt with equal effectiveness. Going into the 1931 season, he was highly optimistic.

"I have five potential triple-threat men in Kohlhase, Feathers, Robinson, [Deke] Brackett, and [John] Bayless," he said. "All can run, pass, and punt. All will play a lot this year. Too, I intend to use McEver for some passing."

With 225-pound senior Herman Hickman anchoring a rebuilt line, the Vols held their 10 opponents to only 15 points. They won nine games, including victories over Alabama, now being coached by Notre Dame alumnus Frank Thomas, and Duke, coached by Wallace Wade. McEver scored three touchdowns against Alabama. The only blemish on another superlative season was a 6-6 tie with old nemesis Kentucky.

Neyland loved to tell about Feathers's punts in that Alabama game: "The greatest of all their punters, Johnny Cain, was keeping our backs to the wall. He was kicking them out on our goal line, and our returns were puny." So Neyland called Feathers to his side: "Get in there, Feathers, and kick that ball out."

Standing three yards deep in his end zone, Feathers received the snap from center.

"That guy put his hand over the top of the ball in that crazy way he always held it," Neyland said. "The second his foot hit that ball, you knew you were in on something special. Well, Alabama's safetyman just turned and ran like an outfielder. When he picked the ball up, he was tackled immediately on his own 25-yard line. Beattie had kicked the ball 75 yards [actually, it was a net 64 yards from the line of scrimmage to the 'Bama 27]." Neyland said that punt, the first of Feathers's varsity career, broke Alabama's back. The Vols romped 25-0.

America was in the grips of the Great Depression in 1931. People without jobs sold apples on city streets. Thousands stood in seemingly endless lines for bread and soup. The morale of the nation plunged.

To raise money for thousands of unemployed, Mayor Jimmy Walker of New York City personally invited the Tennessee Vols to play undefeated New York University in a charity football game on December 5 in Yankee Stadium. Neyland accepted. New York sportswriters called it the Charity Bowl. It was Tennessee's first post-season game.

Feathers broke the game open with a 65-yard touchdown run in the second quarter, and Brackett's 75-yard punt return gave the Vols a 13-0 victory. Herman Hickman's performance was so impressive that he was named to Grantland Rice's All-American team.

One of the spectators was Carl Snavely, the head coach at Bucknell and later at Cornell and North Carolina. "I had never heard much of coach Bob Neyland before that day," Snavely said, "but after watching Tennessee play for about five minutes, I became a Neyland fan."

Gordon Smith, the little lineman, said it was great to play on an undefeated Tennessee team with McEver, Hickman, and Feathers, "but my greatest thrill was after this game when coach Neyland came out on the field, put his arm around me and, as we walked off the field in Yankee Stadium, said 'You're big enough to play on my team.'"

CHAPTER 16

Political Football

1932

After being named district engineer, Neyland assigned his assistant, Captain H. D. W. Riley, to the district office at Florence, Alabama. Riley was given responsibility for navigational clearance of the Tennessee River from Riverton, Alabama, to Chattanooga. Neyland took charge of the river between Chattanooga and Knoxville.

So during the winter and spring of 1932, Neyland supervised the dredges keeping the Tennessee River channel navigable for a sand and gravel company that was shipping materials downriver by barge. He arranged his schedule so he could drill the football team in the spring.

Neyland expanded his coaching staff—adding two of his former players, John Barnhill and Hugh Faust, to help him, Britton, and Parker. Barnhill coached the freshman team. McEver completed his eligibility in 1931, but junior Herman "Breezy" Wynn was ready to start at fullback alongside tailback Beattie Feathers. Joining them in the starting backfield were quarterback Deke Brackett and wingback Dick Dorsey. Neyland had effectively repaired graduation losses in the line. He was ready for another banner year, and that is what 1932 proved to be.

The Vols were undefeated in 10 games, with only a scoreless tie with Vanderbilt marring a splendid year. The season was especially memorable for Vol fans because Feathers took up the pen and became a post-game analyst for the *Knoxville Journal*. The paper gave him a by-line and identified him as a "*Journal* Staff Writer."

"The Vols looked pretty good yesterday in rolling up a 33-0 victory over Ole Miss," Feathers wrote after the second game. "Our play, however, was nothing to get excited over. There is still a lot of work ahead for the Major if we hope to beat

North Carolina and Alabama in a row.

"Although we beat Ole Miss by a decisive score, I am sure that Alabama could have defeated the same team by a much larger margin. I guess I had better not talk so much about 'Bama right now because North Carolina is going to give us a tough afternoon next Saturday."

Beattie Feathers's prognostications were a bit off target. For example, the "tough afternoon" against North Carolina turned out to be a routine Vol victory. The Vols led 14-0 at the half and 20-0 in the fourth quarter. The final was 20-7. Feathers provided the only excitement in an otherwise dull afternoon—a 59-yard touchdown run, aided by a textbook downfield block by team captain Malcolm Aiken.

Then came the game always played on the third Saturday in October—the Vols and the Alabama Crimson Tide, this time at Legion Field in Birmingham. Rain fell steadily through the morning. Conditions were so bad that Neyland and Frank Thomas, Alabama's new head coach, turned almost exclusively to the kicking game. And what unfolded was one of the most memorable punting duels in the history of college football.

Beattie Feathers of Tennessee and Johnny Cain of Alabama, negotiating a treacherous field, punted back and forth throughout the game. Often they kicked on first or second down. Feathers averaged 46 yards on 23 punts, one of them for only 18 yards. Cain averaged 43 yards on 19 punts, but one from his own end zone went only to the Alabama 12 and set up Tennessee's winning touchdown.

Alabama was leading 3-0 at the half, and Tennessee had the option to take advantage of the wind in the third quarter or to receive the kickoff.

"No," Neyland ruled. "We'll give Alabama the wind in the third quarter. They have a lead to protect, and they'll have to be conservative, taking no chances on a sloppy field. Then, when we get the wind in the fourth quarter, we'll be able to strike, and they will be helpless to stop us or retaliate."

Neyland's prophecy was fulfilled. Alabama guarded its three-point lead in the third quarter. In the fourth, Tennessee had the wind at its back and was gaining yardage on every punt exchange.

It appeared for much of the game as if Alabama's second quarter field goal would be the margin of victory—until a Feathers punt in the fourth quarter rolled dead at the Alabama one. Cain tried to punt from the end zone on first down but got a bad snap from center and had to rush his kick, which splashed down in the muddy sod on the 'Bama 12. Feathers scored three plays later, and Wynn's extra point gave Tennessee a 7-3 victory.

"It was one of the greatest games I have ever seen played under such bad conditions," Neyland said.

The Duke game two weeks later ended in extraordinary fashion, but not before some play-making shenanigans. Vol fullback Breezy Wynn recalled how Tennessee, with a 13-0 lead, was driving toward Duke's goal.

"[Deke] Brackett was feeling his oats, so he made a bold move," Wynn recalled. "In the huddle, he told Feathers to switch from tailback to wingback, sent Vaughan to tailback, and left me at fullback." Brackett then proceeded to conceive a play in the huddle.

"Vaughan will fake a pass to Feathers, and I'll slide out into the flat. He'll throw to me, and I'll step over [the goal] for a touchdown," Brackett told his teammates.

Wynn objected, but Brackett was adamant, "I'm running the team," he said. "Be still or I'll send you to the sidelines."

The Vols did as Brackett told them, but the Blue Devils' all-American tackle Fred Crawford intercepted the pass and returned it for a Duke touchdown. After Duke tied the game in the fourth quarter, Neyland called for a field goal attempt by Wynn. But Brackett, the holder, fumbled the snap from center and could only place the ball sideways on the ground. Locked in concentration, Wynn kicked the ball anyway and the unlikely 18-yard field goal gave the Vols a 16-13 victory.

Monday typically was a day when Neyland gathered the team in front of a chalkboard and reviewed their mistakes in the previous game. But not on the Monday after that Duke game.

"Gentlemen," Neyland began, "I have no business up here today. We have a man on our squad far smarter than I am. He is absolutely brilliant. We spend spring drills, [all of] September, and afternoon drills [during the season] to perfect a few plays. But we have a man so brilliant that on the spur of the moment he can make up a play, put it in, and execute it, while I cannot even get you boys to execute a play on which we have worked months."

The tone of Neyland's voice was stern, not sarcastic.

"So, I think Mr. Brackett should stand up here and direct this coaching clinic instead of me. On second thought, Mr. Brackett will be retired to the second team, and Mr. Brackett will run five miles for his brilliant direction of the team."

Brackett's punishment reflected Neyland's law about preparation. "No play is any good until it's been rehearsed 500 times," he often said. "I'd rather have one bad play executed well than 50 good plays executed poorly."

On Sunday morning, November 13, newspaper headlines told of a scoreless tie, a nullified touchdown, and a near-riot at the Tennessee-Vanderbilt game at Dudley Field in Nashville. The two teams were undefeated, and the game was a sellout. Thousands of ticketless fans who were turned away at the gates knocked down the fences. Some dropped into the stadium enclosure from surrounding housetops.

"In a game featured by super-savage tackling and murderous blocking, Tennessee and Vanderbilt waged a defensive masterpiece in their traditional battle here this afternoon before a mad, surging throng of 30,000 fans," the *Knoxville Journal* story said, adding the crowd at times seemed to reach "maniacal proportions."

"Between halves, it was announced that the game would not be continued unless the wild, rabid crowd cleared the cinder path [between the playing field and the stadium seats]," the *Journal* reported. "Both squads left the field, taking all equipment with them." The game was delayed 40 minutes while order was being restored. Throughout the second half, coaches restrained fans along the sidelines. At one point, Vandy coach Dan McGugin warned fans that if they did not retreat within two minutes the game would be forfeited to Tennessee.

The rowdiness erupted again among Tennessee fans in the fourth quarter when Feathers caught a pass from Pug Vaughan and ran 51 yards to an apparent touchdown. But one of the referees, Battle Begley, ruled that Feathers had stepped out of bounds at the Vandy 49. Crowd behavior got so unruly that the referees ended the game with three minutes left on the clock and Vandy deep in Tennessee territory. It was a scoreless tie.

With the Vols riding a 24-game unbeaten streak, jittery fans once more became concerned that Major Bob Neyland would leave Tennessee. Rumors had him taking the head coaching job at Fordham University.

"We discussed it at length," Peggy Neyland said. "I thought he was going to accept the Fordham offer."

On the night before the season finale against Florida in Jacksonville, Neyland was notified that his mother had died in Greenville, Texas. Neyland left Jacksonville at 1:45 a.m. on Saturday to make his way back to Greenville for her funeral.

A sadness settled over the Tennessee football team when news of Mrs. Neyland's death reached the players. Team captain Malcolm Aiken called a meeting of the players. They pledged an all-out effort against Florida as a tribute of respect to the Neyland family.

With assistant coaches Bill Britton and Paul Parker carrying on in Neyland's absence, the Vols defeated Florida, 32-13. Deke Brackett broke Florida's back with touchdowns on an 87-yard kickoff return and a 53-yard punt return. The Vols led 25-7 at the half.

"Tennessee for about a half today was probably the greatest team we have ever coached," Britton said. "They went out to play for Bob Neyland, and I will always admire their attitude."

The victory over Florida gave the Vols another undefeated season—Neyland's fifth in seven years as Tennessee's head coach. The Vols were acclaimed the Southern Conference champion with a 7-0-1 record, but LSU had a 3-0 conference record and Louisiana Governor Huey "Kingfish" Long declared the Tigers the conference champion.

Just a few days after the end of the 1932 season, 13 schools seceded from the Southern Conference and formed the new Southeastern Conference. Charter members were Alabama, Auburn, Georgia, Georgia Tech, Florida, Kentucky, Louisiana State, Mississippi, Mississippi State, the University of the South (Sewanee), Tennessee, Tulane, and Vanderbilt.

Meanwhile, the rumor mill had Neyland leaving Tennessee. Neyland himself confirmed he had been made an offer by Fordham University. "Fordham officials had assured him that they could arrange a transfer from his army post at Chattanooga," Russ Bebb said in *The Big Orange*.

"An unidentified school in Texas also made overtures," Bebb reported. "Neyland's only comment was that the Fordham offer was 'very attractive.'" But Neyland stayed at Tennessee, even though he did not receive a salary increase after another undefeated season.

Meanwhile, the military side of Neyland's life was becoming embroiled in controversy that would reach all the way to the White House, soon to be occupied by Franklin D. Roosevelt.

On October 10, 1932, two days after Tennessee's win over North Carolina, Major T. W. King made an inspection tour at the Corps of Engineers's district office in Chattanooga. Neyland, of course, was not there. He was in Knoxville, coaching his football team and about to become a political football.

"Employees of his office [in Chattanooga] stated that Major Neyland resided at Knoxville, Tenn., a distance of 111 miles from Chattanooga, and handled all the work of his office by mail," King said in a dispatch to the Inspector General's office in Washington, D.C. "As far as known, Major Neyland has no official duties at Knoxville."

On November 15, Neyland received a communique ordering him to respond in writing to King's "discovery." He did so, explaining how he assigned Captain Riley to supervise the lower half of the Chattanooga District while he supervised the upper half. He also noted that most of the recent river improvement had occurred in the Knoxville area.

One of Neyland's superiors, Lieutenant Colonel E. L. Daley, wasted no time firing off a dispatch in support of Neyland's position. Daley was assistant to the division engineer, headquartered in St. Louis, Missouri.

Daley informed the chief of engineers in Washington that Major King had made no effort to obtain available information about the scope of Neyland's duties and work schedule.

"The conduct of the operation of the Chattanooga District by Major Neyland as outlined by him . . . has had the complete approval of the Division Engineer," Daley told Washington.

"In addition to the very efficient discharge of his duties as District Engineer, it is widely known that Major Neyland has been the successful coach of the football team of the University of Tennessee, located at Knoxville, Tennessee. His activity and ability as a football coach have enhanced his reputation as an engineer and have materially increased his effectiveness as a representative of the Corps of Engineers in the large area of which he is District Engineer."

But the controversy would not go away. Major King, in that first dispatch after visiting the Chattanooga office, had raised questions that Neyland and Daley had not addressed in their responses—namely that Neyland "handled all the work of his office by mail."

In short, Neyland was being accused of being an absentee district engineer—having an office in Chattanooga, but living in Knoxville and coaching a college football team on the side.

Major General Lytle Brown, the chief of engineers and the man who made it possible for Neyland to continue coaching the University of Tennessee football team while commanding the Chattanooga District, could not let King's insinuation go unanswered.

"Major Neyland is performing his duties as district engineer efficiently," Brown told the adjutant general in correspondence dated December 5, 1932. "In conference with the Chief of Staff I secured his approval of the present arrangement in 1929, when it was understood that Major Neyland might, on his own time, assist in athletic training at the University of Tennessee at Knoxville provided no interference would occur with his duties at Chattanooga."

Then, the acting inspector general of the United States, Colonel M. G. Spinks, got into the act.

"The War Department should not sanction a system by which a disbursing officer [Neyland] handles all or even a large part of the work of his office by mail," Spinks said in a dispatch to R. P. Palmer, the adjutant general of the army.

In the midst of the dispatches, memoranda, and letters flying back and forth between Chattanooga, St. Louis, and Washington, another curious element was injected into Neyland's volatile situation.

Pelham St. George Bissell, a municipal court judge in New York City, on December 6 wrote to F. Trubee Davison, the assistant secretary of war.

"A large number of my friends are greatly interested in the transfer of Major Robert R. Neyland . . . to the Second Corps Area in the vicinity of New York City," Judge Bissell wrote. "The transfer would be a most popular act from the standpoint of many in the New York area, and I am hoping that you may see your way clear to speak a word in behalf of it to Secretary Hurley."

Fordham University of New York City, desiring Neyland's services as a football coach, had made overtures to him on several occasions in recent years. The Fordham offers were more than rumor. And, while there may have been no link between Fordham and Bissell's letter to the War Department, the timing is at least intriguing.

Bissell's letter set in motion a chain reaction within the War Department.

On December 22, 16 days after Bissell wrote the letter, he received a reply from Davison: "It is found to be impracticable at this time to transfer Major Neyland from Chattanooga, Tennessee, to New York City. This officer is engaged upon very important work, at his present position, and for which he was specially chosen due to his professional qualifications."

Thus, the mission of Judge Pelham St. George Bissell of New York City failed. There would be no transfer of Bob Neyland to New York City.

With Christmas approaching, Neyland relegated his concerns about the "investigation" to the back burner and devoted his attention to Peggy and their son, Bobby, now almost three years old. The Christmas tree. The exchange of gifts between Bob and Peggy. Santa Claus for Bobby. Rest for the Major, a respite from the everyday pressures of football and the river.

But after New Year's Day, Neyland returned to the task of answering the implications of Major King's inquisition.

"The statement that I handled all of the work of this office by mail, attributed to employees by Mr. King, is a mistaken statement," Neyland said in a formal reply. He explained how he handled routine matters by mail, but his work requiring consultation with superiors or assistants was handled in conformity with those requirements. "I understood thoroughly the necessity for producing work conforming in quality and quantity to a high standard and bent every effort toward that end," Neyland said.

Lieutenant Colonel Daley in St. Louis told the chief of engineers in Washington that Neyland had performed the duties of district engineer efficiently, expeditiously, and economically.

"He [Neyland] keeps a close and successful contact with administrative matters in the Chattanooga District," Daley said. "Administrative matters have improved under his direction. . . . He is thoroughly conversant with and efficiently controls the activities throughout his district, in the district office at Chattanooga, sub-office at Florence, Alabama, storehouses, and field operations."

Daley said Neyland's financial and property accounts in the Chattanooga District office clearly showed he performed his duties in a manner that "assured the economical, efficient, and lawful expenditure of funds and property."

So, during the winter months of 1933, the controversy, which threatened to be as volatile as the Tennessee-Vanderbilt crowd, quietly died. The terse letter of Major General Lytle Brown, chief of engineers, was the instrument largely responsible for ending the ruckus caused by Major King. Brown's letter, ultimately reaching the inspector general and the secretary of war, was a ringing endorsement of Neyland's character and military performance.

CHAPTER 17

Neyland vs. Roosevelt

1933

Borrowing a thought from writer-philosopher Henry David Thoreau and telling Depression-scarred America that "the only thing we have to fear is fear itself," Franklin Delano Roosevelt in January 1933 became the 32nd president of the United States and instituted changes that drastically affected the social and economic fabric of the nation.

Events of great importance were occurring in Asia and Europe too. Japan in September 1931 had marched into Manchuria, the first military action leading to World War II, and in January 1933, the Japanese delegation walked out of the League of Nations assembly. Meanwhile, one-time Austrian paper-hanger Adolph Hitler became chancellor of Germany and began to assert dictatorial power to mobilize his country for a brutal war of conquest and genocide.

In the United States, President Roosevelt sent to Congress a steady stream of "New Deal" economic and social legislation designed to put Americans to work, to regulate banking, and to feed, house, and clothe the poor. On April 10, Roosevelt suggested to Congress the creation of the Tennessee Valley Authority (TVA), "a corporation clothed with the power of government but possessed of the flexibility and initiative of a private enterprise." The mission of the TVA was to harness the often-rampaging Tennessee River, to improve navigation, to promote agricultural and industrial development in the Tennessee River valley, and to produce hydroelectric power through a series of dams. The legislation was signed into law May 18, 1933, and before the end of the year construction began on the first dam.

The creation of the TVA, however, disturbed power companies that had for years been generating and distributing electricity within and outside of the Tennessee River valley.

Private power companies in Tennessee and Alabama had made agreements with the War Department to buy Muscle Shoals power. Officials of the new administration, however, claimed the Wilson Dam power plant at Muscle Shoals, operated by the Army Corps of Engineers, was being damaged because the Corps of Engineers was allowing the Tennessee Power Company and the Alabama Power Company to transmit electricity to each other through the plant. The target of the investigation was Major Bob Neyland, the Chattanooga district engineer, whose area of responsibility along the Tennessee River included the Wilson Dam power plant at Muscle Shoals.

The investigation by the Roosevelt administration into alleged sabotage of the Wilson Dam power plant continued into the early summer of 1933, and Roosevelt ordered the removal of Neyland and Captain Riley, whom Neyland had placed in charge of Wilson Dam. Neyland received orders transferring him to Nashville as district engineer. But the chief of the Corps of Engineers in Washington was slow to execute Neyland's transfer orders. In fact, when finally issued, the orders were to become effective "on or about Aug. 1." He officially reported to Nashville July 28.

Meanwhile, in their routine efficiency reports, Neyland's superiors continued rating his performance "excellent." Colonel George R. Spalding, the division engineer headquartered in St. Louis, said Neyland's performance as district engineer at Chattanooga and then Nashville qualified him for promotion in rank. Asked what was the highest command for which Neyland was qualified, Spalding wrote "no limit." He described Neyland as "a fine officer and natural leader."

The Muscle Shoals investigation withered and died in the face of Major General Lytle Brown's letter to Senator George W. Norris of Nebraska demanding, in effect, that the government either charge Neyland and Riley or drop the investigation. No charges were ever formalized against Neyland or any of his subordinates. But Bob Neyland never forgot how he was treated by the New Deal administration. Years later, following his retirement with the rank of brigadier general after World War II, he expressed in clear and strong language his contempt for Roosevelt and New Deal Democrats.

"I was brought up a dyed-in-the-wool 100 percent Democrat," he said in his memoirs. "However, I lived to see the day that Dad said: 'If these damn New Dealers are Democrats, I ain't.' . . . I am 'agin' the New Deal, Fair Deal, or any other sort of Deal that promulgates:

- The national graduated income tax that is Requirement [No.] 1 of the Communist Manifesto.
- The Social Security laws which constitute the most barefaced and gigantic fraud upon our present population and upon millions of those yet unborn.
- The national labor laws which permit and encourage tyrannical union bosses, who falsely claim to represent labor, to make slaves of millions of workers, deny them the right to employment, and

to jeopardize our national safety by stoppage of essential nation wide industries.

- Social concepts which put the federal government in business competition with private industry."

The events of the first half of 1933 left a bitter taste in Neyland's mouth and caused him to begin a new assessment of his career path. Could he continue to mix the army and football or would he have to choose one over the other?

For the present, however, he could continue with both. His army orders permitted him to coach the University of Tennessee football team while serving as district engineer in Nashville.

The magazine section of the *Nashville Tennessean* carried a cartoon drawing of Neyland and the words: "Illustrious Nashville citizen, who as one of Uncle Sam's Army engineers, spends most of his time working to help mariners run over the Tennessee River, and the rest of his time working to prevent anybody (especially Commodores) from running over his Tennessee football team."

The new 13-member Southeastern Conference was preparing for its first season. In a poll of SEC coaches, Tennessee was picked to win the first SEC football championship, mainly because of the veteran backfield of Beattie Feathers at tailback, Breezy Wynn at fullback, Deke Brackett at blockingback, and Charles "Pug" Vaughan or Leo Petruzze at wingback. Neyland, however, disagreed with his colleagues. He picked Vanderbilt first, then Alabama and LSU.

Intrigued by Tennessee's 61 victories in Neyland's seven years as head coach, *Atlanta Constitution* sports editor Ralph McGill visited Neyland before the season started. At dinner, McGill asked Neyland about the origin of the "Neyland system."

"I borrowed something of the strong side play from [Knute] Rockne and from Gil Dobie," Neyland said. "I like some of the features of Wallace Wade's weak side play, and so I borrowed that. I took some of the Army's style and incorporated it into mine. Then, I had some ideas of my own.

"Especially did I stick to the balanced line and the quarter[back] handling the ball. I don't think other coaches had started that when I did. Usually the quarter does not handle the ball in a balanced line.

"And I think we had advanced ideas as to forward passes. In 1931 we completed about 75 percent of our passes. It was considerably lower in 1932, but in 1930 Bobby Dodd completed about 45 percent, and he grounded many of his intentionally.

"Put all that together, and it's the Tennessee system." Neyland went on candidly.

"They have said of us in the past that we have not played a representative schedule and are not entitled to some championship claims. I say to that, 'You are quite right,'" Neyland told McGill. "I do say, however, that we have had a team which on any given day was a difficult team to beat. We have had few big players. I like the Tennessee material. It averages about 180 pounds. We have won with that."

Neyland impressed McGill with his candor.

"There is no modern football team anywhere . . . which can approach this record," McGill wrote of Neyland's 61 victories. "He has good material. He admits it. But it has never been super material. He has made no championship claims."

Ironically, Neyland had beefed up Tennessee's 1933 schedule. It included Virginia Polytechnic Institute, Mississippi State, Duke, Alabama, Florida, George Washington, Mississippi, Vanderbilt, Kentucky, and LSU. "Quite a menu for a team that usually has met about three strong teams a season," said Morgan Blake, sports editor of the *Atlanta Journal*.

"Yes, we'll have a better team than last year," Neyland said. "We've got more reserve strength than we've ever had, but we'll have to have a team three times as strong to win every game on our schedule." It was a prophetic statement.

The 1933 season began on a dismal note for Tennessee. Breezy Wynn, the Vols' first team fullback, suffered a broken ankle in the opener against Virginia Tech. Doctor Robert G. Brashear, the Tennessee team physician, examined the senior fullback in the dressing room and said Wynn's playing days at Tennessee were finished.

"For 12 long months, I dreamed of football and how we would mow down our opponents this fall. Now where am I?" Wynn lamented from his bed in the university infirmary.

For the first time since Neyland had become Tennessee's head coach, the Vols struggled from day to day, trying to find that old magic that had propelled them into the national limelight. But, even with Feathers, the Vols dropped two in a row—to Duke, 10-2, and to Alabama, 12-6—for the first time since Neyland took command in 1926.

The 50-yard-line post-game meeting between Neyland and Duke coach Wallace Wade, and the subsequent scene inside the Vol dressing room, gives an insight into how Neyland handled defeat.

"You deserved that one, Wallace, and I offer my congratulations," Neyland said as they shook hands.

"Thanks, Bob," Wade replied. "I can't quite realize that we've beaten you fellows." They shook hands again, and Neyland rushed to the dressing room where he walked among the defeated Vols, patting some, hugging others. Consoling all

"It just wasn't in the cards," Neyland said of the loss to Duke. "I could almost sense it from the first three plays. Everything we did seemed to go wrong. But we tried hard, and I am proud of the boys in defeat. Duke played inspiring football, and I don't think I ever saw a team make fewer mistakes."

Neyland praised Wade lavishly. "We were beaten by a great team, a team that was excellently coached. Duke didn't 'get' the breaks, they 'made' them and were clever enough to take advantage of them. If I've got to be beaten, I'd rather it be by Wallace Wade than anyone else."

In the Duke dressing room, Wade spoke of Tennessee and his old friend, Bob Neyland, warmly. "If you lose to them, they praise you. If you beat them, they praise you," Wade said of the Vols. "I can never say enough about Neyland's team. I have always said they were the finest coached teams in the country. They are hard fighters and always clean players."

The highlight of the year for Tennessee occurred at mid-season when the Vols traveled to Washington, D.C., to play unbeaten and nationally ranked George Washington University. To mark the occasion, Neyland wrote an article for a Washington newspaper.

"Our team is in excellent physical condition. We have our greatest strength of the year," Neyland wrote. "It is my opinion the morale of the Volunteers undoubtedly is the best it has been all season long."

It wound up being one of the best days in Feathers's career. He averaged 51 yards on 12 punts, one of them for 66 yards. And Feathers and Brackett repeatedly completed passes to ends Cecil C. "Sonny" Humphreys and Louis Pounders.

With a 13-0 victory safely tucked away, Neyland called Feathers to the bench for the final three minutes. At the time, Tennessee had a first down on George Washington's nine-yard line. With his face scratched and his nose bleeding, Feathers left the field with a thunderous ovation ringing in his ears. He had gained 111 yards on 14 carries and had scored both touchdowns. Washington writers described Feathers as the greatest back since Jim Thorpe at Carlisle.

Washington sportswriter Harry Costello, a former player and coach, said Neyland "stands alone at the head of the parade" of football coaches. "Major Neyland stands alone as the man of preparation. No other coach in America ever has achieved Bob's success in planning for a game. Minute details, cumbersome to some others, are personal duties to Major Neyland. Truly he has been, and is, the great master of detailed football."

Costello added that Neyland was more than just a football coach. "He is a scholar, soldier, gentleman, all rolled into one. He is cultured. He is understanding. He is tolerant. He is aggressive. He is intellectually honest. He is loyal, true blue. He is a scientist, which means that facts are his particular fetish. He is a man in whom the university proudly may place its confidence, its respect, its reputation."

No other football coach was more admired and respected, or held in higher affection, "by those who really know him" than was Bob Neyland, Costello wrote. "He has the qualities of mind and heart and soul out of which greatness comes. His practical training, his knowledge, his ideals, his abilities, all contrive to give him that most essential of all desirable characteristics—the mark of a gentleman and sportsman. Tennessee must be proud of this man, Bob Neyland."

The most emotional moment of the 1933 season occurred in the 33-6 victory over Vanderbilt just after Pug Vaughan intercepted a Vandy pass and returned it 79 yards for the final touchdown of the game. Senior fullback Breezy Wynn, who had missed six games because of a broken ankle, was in uniform on the bench. His presence was more symbolic than strategic; no one expected him to play. But as soon as Vaughan scored, Neyland called for Wynn, who rose from the bench and discarded his orange hood.

"The Major is going to send Wynn in to kick the [extra] point," an astonished sportswriter in the press box said. And onto the field trotted Breezy Wynn. A strange quiet settled over the stadium as the teams lined up. Then the snap, and the kick—squarely between the uprights. The quietness instantly became a deafening roar. As Wynn ran off the field, Tennessee fans paid him a hero's tribute.

"That was the greatest thrill in my life," Wynn said. "The Major had told me he was going to put me in the game, so I just waited until he told me to go in and kick."

After the game, Neyland entered the dressing room, smiling from ear to ear, wrapped an arm around Wynn's shoulder and patted the fullback. "Great stuff, Breezy, old boy," Neyland said. Then, to no one in particular, Neyland praised Vaughan's interception return. "Charley followed his interference to perfection," Neyland said. "There wasn't a flaw in the run. Why, he reversed his field three times, and each time he was right behind his interference. I have never seen a prettier run."

Peggy Neyland gave her husband a rousing sendoff for the train trip to Baton Rouge for the season-ending loss to LSU. On December 6, three days before the game, she gave birth to their second child, Lewis Fitch Neyland. Like his older brother, Bobby, Lewis years later would become a letterman athlete at the University of Tennessee—Bobby in football and swimming, Lewis in basketball, golf, and tennis.

Although blessed with talent, the Vols ended the 1933 season with three losses (Duke, Alabama, and LSU)—more losses in one year than Neyland teams had suffered in his first seven years combined at Tennessee.

CHAPTER 18

Final Year on the River

1934

When the winter of 1934 arrived, Major Neyland once more shifted his energies from football to military matters. As Nashville district engineer, he was responsible for navigation along the Cumberland River, whose waters flowed into the Ohio River from Paducah, Kentucky, and eventually into the Mississippi River at Cairo, Illinois.

Neyland's immediate superior, Lieutenant Colonel R. G. Powell of the Ohio River division of the Corps of Engineers, gave him an "excellent" rating in the fitness report for the three months ending March 4, 1934.

Neyland "is a natural leader," Powell said. "He has a kindly manner, is a little too diffident and retiring, also very sensitive and high strung. [He] should have service with engineer troops and at C. & G.S. school [Command and General Staff School]. . . . He is ambitious. Mixes well with civilians. Well qualified for duty with civilian components."

Powell had known Neyland since 1913 when both were cadets at West Point. On the fitness report line asking "What is the highest command he [Neyland] is qualified to hold in war?" Powell wrote: "General officer."

And yet, despite a glowing fitness report, Neyland in the spring of 1934 found himself relegated to "military assistant" reporting to a new Nashville district engineer, Major C. E. Perry. Perry gave Neyland an even better fitness report than Powell had.

"I would especially desire to have this officer [Neyland] serve under my command in peace, in war," Perry said. Asked to give a general estimate of Neyland, Perry wrote: "An officer of the highest mental integrity and of the finest honor and loyalty." Perry rated Neyland's performance "superior."

Neyland, for the moment, had weathered the assault against him by the Roosevelt administration. But he determined to be ever-vigilant, lest the new people in Washington might be aiming at him again. He executed his new Corps of Engineers assignment in the Nashville district efficiently. He conducted spring football practice at the University of Tennessee, did his annual summer tour of duty training younger engineers, and got ready for the fall of 1934.

Gordon Smith, that tiny lineman who had earned three football letters at Tennessee, wrote to Neyland in February 1934 and asked for a coaching job.

"Dear Gordon," Neyland responded. "I have your letter of February 4 in regard to coaching football in the spring and fall at the university. I will be very glad to have you at both times. Of course, you know we do not pay for the spring coaching as we expect the boys [young assistant coaches] to profit by that experience. We will, however, be able to pay $50.00 a month for the three fall months. I have a great deal of regard for your ability and believe you will make a fine coach. For that and other reasons, I will be very glad to have you with us. Sincerely yours."

Neyland signed it: "R. R. Neyland, Major, Corps of Engineers, Head Coach." Notice the two titles.

During the summer of 1934, Neyland began laying plans to house some of the football players in Blount Hall on campus. He offered to pay for the electricity the players used, but school officials quoted him an amount that to Neyland seemed excessive.

"Neyland sent me up to map and count every electrical outlet in the building, which I did," recalled Gordon Smith, also an engineering graduate who eventually would earn a doctorate. "He [Neyland] figured that if a 100-watt bulb burned 24 hours a day in every outlet, the bill would not be as much as they [university officials] claimed."

Neyland computed the data Smith had collected, picked up his papers, and headed out the door to discuss the situation with school administrators. "Now I've got my ammunition," Neyland said to everybody within earshot. "I'm ready to go to war." The administrators capitulated, and Neyland got the dormitory space at his electricity rate.

Tennessee's 1934 football season produced eight victories and only two losses—to Alabama and Fordham, which had tried to hire Neyland—but the War Department had put a damper on the excitement of Volunteer fans. In mid-September, a week prior to Tennessee's first game, Neyland received orders signed by his former West Point boss, General Douglas MacArthur, the army chief of staff.

"Major Robert R. Neyland, Corps of Engineers, is relieved from his present assignment and duty as assistant to the district engineer, Nashville . . . and from additional duty with the Organized Reserves of the Fourth Corps Area," the order said.

Neyland was directed to "proceed to New York and sail on the transport scheduled to leave that port on or about January 9, 1935, for the Panama Canal Department. Upon arrival at Panama . . . report to the commanding general for assignment to duty with the Corps of Engineers."

A two-year tour of duty at the Panama Canal! The Neyland era at Tennessee had come to a temporary end.

"We didn't know any way, really, to keep him from going, because we had exhausted all our methods," lamented Doctor Nathan W. Dougherty, the university faculty chairman of athletics. "By shenanigans of many kinds, we had kept Neyland here for 10 years. He should have been here for [only] three years on his first army appointment, but we had a friend, General Brown, who . . . understood us and understood Neyland." It was Brown who had authorized Neyland's double duty—engineering work along the Tennessee and Cumberland rivers for the army and coaching football for the University of Tennessee.

The War Department said Neyland could take his family with him to Panama. So Peggy began preparations to break up housekeeping in Knoxville and to relocate in the sweltering, mosquito-infested Panama Canal Zone.

News of Neyland's orders began to spread throughout Knoxville and the rest of the state. It cast a gloom over Knoxville and the university campus. After opening with three straight victories, the Vols lost to Alabama, 13-6, on a five-yard reverse by all-American end Don Hutson, more famous as the receiver of Dixie Howell passes than as a runner.

Tennessee rebounded to beat Duke, 14-6, but then lost to Fordham, 13-12, before running off three consecutive victories to set the stage for the season finale against LSU in Knoxville. It was a game Neyland wanted desperately to win because LSU was coached by his former Army teammate Lawrence M. "Biff" Jones, West Point class of 1917, and because LSU had beaten the Vols in 1933.

Bob and Peggy Neyland were honored in a pre-game ceremony on the field. The president of the University of Tennessee Alumni Association, James N. Cox, presented them with a silver service and read a brief statement: "Thousands of others whom we were unable to contact, but who have been watching your career and are just as proud as we, are joining us today in spirit and in truth in wishing for you and your good wife and children safe and successful sojourn in that foreign possession where your country calls; but with this admonition that you make that stay as brief as possible and return to us whenever you can, as we feel that you are one of our very own."

Fred Russell, covering the game for the *Nashville Banner,* was assigned a press box seat next to Tennessee's end coach, Major Bill Britton, and got an extraordinary opportunity to observe the press box-to-bench telephone system that Neyland had introduced to college football. Neyland recognized the value of having an assistant coach watching the game from the press box and communicating with coaches and players on the sidelines to make adjustments during a game.

Britton and Vol freshman coach Hugh Faust were on the press box end of the telephone. Assistant coach Deke Brackett, sitting next to Neyland on the bench, was on the receiving end of the phone line.

"About two minutes before the start of the game, Britton and Faust arrived at their seats and checked the LSU lineups. As the teams arrayed for the kickoff, Britton called to the bench and told them [Abe] Mickal was not starting [for LSU]," Russell said. "Neyland himself no doubt noticed that from the bench, but Britton takes no chances."

As LSU advanced into Tennessee territory, Britton yelled into the phone to Brackett on the sidelines: "Get some information in there for our fullback and center not to play so close to the line. Tell 'em to drop back just a little."

Russell said Britton made another call to the bench 15 seconds later, this time faster and louder and more impatiently: "Tell Crawford to stop talking so much and play football. We don't want to get penalized here." And so it continued throughout the game, Britton delivering information he believed was important for Neyland to have on the sidelines.

Late in the game, with the score tied, 13-13, Vol tailback Pug Vaughan handed off to wingback Toby Palmer on the Statue of Liberty play. The Vols set the same play in motion once more, but this time Vaughan faked the handoff, LSU converged on Palmer, and Vaughan threw a 21-yard touchdown pass to Gene Rose to win the game, 19-13.

Neyland and Biff Jones spent some time at midfield, old West Point buddies sharing a few private thoughts. Jones wished Neyland well in Panama.

The season over, Neyland cleaned out his desk at the university and pitched in to help Peggy finish the packing and make arrangements for storing furniture in Knoxville. In nine years as head coach of the Tennessee Vols, his football teams had compiled a phenomenal record of 76-7-5.

That record was not lost on Congressman Will M. Whittington of Greenwood, Mississippi. Folks in his district were not too happy when Mississippi State's football team failed to win a Southeastern Conference game in 1934. In fact, State's head coach, Ross McKechnie, was on his way out. So Whittington wrote to Major General James F. McKinley, the adjutant general, in Washington.

"In view of the fact that Major Bob Neyland, the head coach at the University of Tennessee, is leaving Tennessee at the close of this year, the people of Mississippi are very anxious that he be given an assignment in the ROTC unit at Mississippi State College," Whittington wrote. "I will appreciate it very much if you will advise me whether or not Major Neyland might be available for this detail and the necessary steps to be taken in the matter."

General McKinley politely notified Congressman Whittington that Neyland could not be spared to coach at Mississippi State. One month and a day from the victory over LSU, Neyland reported to Governor's Island at New York City to sail for the Panama Canal Zone.

1935-1940

PART V

CHAPTER 19

Assignment in Panama

1935

On January 29, 1935, a month before Major Bob Neyland arrived in Panama, the U. S. Senate fell short of the necessary two-thirds vote to ratify U.S. participation in the World Court. The vote sent a message of U.S. isolationism—a message which would not go unnoticed by Adolph Hitler in Nazi Germany or by the militarists who had seized control of Japan.

In the United States, military leaders increasingly worried about the defense of Panama in the event war broke out in Europe or Asia. The Panama Canal, built by the United States, was crucial to the flow of naval traffic between the Atlantic and Pacific oceans.

In 1935, when Neyland arrived at the Panama Canal, only a few thousand Americans lived in Panama—mostly government personnel, private contractors and their families, and units of the Corps of Engineers responsible for canal maintenance and security.

Neyland was made commander of the 1st Battalion, 11th Engineers, stationed at the town of Corozal, seven miles north of Balboa and Panama City on the east side of the canal. It was the beginning of the "lost year" of Neyland's military and coaching careers.

"I served near him when he commanded a battalion of combat engineers in Panama," Colonel Russell P. Reeder said. "The soldiers adored him. They were his boys and could do no wrong. Nobody picked on his boys."

Major Neyland, in the first few months, actually enjoyed having an "overseas" command. But Peggy and the boys, Bobby and Lewis, were sick much of the year with illnesses largely attributed to the climate of Panama. Neyland himself was placed on sick leave for five weeks between February 25, 1935, and the following June 30.

When fall arrived—the time he would be with his football team if he were still in Knoxville—Neyland began to miss the game he had grown to love. At 43 and in good health, with the best won-lost record in college football, Neyland saw himself as a "has-been," his coaching career behind him. And that might have been the case if not for a series of coincidences. Congress had passed a law allowing army officers with fewer than 30 years of service to retire on partial pension. Congress also had passed a law prohibiting military personnel from accepting head football coaching jobs while still in the armed forces, so Neyland would have had to resign his commission to return to coaching.

After the Vols lost five games in 1935, university officials and alumni cabled Neyland an offer of $12,000 a year to return as head coach.

"At the time, my wife was in the hospital [in Panama] with pneumonia," Neyland recalled. "The day she left, Bobby [age 5] entered. When my youngest boy [Lewis, age 2] showed symptoms, I didn't have to decide between Tennessee and Panama, coaching or the army. What had happened to my wife and children decided against Panama and for Tennessee."

But voluntary retirement from the army was not as easy as it sounded. The War Department had gotten wind of Neyland's desire to retire from the army, leave Panama, and return to coaching. He had discussed the matter in letters to several close friends, including Paul Parker, his old West Point classmate and long-time assistant coach at Tennessee who became athletics director when Neyland resigned to go to Panama. In fact, Neyland expressed to Parker a wish to leave Panama as early as mid-September 1935.

"I strongly urged him to do it because I felt the army was stagnating, and I did not foresee World War II," Peggy Neyland later confided. "He later regretted this [decision], and so did I." But in the fall of 1935, retirement seemed the best course of action.

Rumors about Neyland's dissatisfaction in Panama were so widespread that Major General E. T. Conley, the acting War Department adjutant general, phoned Tennessee Congressman Sam D. McReynolds about the situation.

"I appreciate it [sic] very much your kindness in advising me over the telephone this afternoon with reference to the report concerning the alleged effort being made by Major Robert R. Neyland to retire from the service on September 15, 1935, and it was especially nice of you to agree to immediately telephone this office in the event his application for retirement is received by you," McReynolds's secretary, David Manker, wrote to General Conley.

While letters were flying back and forth between Neyland in Panama and the War Department and McReynolds's office in Washington, the Tennessee Vols were struggling on the football field.

Bill Britton had taken over as head coach when Neyland left for Panama. Some key players suffered disabling injuries early in the season, and Tennessee in 1935 found itself with a losing record for the first time since before Neyland arrived at Tennessee as an assistant coach in 1925.

Meanwhile, Neyland's efforts to get out of Panama and return to Knoxville began to build momentum. Congressmen and influential Knoxvillians swung into action on Neyland's behalf. They wrote letters and made verbal contacts with the War Department.

In December 1935 a rapid sequence of correspondence pointed clearly toward retirement for Bob Neyland within a matter of months.

Neyland, in a December 16 letter to General Conley, the adjutant general, requested "that I be placed on the retired list effective February 29, 1936, at which time I will have completed over 23 and a half years service.

"In the event this application is approved, it is requested that I be granted leave of absence for one month effective upon arrival in the United States, with permission to sail from the Panama Canal Department for New Orleans, Louisiana, on or about January 25, 1936, by commercial vessel without additional expense to the Government.

"I have sufficient accrued leave to cover the period involved.

"My address while on leave will be: Knoxville, Tennessee." On January 20, 1936, Neyland got the word—a radiogram from the adjutant general's office.

"Inform Major Robert R. Neyland, Engineers, his request for retirement has been approved effective February 29, 1936," the message said. "He is authorized to return to continental limits of United States by commercial liner without additional expense to the Government."

Orders issued the same day made it official: "Major Robert R. Neyland . . . is relieved from his present assignment and duty in the Panama Canal Department, effective on or about January 25, 1936, and for the convenience of the Government will then proceed to his home [in Knoxville] and await retirement."

So in late January, Major Bob Neyland boarded a ship with Peggy, Bobby, and Lewis, and they sailed for home.

Two months later, a letter arrived in Knoxville for Neyland.

"My dear Major Neyland:

"At this time of your retirement from active service upon your own request, I wish to express the appreciation of the War Department for the faithful service you rendered the country as an officer in the Corps of Engineers of the United States Army

"The military record you leave in the Department discloses that you performed your duties with efficiency and zeal during your service of twenty-four years, thereby winning the commendation of your superiors.

"As you now enter a new sphere of life, I hope that the future will bring you happiness and success.

"Sincerely yours, Malin Craig, chief of staff."

CHAPTER 20

The Road Back

1936-37

The nation was still struggling to free itself from the grip of the Great Depression in 1936. The new Social Security law went into effect on the first day of the year. Margaret Mitchell's new book, *Gone with the Wind,* sold a million copies in the first six months after it went on sale. Boulder Dam, later renamed Hoover Dam, near Las Vegas, Nevada, was completed. Clark Gable and Jeanette MacDonald starred in the motion picture *San Francisco.* In the tense atmosphere of the Berlin Olympics, Jesse Owens won four gold medals in track and field.

Radio was in its heyday, singer Kate Smith ("When the Moon Comes over the Mountain") and newscaster Boake Carter were two of its top personalities, and "Gang Busters" was its newest hit program. President Roosevelt defeated Kansas Governor Alfred Landon for a second term in the White House. Across the ocean, Adolph Hitler's German armies marched unopposed into the demilitarized Rhineland, Benito Mussolini of Italy completed his conquest of Ethiopia, civil war erupted in Spain, and Germany signed pacts with Italy and Japan.

And the Neylands, back from a year in Panama, moved into their home in Westmoreland Heights off Kingston Pike in Knoxville. Bill Britton stepped aside as head coach to resume his old job of coaching the ends. John Barnhill coached the Tennessee line, and Hugh Faust handled the freshman team.

Paul Parker, the Vols' line coach since Neyland became head coach in 1926, resigned the athletics directorship at Tennessee to become AD at Mississippi State.

Chester L. Smith, a sports columnist for the Newspaper Enterprise Association, a feature service, noted that "one of the most powerful football dynasties the southland ever knew takes up the march that was halted in 1934" when Neyland left for Panama.

Nashville Banner sports editor Fred Russell said Neyland applied the principles of army engineering to the task of rebuilding Tennessee's football program.

"Taking over a football squad offers the same problem as taking over a company of engineers," Neyland told Russell. "With both, the most important things are morale, physical condition, and technique. Morale must be developed from the very first day. The matter of physical condition must not be overdone. Both football players and soldiers go stale. As for technique, you can never get too much of that, but it must be well-balanced. Your company of engineers must know more than just how to build bridges. They must know how to tear them down. Likewise, your football team must know more than just how to advance the ball. It has to know how to stop the other fellow from advancing it."

Neyland assembled his staff in early February to assess returning personnel and to plan for spring practice. It was a roster with few seasoned veterans—among them senior tailback Phil Dickens, junior tailback Thomas "Red" Harp, senior fullback Joe Dougherty, senior guard and captain DeWitt Weaver, and junior guard Joe Black Hayes. But Neyland quickly saw he would have to rely on the 1936 sophomores to begin rebuilding Tennessee's football fortunes. That group included ends Bowden Wyatt and George Hunter, tackle Bob Woodruff, center Joe Little, and tailbacks Walter "Babe" Wood and Robert "Doc" Sneed.

Dickens, because of that injury his junior year, never regained the 1934 form when he led the Vols in scoring. His presence alone was reassuring to the 1936 team, but he also was the team's leading ground-gainer. Harp and Sneed, meanwhile, shared tailback time with Dickens and made significant contributions to a 6-2-2 record.

An unheralded hero of the 1936 Vols was end Dick Porter, whose two touchdown pass receptions from Sneed enabled Tennessee to beat Chattanooga, 13-0, in the opener. Porter ultimately led the team in scoring that season.

But the season got off to a rocky start, back-to-back losses to North Carolina and Auburn. The Auburn game was scoreless until the final two minutes when Auburn's Joel Eaves, who later became basketball coach at Auburn and then athletics director at Georgia, caught a touchdown pass from Robert Blake.

The only blemish on Alabama's 1936 record was a scoreless tie with Tennessee the week after the Vols lost to Auburn. The defenses dominated the Alabama game so thoroughly that Tennessee fullback Marion Perkins pointed to the 10-yard-line and said to his teammates, "Let's pitch a tent here. Looks like we'll be here all day." And, indeed, that's where most of the game was played, deep in Tennessee territory. The Vols could not score, so they refused to let Alabama score.

After four games, the 1936 Vols had two losses, a tie, and only one victory. The fifth game—against Duke—turned Tennessee's season in the other direction. Duke, led by all-American tailback Ace Parker, was heavily favored over the Vols and hoping for a Rose Bowl invitation.

In the third quarter, with Duke leading 6-0, Tennessee tackle Frank Crawford and end Bowden Wyatt nailed Parker in the Duke end zone for a safety. But Duke was still leading 13-9 with only two minutes left in the game when Tennessee's Harp got behind a wall of orange-clad blockers and scored on a 70-yard punt return. Parker, the Duke punter, was the last man with a chance to make the tackle, and he was assaulted almost simultaneously by four Vol blockers—Joe Black Hayes, Ike Levine, Jim Porter, and Gerald Hendricks—and Tennessee won 15-13. Hayes, who became a distinguished line coach at Middle Tennessee State University, called that block the greatest thrill of his football career.

"Most football players know how to block," Neyland said. "Few know when to block. What might be an excellent block is useless if it comes too soon or too late. It's all in the timing. Our boys block, block, block every afternoon. They either get good at it or they don't play for Tennessee. The best ball carrier in the country can't play for us unless he can block."

Precision blocking was a Neyland trademark and the basis for one of his football axioms: "One good blocker is worth three ball carriers." The Vols won four more in a row, then with a chance to go to the Orange Bowl hinging on a victory in the final game of the season against Mississippi, struggled to another scoreless tie. Senior guard Austin Shofner remembers the day: "We appeared to be headed for the Orange Bowl, but Neyland ended those hopes in the dressing room after the last game." Shofner remembers Neyland saying: "You tied Mississippi, so you're not going to the Orange Bowl."

Shofner, from Shelbyville, Tennessee, went into the U.S. Marine Corps immediately after graduating from Tennessee and became a World War II hero when he led a 10-man escape from a Japanese prison camp on the Philippine island of Mindanao in 1943. He had been captured shortly after the war began and was one of the survivors of the infamous Bataan "death march." He led an American-Philippino guerilla team for a year before being picked up by submarine and taken to Australia.

"After the war, I visited Neyland in Knoxville and told him that the training I received under him at Tennessee helped me survive in the prison camp and in the jungle of Mindanao after my escape," Shofner said. "He thanked me and said how much he appreciated being told. I learned then that there was a General Neyland I hadn't known at Tennessee. He had a soft spot in his heart for his former players, especially those who had fought in the war." Like Neyland, Shofner became a brigadier general.

In the valley of east Tennessee in 1937, it was more fun to contemplate Bob Neyland's rebuilding program than to be concerned about the growing menace abroad. The nation was in an isolationist mood, and Franklin D. Roosevelt was inaugurated for his second term as president. Joe Louis won the world heavyweight boxing championship. During an approach to a mooring berth at Lakehurst, New Jersey, the German dirigible "Hindenberg" exploded and burned, killing 36 persons. And American aviator Amelia Earhart, attempting an around-the-world flight, vanished over the Pacific Ocean.

Meanwhile, Bob Neyland expressed concern to himself about the potential of his 1937 squad. After spring practice, he wrote in his private notebook that "all [tackles] are poor, defensively and offensively. Not a good charger or open field blocker in the crowd." He described the guards as "poor at line charge, running interference, open-field blocking. Mediocre defensively." He said the centers could play in the defensive line and were "only fair" at linebacker.

Neyland expressed confidence in Tennessee's ground attack, especially the possibility of long runs by Harp, but he was concerned about the Vols' ability to pass.

"We are going to win or lose, depending upon our passing attack," Neyland scribbled in his notebook. "We have no great passers and few good receivers. Therefore, the success of our passing attack will depend [on] the deception of our passing plays . . . proper understanding of passing . . . faultless protection of passer . . . covering after pass is thrown. . . . Our concentration must be to perfect the protecting, faking, and timing of the plays, and thorough understand by passers and receivers of what we are trying to do and why."

Neyland also reminded himself: "We must carry on theoretical instructions increasingly from now on. Full advantage must be taken of every possible opportunity in the fall to practice passing under game conditions."

These were still the days of single-platoon football. A player went both ways, offensively and defensively. So Neyland's private ledger contained notes about off-season conditioning, the building of endurance, and the method of evaluating and treating injuries.

He prescribed certain types of summer exercises and running to get players into shape for the football season. But in the final analysis, he said, one can get into condition to play football only by playing football.

"At least two scrimmages under game conditions are required before the first game. Then you must permit the men whom you are to depend on in the big games to play enough in the small ones to get ready," Neyland said. "The only way they can get rid of that smothered feeling which pulls their wind so completely is to play a lot of football. After the sixth game, a good man should be able to play 50 minutes at least."

The key to effective management of injuries, Neyland said, is early diagnosis. He specified that injuries defined by the team physician as minor be treated by the assistant trainers. Serious injuries receive "prompt, unremitting treatment and [players] are not discharged from treatment until cured," he said. The final decision on whether an injured player would be cleared for practice or a game belonged to the team physician, Dr. Robert Brashear.

Neyland also had his eye on effective management of another aspect of the athletics department—finances and ticket sales. Even though he was athletics director, he did not like handling tickets and contracts or balancing the books. So he hired the first full-time business manager in the department—Edna Callaway, for nearly two decades the only woman holding the position of athletics business manager at a major university. She would handle those duties for the University of Tennessee for 37 years—retiring in 1974.

The Vols lost three games in 1937, but Neyland had begun to see quality depth. The 1936 freshmen were now sophomores—tailback George Cafego, fullback Leonard Coffman, blockingbacks Sam Bartholomew and Billy Barnes, and linemen Boyd Clay, Al Thomas, Jim Rike, and Tom Smith, to name a few. The 1937 freshmen included names that would become legendary in Tennessee football lore—guards Bob Suffridge and Ed Molinski, tackle Abe Shires, and wingback Bob Foxx.

Also, Neyland made a personal sacrifice. When not in his office or on the practice field, Neyland often could be found at Cherokee Country Club playing bridge with a few close friends. But after the 1937 season, he called a team meeting and told his returning players: "I may have had a part in our poor showing last season. I've been accused of spending too much time at the bridge table. If the squad will make an all-out effort to have a great year [in 1938], I will not play bridge a single night during the season."

Exciting days—a spectacular string of 33 consecutive regular season victories—were just over the horizon.

CHAPTER 21

The Glory Years

1938

In 1938 German troops marched into adjacent Austria, and Hitler told the world the "annexation" was necessary to "preserve order" and reunite the two Germanic nations. The Chinese capital of Hankow fell to the Japanese army. The United States observed the 75th anniversary of the Civil War battle of Gettysburg, and President Roosevelt dedicated a memorial in the presence of many Civil War veterans. A hurricane ravaged the Atlantic Coast, killing 700 people. Actor Orson Welles's radio program, "Invasion from Mars," was so realistic that it caused panic among many who heard the broadcast. In sports, Cincinnati pitcher Johnny Vander Meer hurled back-to-back no-hitters.

On September 30, 1938, British Prime Minister Neville Chamberlain, Benito Mussolini of Italy, Edouard Diladier of France, and Hitler signed the Munich Pact, which granted Germany the authority to occupy the Sudetenland in Czechoslovakia. The following day, while Tennessee was defeating Clemson, 20-7, in Knoxville, German troops were occupying the Sudetenland and bringing Europe closer to war. John D. McCallum, a New York writer and author of a history of the Southeastern Conference, poignantly observed "the world passed from one period to another almost between the opening kickoff and the final whistle" on October 1, 1938.

During the winter of 1938, Tennessee's Bob Neyland began preparing for the upcoming season as if it were war. To him, it was war. The Vols had lost three games in 1937, and the experience was unacceptable to Neyland. He had lost only nine games in his first 10 years as a head coach, and he did not like to lose. So he began 1938 spring practice in the dead of winter, January 9, and continued it through the spring academic term. The coaching staff went to work each morning before daylight.

But even through the gloom of darkness, they must have seen a glimmer of future promise in the athletes who had been gathering at Tennessee. Among the brightest stars in the firmament of the "glory years" that would follow were three very different fellows: Bowden Wyatt, Bob Suffridge, and Ed Molinski.

Wyatt, the 1938 captain from Kingston, Tennessee, had arrived on campus in 1935 when Neyland was in Panama. When Neyland returned from Panama in 1936, Wyatt was working two part-time jobs to earn money for additional food and incidental expenses. "I went to Major Neyland and told him I was hungry," Wyatt said, recalling meals of bread and catsup. "If you feed me, I'll make you a good football player," he told Neyland.

Vol coaches moved Wyatt from fullback to end. He studied the game intensely, sharpened his ability to execute assignments, and, perhaps most importantly to Neyland, emerged a leader. In 1938 Wyatt earned all-American honors. Wyatt would go on to a successful head coaching career with stops at Wyoming, Arkansas, and ultimately Tennessee.

The 1938 sophomore class was potentially the best Tennessee had assembled since the McEver-Dodd-Hackman bunch a decade earlier, but Neyland saw too many individual weaknesses in spring practice to be very encouraged about the upcoming season. His notes evaluating spring practice reveal his innermost thoughts. For example: "Wyatt—good blocker, good kick coverer, fair pass receiver, in and out at defensive end."

The notes reveal little of Neyland's opinions about sophomore guard Bob Suffridge. Still, Neyland penciled Suffridge's name into the starting lineup at the end of spring practice. "Suffridge is a slicer," the coach said. "[Ed] Molinski may be better than we think." Both were starting guards as sophomores. Suffridge was named all-American in 1938 and 1940, Molinski in 1939.

Two months prior to the 1938 season, when Suffridge was a sophomore, he and end Jimmy Coleman, also a sophomore, were told by Neyland that they could not room together as they had their freshman year. "You just get into too much trouble, and you're causing the whole coaching staff a lot of grief," Neyland said. "So see [coach] Britton and have him give you another roommate."

"I sure will, sir," Suffridge replied. "I don't like Jimmy anyway. He's always getting me into trouble."

A few days after fall practice began, Neyland approached Suffridge and asked: "Who are you rooming with now, Bob?"

"Jimmy Coleman," Suffridge answered.

"What?," Neyland barked sharply. "I thought I told you that you had to have another roommate."

"Nobody else would room with me," Suffridge replied. "And nobody would room with Coleman."

Ed Molinski, from Ohio, played high school football at talent-rich Massillon High. "I desperately wanted a college education, but I was a poor boy. I didn't have any money," he said. "The only way I was going to get to college was a football scholarship. Coach Neyland came up to see me. He told me what he was offering, and said I could be a doctor or anything else I wanted to be if I came to Tennessee, played football for him, and studied hard." Molinski did all three—went to Tennessee, played football, and studied hard—became a doctor and practiced many years in Memphis.

In addition to playing football, Molinski was a member of the Tennessee boxing team. "Major Neyland came into the gym one day while we were sparring, and I asked him to put the gloves on and go a few rounds with me. I knew he had boxed at West Point, but he was 46 or 47 years old, and I was only 20," Molinski said.

Neyland demurred, "I don't want to hurt you, Molinski."

"But I insisted, so Neyland put on the gloves," Molinski said. "After feeling each other out for a minute or so, I began to throw some punches. All of a sudden, I was flat on my back."

"I just wanted to show you what a left jab followed by a real left hook could do," Neyland said, looking down at the sprawled and bewildered Molinski.

"I didn't see it coming," Molinski recalled. "Fastest left hook I ever saw. I didn't spar with the Major any more after that."

Two decades after Neyland died, Molinski was asked what the General meant to him. "Oh, shoot," Molinski said, trying to choke back the tears. "I couldn't have made it without him."

Neyland saw the backfield as the 1938 team's strength—Cafego and Wood the tailbacks, Leonard Coffman at fullback, Bartholomew at blockingback, and Bob Foxx or Bob Andridge at wingback.

"Foxx is a great athlete with no apparent weaknesses," Neyland wrote in his notebook about the flashy sophomore wingback. "Kicks and passes well. Good blocker and tackler. Excellent runner and pass receiver. Needs defensive experience."

About tailback Babe Wood: "Slated for a good year. Great 'spot' man. Good kicker, fair passer, excellent runner."

And then there was sophomore tailback George Cafego from Oak Hill, West Virginia. He would become one of the all-time great tailbacks in Tennessee football history, but nobody knew that in 1936 when he was a freshman. He enrolled at Tennessee because other universities were not exactly falling over themselves to sign him. His high school coach, Russ Parsons, tossed Cafego's name at West Virginia, Notre Dame, and Ohio State. Cafego heard nothing from them.

"Hell, nobody wanted me," Cafego said. "I guess because I was too small. I only weighed 148 pounds. Coach Parsons told Tennessee about me. It was Tennessee or the coal mines."

Two Tennessee assistant coaches, Britton and Barnhill, went to West Virginia to see Cafego play basketball. "They didn't offer me a scholarship, just said I'd probably be hearing from Coach Neyland," Cafego said. "Several months later, I was playing baseball with the town team, and we were out on the field practicing. I noticed this man sitting in the stands; he had been watching me for about an hour. Finally he came down on the field, and it was Neyland. He asked me what I thought about going to school, and I told him I wanted to but couldn't afford it."

"If you want to come to Tennessee," Neyland said, "you come on, and I'll take care of everything."

The rest is history. Cafego became an all-American at Tennessee, ultimately was inducted into the college football Hall of Fame, and spent 30 years on the Tennessee coaching staff.

During 1938 spring practice, some of those future stars decided they deserved more than the $10 per month they were allowed for spending money, and they delegated Captain Wyatt to broach the subject with Neyland.

Neyland told Wyatt how tight the athletics department budget was and, in effect, denied the players' request for more money. When Wyatt informed his teammates, some of them wanted to strike, but fullback Joe Wallen did not. "I'm eating better than I would at home, so I'm staying," he said.

When Neyland heard about the possibility of a players' strike, he summoned Wyatt and seniors Bob Woodruff, Joe Little, and Cheek Duncan. "If you're not satisfied, then the school and the team will be better off without you."

Wyatt called another squad meeting, informed his teammates of Neyland's threat, and they decided that continued talk of a strike was not such a good idea.

In their annual pre-season ritual, the Southeastern Conference football coaches voted on the order of finish in the 1938 league race. They picked Alabama to win the SEC, followed by LSU, Auburn, and Tennessee in that order. The University of Mississippi's coach, Harry Mehre, said Tennessee would finish second because of its easy schedule.

A week into fall practice, Neyland was concerned about his team's 1938 prospects. "The offensive play of the line from tackle to tackle has been terrible," he said. "The situation as a whole is bad, and unless it improves we won't have as good a year as we did in 1937."

But on Gay Street in downtown Knoxville, the expectation of Vol football fans was high. Tom Anderson, a new sports columnist for the *Knoxville Journal*, predicted an outstanding season for Tennessee. Anderson did not endear himself to Neyland with that forecast; Neyland did not approve of pre-game or pre-season hype. And he did not exactly trust newspapermen, especially Anderson, whom Neyland learned had once played football at Alabama.

As the season approached, contractors were putting the final touches on a 10,000-seat addition to the University of Tennessee football stadium, raising the capacity to 31,390. When Neyland had arrived at Tennessee in 1925, the concrete stadium had only 17 rows on the west side of the playing field and 3,200 seats.

The Vols rolled over Sewanee in the 1938 season opener and then handled Clemson with relative ease. But the third foe, Auburn, was another matter. Auburn had been picked in some pre-season polls to finish among the top five teams in the nation. "I don't see how we can possibly beat them," Neyland said. But the Vols did win 7-0 by holding Auburn to only five first downs. Sophomore tailback Buist Warren directed a fourth quarter touchdown drive, but it was the steady productivity of junior George Cafego through most of the game that impressed a young enemy scout in the press box. "I learned one thing today if I found out nothing else," said Alabama scout Paul "Bear" Bryant. "If we want to beat Tennessee, we will have to stop that Cafego."

The week before an Alabama-Tennessee game was always intense in the Vol football camp. Neyland considered Alabama THE game on Tennessee's schedule. He often said a young Tennessee player could not be evaluated accurately until after being tested in battle against Alabama.

When the day of the Alabama-Tennessee game in Birmingham arrived, both teams had 3-0 records. The Crimson Tide, unbeaten in 21 regular season games, was a heavy favorite. But Bear Bryant's scouting opinion of George Cafego proved prophetic. Cafego had a great day against Alabama. He carried 19 times for 145 yards and set up one touchdown with a 33-yard jaunt to the 'Bama one-yard line.

"All my boys played well and made few mistakes," Neyland said. "I was impressed with the way our line opened the way for the backfield. The play of Cafego, I thought, was one of the features of the game. He is a fine back." The Vols won 13-0. "We were defeated by a great football team," Alabama coach Frank Thomas said. "It was as fine a team as I have seen since my Alabama team in 1934."

The following day at 6:30 a.m., Tennessee Governor Gordon Browning and an estimated 3,000 fans greeted Neyland, his staff, and his 37 players as they stepped from the Vol football train at the Southern Railway depot. In Sunday morning newspapers, many national sportswriters proclaimed the Tennessee Vols among the best in college football. "It is the best Tennessee team I have ever seen," said LSU scout J. B. Whitworth, who had played against the 1929-30-31 Vols.

Tennessee's fifth game was a 44-0 waltz over the Citadel, in which Neyland used his third team most of the game. Fans who stayed until the end that day could not believe their eyes. After the game, Neyland kept his first and second units on the field for *post*-game practice, giving them some work since they had not played much against the Citadel.

On the eve of the game with LSU, Neyland attended a Vol pep rally. "This LSU game will be won or lost by spectators in the stands as well as by the players on the field," Neyland told approximately 3,000 students and townspeople. "I don't know to what extent you supporters helped win the Alabama game two weeks ago, but I do know your spirit and cooperation played a major part in the victory."

Most of the LSU game was played on LSU's side of the 50, and Neyland said the Vols were lucky to win 14-6. Tennessee's "luck" was recovering two LSU fumbles and blocking three LSU punts—proving once again Neyland's maxim that the team making the fewest mistakes wins. "We played some awfully good football in spots and some awfully ragged football in others," Neyland said. "Cafego played a wonderful game. Our sophomore guards [Suffridge and Molinski] were particularly outstanding."

The Vols outscored their next four opponents, 152-0. "I won't say yet it is the greatest team we've ever had at Tennessee, but certainly it's the best-balanced,"

Neyland said. "This team has fewer weaknesses than any I have ever coached. The chief factors in our success have been the surprising development of several sophomores into fine players, the splendid and persistent morale of the squad, the remarkable unity of the team, and the high quality of leadership of captain Bowden Wyatt." Neyland said the shift of Bartholomew from fullback to blockingback was significant. He recognized early the skills that made Bartholomew one of the finest blockers in Vol history.

The weekend of November 19-20 generated a flood of "Neyland news." Immediately after the Vols beat Kentucky on Thanksgiving Day, the Major went to Durham, North Carolina, to see Duke, coached by his old friend Wallace Wade, play powerful Pittsburgh. Duke won en route to an undefeated season in which the Blue Devils held regular season opponents scoreless.

Two days later, a newspaper in Montgomery, Alabama, reported that Neyland would leave Tennessee and become head coach at Florida. The story also carried Neyland's denial. "This makes the fifth or sixth college which has 'signed' Neyland within the past few weeks," Tom Anderson wrote in his *Knoxville Journal* column. There also were published reports that Neyland would succeed Bernie Moore at LSU. Neyland, who had two years remaining on his $12,000-a-year contract, declared he had no intentions of severing his connections with UT. "I only hope Tennessee is satisfied with me," he said.

Meanwhile, after polishing off 10 opponents and yielding only 16 points all season, the Vols anticipated an invitation to play in the Rose Bowl. But the invitation went instead to Duke. Tennessee players and fans were angry and hurt, but Neyland accepted the Rose Bowl committee's decision with characteristic poise and graciousness.

"Duke was the natural choice on the strength of their fine record for the season and the victory over Pittsburgh," he said. "I am sure Wallace Wade's team will be a worthy representative for the South."

The Orange Bowl immediately invited the Vols to play Oklahoma, and Neyland accepted. It was to be Tennessee's first bowl game, and it had the earmarks of a ferocious battle. The Vols were ranked number two by the Associated Press, and unbeaten Oklahoma was number four. The Sooners had allowed opponents only 12 points in 10 games. Both teams had all-American ends—Waddy Young of Oklahoma and Wyatt of Tennessee.

As excitement about the bowl trip mounted, so did concern that Neyland might be leaving Tennessee after the encounter with Oklahoma. University officials met with the Major behind closed doors. And on December 5, Tennessee President James D. Hoskins ended the speculation by announcing a five-year extension of Neyland's contract. Although terms of the agreement were not made public, Knoxville newspapers quoted "sources" as saying Neyland would be paid $15,000 annually under the new contract.

Concerned about the difference in Knoxville and Miami weather conditions, Neyland decided to take the team to Florida nine days in advance of the Orange Bowl game, scheduled for Monday, January 2. So the Vols enjoyed a Christmas Eve dinner at Ma Brann's training table, then departed by train at 2:11 p.m. Christmas Day for Miami. About 1,000 fans were there at the L&N Railroad terminal to give the team a rousing sendoff. The official team party included 41 players, the coaches and their wives, Knoxville sportswriters, and others closely connected with the team.

Never one to leave the slightest detail to chance, Neyland arranged for more than 500 gallons of "Knoxville water" to be stored on the train for the team's trip to Florida. The Major feared a change in water might upset the players' stomachs. Workmen drained two pullman water tanks and the diner tank and filled them with Knoxville water. In addition, extra five-gallon jugs of "good" water were loaded onto the train.

When the train pulled into the Miami station the day after Christmas, CBS sports commentator Ted Husing was waiting with a "live" microphone to do something nobody else ever had done—interview Bob Neyland on radio. Neyland responded by saying that he was happy to bring the Tennessee Vols to the Orange Bowl, that he anticipated a great game.

"That was the first time that the Major ever made a real talk over radio, and I must say that he wasn't at all gun-shy," Knoxville writer Bob Wilson said. "In fact, he talked with ease and poise."

On the morning of their first full day in Miami, Neyland met with his squad on the veranda of the Venetian Hotel and outlined the training rules for the week. The players were free to take advantage of the scheduled team parties and to see the sights of Miami Beach, so long as they complied with his curfew. "Coach Neyland was very lenient with us," Bob Suffridge said sarcastically years later. "We could walk around the block only with a coach in sight. [Trainer] Mickey O'Brien was generally hidden in some palm tree and acted as a detective."

Actually, Neyland did allow his players to enjoy the sights, but he forbade them to go swimming in the ocean or the hotel pool until after the game with Oklahoma.

"A few years ago, Major McEwen, who was a teammate of mine at West Point, brought his Oregon football team here for a game with Florida," Neyland told his Vols. "He let them go in swimming and, when time for the game rolled around, his players were so badly sun-burned that they couldn't bear to wear their jerseys after the first half. It was misery for them. I don't want that to happen to you fellows."

While most of the Vols enjoyed their free time all week, all-American Suffridge was confined by Neyland to the hotel for two days for wise-cracking after a missed assignment in practice. Years later, Suffridge conceded that discipline was Neyland's great asset as a coach. "The General helped me to become a football player," Suffridge said. "He taught me that despite how good I thought I was that he was still the boss. That helped me later when I was in the coaching business. You have to make the players believe in you, and you have to teach them to respect your judgment."

Syndicated columnist Grantland Rice, a native Tennessean and Vanderbilt

University graduate, applauded the Tennessee-Oklahoma matchup in the Orange Bowl. "I doubt that the nation at large has any better all-round football team than Bob Neyland's Volunteers," Rice wrote. "Tennessee comes close to being the best-rounded squad in the country when it comes to both offense and defense and variety of play. Back of a big strong line it has the ball carriers, the blockers, the passers, and the kickers."

It did not take long for controversy to surround the upcoming game. First, Neyland denied Oklahoma writers an opportunity to watch the Vols practice. "What the hell could we take back to the Sooners, and what coach would pay any attention to our scouting report, anyway?" wrote Bus Hamm of the *Daily Oklahoman.*

The two teams were not supposed to practice in the Orange Bowl, known then as Burdine Stadium. But late in the week Neyland learned Oklahoma had arranged with the Miami Park Commission to practice there since that Wednesday. Vol coaches demanded equal opportunity, moved into the Orange Bowl on Friday, and held their remaining workouts there. The stadium controversy was an omen of things to come.

Actually, Neyland knew more about Oklahoma than the Sooners knew about his Vols. Anticipating the possibility of a bowl meeting with Oklahoma, he had sent Hugh Faust to scout the Sooners late in the season. As a result, the Vols had a solid game plan for the Orange Bowl game.

"You boys know that a team's weakness often lies in its greatest strength," Neyland told the Vols in his brief pre-game talk. "Hit for the strong point, break through that, and the rest is easy. You're going out there to play a fine ball team. They have an all-American end named Young. You'll find him at your left."

Fred Russell, sports editor of the *Nashville Banner,* said the kickoff was the tipoff to what was to come: "It was devastating. Heads bumped, bodies crashed together, and teeth rattled. Never have two teams hit as hard."

On Tennessee's first play from scrimmage, Vol tailback George Cafego peered from the huddle and saw a 6-2, 200-pound hulk wearing crimson pants and white jersey. It was Waddy Young. Cafego called for formation right, a reverse by wingback Bob Foxx to the left on first down. The snap went to fullback Len Coffman, who spun and handed the ball to Foxx, swinging left from his wingback position. Young crossed the line of scrimmage to turn the runner inside, but the hard-nosed Cafego sent him flying with a crushing head block square in the all-American's chest. Writers in the pressbox said Young had gone six feet into the air. Others said he bounced along the ground for six or eight feet.

"Old George really laid the wood to that all-American," Wyatt said. "That was a solid, legal lick in what was to be the roughest, toughest physical contact football game I ever played or saw. It almost turned into a brawl."

"When Waddy Young fell with his great limbs asprawl, Oklahoma fell with him," wrote Walter Stewart, sports editor of the *Memphis Commercial Appeal.* "It isn't that Oklahoma isn't equipped with boys just as brave and fierce as any other boys. It's just that everyone is rather alike. . . . You have seen the best man on your team go down—the war god who spread havoc all year."

Stewart continued the litany: "You have seen him [Young] cut down on the first play of the game—whirled to the ground like an old hat. If they can do that to Waddy, what will they do to me?"

Foxx cut inside Cafego's tumultuous block for a 14-yard gain, and tempers flared immediately. Fists flew on practically every play. Each side blamed the other. Oklahoma writers called Tennessee "dirty." Tennessee writers said the Vols only retaliated. The Vols were penalized 130 yards, Oklahoma 90. Things got so bad that Neyland called reserve center Joe Little off the bench. "Joe, you're older than most of these boys. Get in there and settle them down," Neyland said. On the next play, Little was ejected for slugging. In addition, Tennessee's Ed Molinski and two Oklahoma players were ejected.

"The officials let the game get away from them," one of the Vol coaches said afterward. "If they had called a few harsh penalties . . . early in the game, all that later slugging wouldn't have taken place."

Between fights and 15-yard roughness penalties, the Vols scored 17 points. The breaks were going Tennessee's way. Cafego's 61-yard quick-kick in the first quarter put Oklahoma in a deep hole, and the Sooners had to kick back to Tennessee. Cafego returned the punt to Oklahoma's 27, and Foxx scored on a reverse five plays later. Bowden Wyatt's extra point kick was blocked, but he grabbed the ball in mid-air and ran around left end and scored. Wyatt also kicked a field goal in the second quarter and an extra point following Babe Wood's 15-yard touchdown run in the fourth period. The Vols won 17-0.

"The Tennessee team is the nearest thing to greased lightning we have ever seen on a football field," wrote Everett Clay of the *Miami Herald*. "The Vols are not only as fast as slick electrical charges, but are just as powerful."

"Tennessee presented a five times better team than I expected to see," wrote Jim Hopkins of the *Oklahoma News*. "Oklahoma never had a chance. I am also convinced that Major Bob Neyland's Volunteers could beat TCU and Southern California, and is [sic] the best football team of the 1938 season."

In the days immediately following the bowls, sportswriters from coast to coast tried to drum up enthusiasm for a second post-season game between Tennessee and Texas Christian University for the national championship. The Associated Press and the Helms Athletic Foundation ranked TCU number one. Two mathematical systems ranked the Vols first. Each of the two schools denied challenging the other. It was a game the fans and sportswriters wanted, but not the two schools.

Neyland remained in Florida nearly two weeks after the Orange Bowl game to do some deep-sea fishing with friends. Next to football, fishing was the sport Neyland loved best. He loved baseball too and enjoyed tennis to keep down his waistline, but he was never able to master the game of golf and wound up hating the sport.

In the weeks before and after the Orange Bowl, Neyland's critics and detractors assaulted his won-lost record, or more specifically Tennessee's schedule. They wanted to know why the Duke series was discontinued and why the Vols were playing "breathers" such as Sewanee, the Citadel, Mercer, and Chattanooga.

"When I returned from Miami, I wasn't met with a clashing of cymbals and the booming of drums," Neyland said. "On my desk was a big stack of letters protesting our 1939 schedule."

One reader wrote to Bob Wilson, sports editor of the *Knoxville News-Sentinel:* "The University must have been ashamed when they released the 1939 schedule with 40 percent breathers on it! No wonder other sections ignore the South when every Saturday their papers say Alabama swamps Howard, Tennessee crushes Sewanee."

Atlanta columnist Ed Danforth labeled Tennessee's 1939 schedule "a crime." Knoxville fans, he said, "want a winner at any price, and Major Neyland is taking no chances. The Vols play Alabama, LSU, Vanderbilt, and Auburn with strange interludes before and after each of those dates for rest and reorganization."

However, *Chicago News* sports editor Marvin McCarthy, in an open letter to Neyland, said Tennessee's 1938 record "should be a silencer to scoffers who until now have rated your football club as just another jerkwater eleven getting by simply because the opposition was not so hot. It looks like Tennessee may have absolutely the best football team in the land this year."

McCarthy told Neyland that Tennessee and other great Southern teams were victims of their geographic location. "If your ball club operated out of Chicago, New York, Detroit, Washington, Philadelphia, or some such place, it would be the talk of every fan in the United States," McCarthy said.

At the January 16 Vol football banquet, Neyland addressed the schedule issue. "I can't take time now to try to give you my side of the schedule, but there are some things I do want to say about it," he said. "In the first place, we did not drop Duke off our 1938 schedule. They dropped us."

Neyland said he had long wanted to play Georgia Tech, but that Tech until recently had shown no interest in a game with Tennessee. "About intersectional games for 1939," he said. "We've approached Princeton, Yale, and several of the outstanding Eastern schools, but we have met with no success. I've heard a lot about the fans wanting intersectional games. This talk in the newspapers is just like a bunch of old women chewing on some juicy gossip."

Neyland then called on assistant coach Bill Britton. "We have prospects of having another fine team next fall," Britton said. "If we tear down this team with an over-loaded schedule, it's a crime. We purposely set up our schedule with three weak opponents before the Alabama game so that we could meet Alabama on even terms." Alabama in 1937 had scheduled Howard, Sewanee, and South Carolina for the three weeks immediately preceding the Tennessee game.

Dr. N. W. Dougherty, faculty athletics chairman, told the banquet crowd that Tennessee had tried unsuccessfully to schedule teams such as Ohio State, Pittsburgh, Southern Cal, Princeton, and Army for the 1940-41 seasons. And, unknown at the time, Neyland was trying to schedule Michigan on a home-and-home basis beginning in 1940, but the two schools were unable to reach an agreement on dates.

Commenting on the schedule controversy, Tennessee President James Hoskins said: "I'll leave it to these other gentlemen [Neyland and Dougherty], but whatever it is, I say to them—WIN!"

Newspapers continued to fan the flames of the scheduling controversy, and Neyland finally counter-attacked in the January 19 issue of the *Knoxville News-Sentinel.*

"The 1939 schedule was made two years ago," Neyland said. "The contracts have been signed, and it can't be changed. We're going to play every game as it comes up. Two things are taken into consideration in working out the football schedule. We don't want too hard a schedule from the standpoint of the boys. We've got to protect them against overwork and injuries. In the second place, we try to make a financial success of the football team because it pays the way for other sports at the University."

Neyland warned that agitation by sportswriters and fans was resulting in a harmful team attitude of overconfidence. "The seeds of a lousy team are being sown right now by our own press and people stewing about something we can't help. It is most unfortunate that the fans don't like the schedule, but we can't do anything about it."

Neyland was being truthful, hiding nothing about his scheduling philosophy. "We have never tried to arrange a schedule so as to go through the season undefeated," he said. "The fans insist that Tennessee beat Alabama and Vanderbilt. As long as they [Alabama and Vandy] play breather games before they play us, we've got to do the same to have any chance at all of winning."

Neyland had stated his position and refused to discuss the scheduling issue any more. He focused his attention on 1939 spring practice, which began January 15.

CHAPTER 22

Undefeated, Untied, Unscored On

1939

The United States had been trying to maintain neutrality since World War I, but the aggressions of Japan in the Far East, Italy against Ethiopia, and Germany in Central Europe began to make lasting neutrality unlikely. Then on September 1, 1939, the Germans invaded Poland. Two days later, Britain and France declared war on Germany. Seven years of a war that would engulf the world had begun. By the end of 1939, German bombs were falling on cities in England.

In the United States, baseball was observing its 100th birthday. And, although New York Yankees fans had not forgotten home run king Babe Ruth, fourth-year outfielder Joe DiMaggio made them miss Ruth a little less each day. Cleveland Indians pitcher Bob Feller, only 20 years old, won 24 games. Millions of Americans packed motion picture theaters to see Judy Garland walk the yellow brick road and sing "Over the Rainbow" in the hit musical *The Wizard of Oz*. The motion picture *Gone with the Wind*, starring Clark Gable and Vivian Leigh, premiered in Atlanta at Loew's Grand Theater. And in 1939, a first-class stamp cost three cents.

On Gay Street in Knoxville, and indeed throughout the country, Tennessee coach Bob Neyland was the toast of the sports world. His University ofTennessee Volunteers had smashed Oklahoma with surprising ease in the Orange Bowl, had shared national championship acclaim with Texas Christian University, and were expected to be as good, possibly better, in the fall of 1939.

But, to Neyland, spring practice was not a continuation of 1938 into 1939; it was a whole new beginning. In his conservative thinking, the Tennessee Vols were starting from scratch. Never mind that they had lost only three players—tackle Bob Woodruff, and ends George Hunter and Bowden Wyatt—from the 1938 starting lineup. Handwritten notes in the Major's private football ledger listed Tennessee's spring depth chart and reflected his conservatism.

He penciled in his projected starting lineup for the fall—Ed Cifers [he spelled it Ciphers] and Mike Balitsaris at ends, Abe Shires and Bill Luttrell at tackles, Bob Suffridge and Ed Molinski at guards, Jim Rike at center, and a backfield of Bob Foxx, Sam Bartholomew, Len Coffman, and George Cafego. Neyland's highest evaluation of individual players, based on spring practice, was "adequate." He listed eight players as "adequate," twelve as "fair," two as "possible," and four as "hopeless."

Always ready to learn from past performance, Neyland analyzed various aspects of the 1938 team's execution. He noted vast improvement in the running attack—better ball handling and blocking. "Passing attack retro-graded to some extent, mainly in . . . choice of passes. However, many were badly thrown, and an unusual number were missed by receivers. Saving grace was [the] small number thrown for interceptions [three].

"Kicking game not up to standard. Flubbed kicks were numerous in the first half of season. Quick kicks, which were uniformly successful during the season, kept our average [yardage] up. Our kicking for coffin corners was very poor. On the whole, poor kicking kept us in trouble during the greater part of the season. In the main, our covering of kicks was good, but we almost let Kelly of Auburn get away with one for TD," Neyland wrote.

The Major gave "excellent" ratings to Tennessee's kick returns, kickoffs, and kickoff coverage. The defense, he said, was the best it had been in several years.

"Spirit and morale—best ever," he wrote. "Squad got 'will to win' early and held it."

Then came his assessment of how well the team executed in response to what the opponent did during the game. "Generalship in most cases good, if not brilliant," the major said. "Many times could be called brilliant. Helped a lot by preseason analysis of defenses, sound pre-game plans, and definite information early in each game as to defensive distributions and probable plans."

Neyland also assessed the performance of his staff. He was particularly pleased with the "meticulous analysis of all possible defensive distributions [of players] against the Tennessee offense and listing [offensive] plays which should go against each [defense]."

Mickey O'Brien, a tall, imposing physical therapist, had been hired by Neyland in 1938, and the results were noticeable. O'Brien was a taskmaster who made certain players did the exercise routines prescribed for them, including running laps and up and down the steps of the stadium.

The Major was pleased with the execution of game-day duties he had assigned to his assistant coaches—Hugh Faust and Murray Warmath scouting the next opponent and preparing the freshman team to employ the opponent's offense and defense against the varsity, and Britton sitting in the press box and communicating with the bench by telephone. Neyland and the staff had simplified and refined their methods of getting "proper information" to the team on the field from the press box via telephone to the bench.

Neyland believed in the use of still photographs as teaching tools. As early as the late 1920s, he had been marking game photographs with circles and notations to show examples of good and bad execution. By 1939 he was using photographs of each play as a teaching tool in practice, what he called the "psychological use of pictures."

Also in 1938, Neyland had refined the use of notebooks by coaches and players. The notebooks contained detailed information about Tennessee's offensive and defensive schemes, offensive play diagrams, and specific information about the assignments of each position in varying situations. Coaches and players alike studied their notebooks and added to them as necessary.

So, on September 1, 1939, the stage was set for the opening of Tennessee's pre-season football practice. It also was the day World War II began in Europe. Newspaper headlines that day proclaimed:

"WAR!" "HITLER SMASHES INTO POLAND."

"WARSAW BOMBED."

"POLISH SEAPORT IS BLOCKED."

"'GET OUT OR WE'LL FIGHT,' BRITISH WARN."

But Europe seemed so far away, and the United States had adopted a mood of isolationism. Major Bob Neyland, U.S. Army, retired, read the newspapers that day, but he had put the military behind him three years earlier. His thoughts on September 1, 1939, focused solely on his Tennessee football team, which many national writers were predicting would go to the Rose Bowl.

"Tennessee is expected to dominate the Dixieland gridiron picture again," wrote Jerry Brondfield of the Newspaper Enterprise Association.

"The best college football team in the U.S. this fall will be Tennessee," declared Dick Dunkel, a sports statistician who had been 80 percent accurate in predicting winners of 27,000 football games during the 1930s. "Tennessee should be the greatest team we have seen in recent years. Only one key man was lost from last year's championship outfit, and there are at least three good players for every position."

"Our players show no signs of over-confidence," Neyland told reporters after two days of practice. "Our coaching staff has learned to emphasize the fact that we have definitely been placed on the spot, and we all know that our major opponents are primed and ready for us."

Film crews from Fox Movietone and Universal, which produced the newsreels shown in motion picture theaters, showed up on Tennessee's opening day of practice. Somewhat surprisingly, Neyland cooperated. He directed some staged exercise drills. The cameramen filmed all-American guard Bob Suffridge making a bone-rattling tackle on all-American tailback George Cafego. Wingback Bob Foxx missed the first pass thrown to him, prompting Neyland to chide, kiddingly: "Get in front of the camera and miss the ball." It was all great fun.

But as he got deeper into fall practice, Neyland became more and more concerned about Tennessee's ability to duplicate its 11-0 record the previous season. "I do not see how our team can hope to be as effective as it was last year," he said. "It was well-nigh perfect then. We have lost the two best ends Tennessee ever had in [Bowden] Wyatt and [George] Hunter and one of the best tackles in [Bob] Woodruff. Our opponents are all stronger. It is doubtful if the softening effect of all this 'championship' propaganda can be overcome."

Tennessee's 1939 opener was at North Carolina State, whose coaching staff included two former Neyland players—Herman Hickman and Babe Wood. Knowing that Wood was familiar with much of Tennessee's personnel and its offensive and defensive schemes, Neyland had decided on a little fact-finding espionage. He had sent four assistants—Bill Britton, Hugh Faust, Bob Woodruff, and Talmage Maples—to scout N.C. State's opener against Davidson a week earlier. It was Woodruff's first coaching job; Neyland had hired him the day after Woodruff graduated. "My specific instructions were to scout a great N.C. State all-American tackle by the name of Ty Coon," Woodruff related. "I came back and gave a glowing account of his activities and performance and a solution of how we could block him. I also added that he was the fastest and first man down the field on punt formation"

"Where did Coon line up on punt formation?" Neyland asked Woodruff.

"I stammered and said, 'They use an unbalanced line, and he lined up at strong side tackle,' hating to admit I wasn't sure where he lined up," Woodruff said.

"You mean they kicked from an unbalanced line?" Neyland asked.

"Yes, sir!" Woodruff answered emphatically.

"Without hesitation, Neyland picked up the phone and called Herman Hickman (the N.C. State line coach) and asked him where Coon lined up on punt formation," Woodruff said. "My ego shrank as Neyland repeated Hickman's conversation."

"At left tackle from a balanced line," Neyland said, repeating Hickman's words.

"Neyland hung up the phone and looked at me with his penetrating cold black eyes," Woodruff remembers.

"Woodruff, you did a good scouting job," Neyland said. "We'll put in the Coon block for the State game. However, you remember this. I don't want anyone working for me that has a wrinkle in the back of his neck from saying 'Yes, sir.' From now on, if you don't know the answer, say so!" As the Vols boarded the train for the trip to Raleigh, blockingback Sam Bartholomew showed news photographers a "good luck" four-leaf clover. Neyland, probably the coach least likely to rely on luck in the history of college football, had planted clover seeds outside his office window, and they had produced a patch of four-leaf clovers.

"Lucky" Bartholomew returned the opening kickoff 79 yards to set up Tennessee's first touchdown. The Vols' defense limited State to 85 yards and won 13-0.

Jack Horner, then sports editor of the *Greensboro Record,* had dined with Neyland when the Tennessee train made a noon stopover in Greensboro en route to Raleigh. "I found him to be a friendly, warm, and kind-hearted individual, despite all I had heard to the contrary," Horner said. "The next afternoon, he revealed what a truly soft heart he possessed. . . . I honestly believe Tennessee could have scored any time it wanted to. . . . He called off the dogs after scoring two quick touchdowns."

Easy victories over Sewanee, 40-0, and Chattanooga, 28-0, set the stage for what turned out to be, up to that time, the most ballyhooed football game in Tennessee history—the Vols versus Alabama, the clash of two nationally ranked Southern powers.

The Tennessee-Alabama game of 1928 had thrust Tennessee into the national spotlight, but the 1939 Tennessee-Alabama game made Bob Neyland a legend in his own time.

A horde of newspaper writers from across the nation converged on Knoxville the week of the big game. And the two major radio networks decided to broadcast it. The most famous sports announcers of that day—Ted Husing of CBS and Bill Stern of NBC—arrived in Knoxville on the same plane from New York City.

The press entourage read like a "who's who" of the sportswriting world—Grantland Rice, syndicated columnist and sports editor of *Collier's* magazine, Joe Williams of the *New York World-Telegram,* Henry McLemore of United Press, Francis Wallace of *Saturday Evening Post,* former Pittsburgh coach Jock Sutherland of the Pittsburgh Press, Fred Russell of the *Nashville Banner,* Raymond Johnson of the *Nashville Tennessean,* Walter Stewart of the *Memphis Commercial Appeal,* and, of course, the Knoxville writers and many more from other cities.

"Isn't it time that Tennessee was broken up along with the Yankees?" McLemore wrote. Williams called Neyland one of the great sports personalities in America. Jerry Brondfield of the NEA said Tennessee's wealth of material and "the genius of Major Bob Neyland" added up to something special.

The 1939 Tennessee-Alabama game produced an extraordinary storyline, even before the game was played. Even though it was early in the season, the national writers predicted the Tennessee-Alabama winner would play in the Rose Bowl. And they may have had some justification. On hand for the game were Tennessee graduate Clarence Brown, the famed Metro-Goldwyn-Mayer film director, and Rose Bowl representative Drummond McCunn.

"It's practically all set for Tennessee to go to the Rose Bowl," Brown said brashly, not waiting for the game to be played."This one may produce the Eastern representative for the Rose Bowl," wrote Harry Ferguson of United Press.

Like Tennessee, Alabama carried a 3-0 record into the game—two of the victories at the expense of so-called "breathers." But Alabama had a fight on its hands beating nationally ranked Fordham, 7-6. Since their modern rivalry had begun in 1928, Alabama and Tennessee had won five games each, and one had ended in a scoreless tie. Alabama was undefeated in its last eight games; Tennessee had won 16 straight. Both were ranked in the Associated Press Top Ten.

Most of the writers picked Tennessee to win, but Neyland expressed cautious optimism.

"We aren't as good as we were last year, but we have a good ball club," he said. "I think we'll win, but we haven't been tested yet. Alabama comes here to give us the answer. Somehow, I think the answer will be satisfactory."

The stadium at Tennessee's Shields-Watkins Field officially could seat 31,390 people, but there were predictions that 40,000 would see the game. Shortly before the kickoff, several hundred fans, who were unable to obtain tickets, crashed the cyclone fence at the north end of the stadium grounds and rushed past police to claim standing room around the north bleachers. A second wave of gate crashers, men and women, got inside before police closed the breach. Officials later estimated the crowd at 35,000.

"We would have had 75,000 persons for the Alabama game if we'd only had a place to seat them," Neyland said. "The concrete stands were sold out a month before the game, and the end zone tickets were taken even before we had them printed. If our stadium had been a bowl so we could have offered end zone tickets for $1.50 or $1.65 each I think we would have filled it. We turned down thousands of requests for tickets."

Vol tailback George Cafego was the focus of most pre-game stories about the star-studded Vols. Cafego had made several all-American teams the previous year as a sophomore, and in 1939 was regarded as one of the better running backs in the nation. But as kickoff hour approached, the *Knoxville News-Sentinel* predicted: "This May Be Johnny Butler's Day To Shine." It was.

The game was scoreless—a defensive standoff—until midway in the second quarter when sophomore tailback Butler circled left end, cut inside a block by Ike Peel, then swung back to his right to begin a serpentine run that ended 56 yards later in the Alabama end zone.

"They came to see George Cafego, but they saw Johnny Butler . . . who runs as cunning as a fox, and with the elusiveness of an eel," wrote *Knoxville News-Sentinel* sports editor Bob Wilson.

"That was the greatest piece of open-field running that I've ever seen," declared Jock Sutherland, who had retired from coaching a year earlier after directing the University of Pittsburgh to a 110-17-12 record and a 1937 national championship.

"I don't want to take anything away from Butler," Neyland said after looking at the game film. "His run was one of the most remarkable I ever saw, but the movies plainly show he had at least a dozen would-be Alabama tacklers cleared from his path by blocking. Johnny couldn't possibly have made a more beautiful run, but his teammates deserve some of the credit. There were more players down the field trying to block on that play than any I have ever seen."

Indeed, the movies show 11 blocks, two of them by guard Al Thomas. There were the blocks along the line of scrimmage and Peel's block on the end, followed by a second block downfield by Peel, and others by tackles Don Edmiston and Bill Luttrell and wingback Bob Andridge.

Tennessee's defense dominated the game, Cafego repeatedly tore holes in the Alabama forward wall, and the Vols in the fourth quarter scored two more touchdowns to win 21-0. And, while Butler's run was the most spectacular play of the game, the writers wrote glowingly of Cafego's performance. "He's the back of the year until they dig up a better one," Francis Wallace said.

"I honestly think the Volunteers would beat any team in the country, and that goes for the pro teams," Sutherland said. "They have speed, power, finesse, and reserve strength, plus individual greatness. What else could you ask for in a football team? I'm not sure but what it might be the best football club I ever saw. . . . And it is superbly coached."

Sutherland went further. "After seeing the game, I'm quite certain I don't belong in this coaching game. Major Neyland's job at Tennessee exceeds anything I've ever seen in all my football experience. There were no flaws in the Tennessee team on either offense or defense."

Asked if any of his Pittsburgh teams could have beaten the 1939 Vols, Sutherland replied: "We might if Tennessee let us recover a fumble in the end zone."

"Tennessee has taken the place formerly held by Pitt as the perennial dominator of the national gridiron," wrote Francis Wallace. "This squad has everything a great team needs. It has a fine line and great backs, game-breaking backs. It is smart, and above all it is poised. It has the poise of a great Rockne team."

Alabama's coach, Frank Thomas, said the 1939 Vols are on a par with the Alabama teams of 1930 (coached by Wallace Wade) and 1934 (coached by Thomas), and Georgia Tech's 1928 Rose Bowl team. Sutherland rated the Vols alongside "three great teams I have seen in the past—Minnesota in 1934, Notre Dame of 1930, and Southern Cal of 1929."

"Open the portals of the Rose Bowl," Joe Williams wrote. "There's a pretty fair country football team heading out that way—the Tennessee Volunteers."

Neyland was paid the biggest tribute of the weekend by Alabama's Thomas: "I hope the war gets tougher so the Government will call that fellow back to the colors," Thomas said. "I can see I'm not going to have much fun coaching down here as long as he is around." Thomas and Neyland teams met 10 times. Thomas won three and tied one.

After Alabama, the Vols polished off Mercer and LSU. None of those first six opponents was able to penetrate Tennessee's 20-yard line. But the next two weeks caused big headaches for Tennessee. George Cafego, a senior, injured a knee in the game with the Citadel and was ineffective the remainder of the season. Against Vanderbilt, the Vols made no first downs in the first half and no rushing first downs for the entire game, but they managed to win 13-0 with two second half touchdowns—a pass completion and a 64-yard interception return. "I feel that Vandy deserved the victory," Neyland said. "We won the game, but Vandy was the best team on the field."

That was the day Peggy Neyland rolled out of her bed at Fort Sanders Hospital, six blocks from the Tennessee campus, and went to the stadium to lend moral support to her husband's team. She had been hospitalized since becoming ill at the Tennessee-LSU game two weeks earlier. She got more and more nervous listening to the Vandy game on the radio. Things were going badly for the Vols, and Peggy could stand it no longer. She asked the nurses for her clothes, but they hesitated. "She said she was going in her gown if somebody didn't bring her clothes," the nurse said. Peggy got her clothes, called a taxi, and went to the game, accompanied by a hospital orderly. After the Vols won, she dutifully returned to her hospital bed.

The Vols knocked off Kentucky, then finished another unbeaten season by beating Auburn, 7-0, on Johnny Butler's 40-yard touchdown punt return.

Like the Duke Blue Devils the previous year, the 1939 Tennessee Vols had held 10 regular season opponents scoreless. It has not happened since.

A few hours after Tennessee's victory over Auburn, reporters and coaches, Neyland among them, gathered in a large room in Knoxville's Farragut Hotel to listen to Bill Stern's broadcast of Southern Cal's game with UCLA. It was assumed that Southern Cal, if it won, would oppose Tennessee in the Rose Bowl. Most of them believed Neyland already had a Rose Bowl invitation in his pocket. Southern Cal won, but the writers were disappointed when Neyland rose to leave the room: "Gentlemen, I have no news to give out. We'll just have to wait."

Lindsey Nelson, then a junior at Tennessee and later a famous sportscaster, went with some of the Vol football players to the Tennessee Theater. "When we came out of the theater onto Gay Street near midnight, there was a carnival scene," Nelson said in his autobiography, *Hello Everybody, I'm Lindsey Nelson.* "People were literally dancing in the street, and we soon joined them. The Sunday newspapers were out, and they proclaimed in screaming black headlines that Tennessee was going to the Rose Bowl."

Neyland, waiting at home that night with Peggy and some of their friends, finally received a phone call from Bill Hunter, the athletics director at Southern Cal.

"We are inviting Tennessee to play Southern California in the Rose Bowl," Hunter said tersely.

"We are happy to accept the invitation," Neyland replied. And that was all there was to it.

CHAPTER 23

The Rose Bowl

Howard Harding Jones, the coach of the Southern California Trojans, began his head coaching career at Syracuse University in 1908 when Bob Neyland was still in high school. Jones returned to his alma mater, Yale, as head coach in 1909, and Yale that year won 10 games and was recognized as the national champion of college football.

After stints at Ohio State, Iowa, and Duke, Jones became head coach at Southern Cal in 1925, and his teams there won national championships in 1928, 1931, and 1932. Jones's won-lost record at Southern Cal, going into the January 1, 1940, Rose Bowl game with Tennessee, was 117-32-11. Neyland's pre-Rose Bowl record at Tennessee was 109-13-8.

As the Tennessee Vols boarded a Southern Railway train for the trip across the continent, Major Bob Neyland weighed two big questions. Would tailback George Cafego's knee injury keep him out of the Rose Bowl game? Would the Vols' defense be able to stop Southern Cal's aerial bombardment?

Cafego's knee seemed to respond to rehabilitation, and trainer Mickey O'Brien had designed a special brace for it. Neyland decided to test Cafego's knee in scrimmages once the team reached California. Sportswriters openly speculated that the Vols could not win withoutCafego.

The other question—about shutting down Southern Cal's passing—troubled Neyland greatly, mainly because of what had happened to Duke, coached by his friend Wallace Wade, in thc previous Rose Bowl. Duke had led, 3-0, until the final two minutes and 20 seconds, when fourth-string Trojan quarterback Doyle Nave entered the game and completed four consecutive passes to end Al Krueger, the last for the game-winning touchdown with 40 seconds left. Duke lost 7-3.

Neyland personally mapped out the train trip westward—first to Memphis, then to his hometown of Greenville, Texas, on to San Antonio and El Paso, and finally to Pasadena. He selected the Huntington Hotel in Pasadena for the team's headquarters, unaware that no team staying there had ever won the Rose Bowl.

Neyland had planned a brief layover in Greenville for a team practice at Phillips Field, where he had played years earlier. But a heavy rain was falling when the train pulled into the tiny station, so Neyland and his assistants decided to forgo a practice there and hold one instead at El Paso the following day.

Neyland was the first person to step from the train in Greenville, and he was greeted by a chorus of "Hello Robert, Hello Robert" from several hundred townspeople." Ignoring the downpour, and loving every minute of it, Neyland shook hands with friends who had known him as a boy. Newsboys milling in the crowd hawked the *Greenville Morning Herald:* "Extra! Extra! Read all about Major Neyland."

"Hey, Robert, I want you to sign these," yelled one native, waving some photographs. Neyland looked at them. "What do you know about that?" he said, somewhat surprised. "That's the picture of the first high school team I ever played on." Neyland jubilantly held the picture aloft and remarked, "Look how skinny I was then."

Soon Neyland was surrounded by relatives—his uncle Mayo Neyland, a 77-year-old attorney; his brother, Mayo; and his sister, Carroll Robinson. They huddled in a corner of the station and talked for about a half-hour. Then, the party reboarded, and the train pulled out of the station, heading southward toward San Antonio. Before leaving his beloved Texas, the train stopped briefly in El Paso so the team could work out at Kitts Field, site of the Sun Bowl game.

The trip was captured on film by J. Pat Roddy, Jr., a University of Tennessee alumnus, camera buff, and lover of Vol football. "Neyland let me hang around and take pictures," Roddy recalled. "Color film was new, and I shot the entire trip in color." Sam Bartholomew, the Vol blockingback who had picked a four-leaf clover for the Alabama game, wore a rabbit's foot bracelet on his wrist during the trip to California. Preparation on the practice field was fine, but Bartholomew was not taking any chances.

On the fourth day of their trip, the train stopped briefly at Colton, California, 50 miles from Los Angeles, to let MGM film producer-director Clarence Brown and some Rose Bowl representatives board to accompany the team on the final leg of the journey.

More than 5,000 cheering fans and a band playing "Dixie" greeted the Tennesseans as their train pulled into the station at Pasadena. "Hello, California," Neyland yelled as he stepped from the train onto the station platform, doffing his hat in salute.

After appropriate acknowledgments, Neyland took the team to the Rose Bowl stadium. As he walked onto the soft natural grass carpet, Cafego turned 360 degrees, a pirouette captured by Roddy on film. Neyland walked to the 50-yard line, looked toward both end zones, then gazed thoughtfully toward the San Gabriel Mountains, which form a backdrop for the Rose Bowl. "It's a beautiful setting, isn't it?" he said to no one in particular.

On Christmas Day, Clarence Brown threw a party at his Canoga Park ranch in the San Fernando Valley. Several dozen cowboy stars, including Tom Mix, Roy Rogers, Ken Maynard, and Gene Autry, staged a Wild West rodeo. In addition to Brown and MGM president Louie B. Mayer, the host party included actor Robert Montgomery and actresses Gail Patrick, Lana Turner, Laraine Day, Marjorie Weaver, Florence Rice (Grantland Rice's daughter), and Ann Morris.

The Tennesseans mingled with the movie stars and lounged around the swimming pool and lush gardens of the Brown estate. Prior to his death 40 years later, Brown gave his Tennessee alma mater more than $500,000 and made possible the $2 million state-of-the-art Clarence Brown Theater.

The Vols were entertained one night by puppets Charlie McCarthy and Mortimer Snerd at the home of ventriloquist Edgar Bergen. Actresses Ann Sheridan, Myrna Loy, Ann Rutherford, Jean Arthur, and Brenda Joyce joined the festivities there. But Cafego, who had reinjured his knee in practice earlier that day, was confined to the hotel and missed the fun.

The following morning the Vols, accompanied by the movie starlets, toured the MGM studios. They visited the set where Hedy Lamarr and Spencer Tracy were filming *I Take This Woman*. Then to the set of *New Moon*, starring Jeanette MacDonald and Nelson Eddy. But the end of that day marked the end of the gaiety and entertainment for the Vols until after the Rose Bowl game. Neyland closed his Rose Bowl practices to all reporters, including those from Tennessee newspapers. "We are going to work on a lot of new stuff for the Rose Bowl game," Neyland explained. "We may have some hidden ball tricks and a lot of other black magic to pull on January 1. We would rather not have any scribes looking on, so in order not to make the California writers feel that we are discriminating against them, we have decided to make our drills strictly private."

Lindsey Nelson, in his autobiography, tells about one afternoon at the Brookside Park practice field when Neyland thought he saw spies. "The Major called Billy King and me to his side," Nelson recalled. "He handed Billy the keys to his rented car and explained that he left his army field glasses on the dresser in his room at the Huntington Hotel. He wanted us to fetch the glasses, and we did. The Major spent the next hour training the powerful glasses on the distant mountainous terrain. But he never found anything that he could identify definitely as a Southern Cal spy."

Meanwhile, on December 26, a second train, "The Volunteer Special," left Knoxville with several thousand Tennessee fans aboard. The round-trip fare on a Pullman car was $96.42, including $10 a night for a room at the New Rosslyn Hotel in Los Angeles, $4.40 for a Rose Bowl ticket, and $1 for a sight-seeing excursion to Juarez, Mexico, just across the Rio Grande from El Paso during the trip.

New Year's Day weather was cool and sunny. Peggy Neyland sat with Clarence and Alice Brown at the game. Tennessee fans found themselves sitting among such Hollywood stars as Bing Crosby, Deanna Durbin, Clark Gable and wife Carole Lombard, Robert Taylor and wife Barbara Stanwyck, Jack Benny, Guy Kibbee,

Oliver Hardy, Connie Boswell, and many others.

"There was Tyrone Power sitting on one side of us and Robert Taylor sitting on the other," recalled Emily Faust, wife of Tennessee assistant coach Hugh Faust. "We scarcely got to see the game, with all the fans coming to ask the stars for autographs."

The game was almost anticlimactic for Vol fans who had traveled 2,500 miles for a football game only to become mesmerized by the glamour of Hollywood. The game see-sawed between the 20s until late in the first half when Southern Cal's Ambrose Shindler returned a punt past midfield. After marching deeper into Vol territory, a 10-yard penalty gave Southern Cal a first down at the Vol one. Shindler scored the first touchdown of the game two plays later.

"If it hadn't been for that penalty, they would have never scored on the Vols," said Jack Troy of the *Atlanta Constitution*.

Cafego played only sparingly. "Neyland sent me into the game just so I could say I was in the Rose Bowl," Cafego said. "My knee was still injured, and I wasn't effective when I was in there."

Early in the fourth quarter, the Vols drove 84 yards only to lose a fumble at the Southern Cal 15. It was Tennessee's deepest penetration and only scoring threat of the game. With Shindler at quarterback, Southern Cal drove back down the field for the only other touchdown of the game, and the Vols lost 14-0. It was Southern Cal's sixth consecutive Rose Bowl victory.

"We got beat by a better football team," Neyland said. "The Trojans were hot. They took advantage of our mistakes, and they didn't make any themselves. They had a tremendous line and more hard-running backs than the world ever saw before. I want to congratulate Howard Jones and his staff."

"The best story about the whole trip and game is that Tennessee could lose as well as win in a very sportsmanlike manner," Nashville columnist Fred Russell said. "Don't forget, they rolled up 23 victories before being checked, and it is very surprising that they were able to accept defeat as they did."

The following morning, the team boarded the train and headed back toward Knoxville. During a two-hour stop at El Paso, the Tennesseans crossed the border into Juarez on a shopping excursion.

The two trains—the Southern carrying the Tennessee fans, and the L&N with the team and coaches—arrived at Knoxville within 80 minutes of each other. The 500 people waiting for relatives on the first train then drove to the L&N station a mile away to welcome the team.

Reflecting on the game, Henry McLemore of United Press said Tennessee could have salvaged a tie if it had not been for the slugging penalty that set up Southern Cal's first touchdown or the fumble that cost the Vols a chance to score late in the game. Elmer Disspayne, a reserve end, had thrown the punch and blamed himself for the loss. On the return trip home, Neyland called Disspayne to his stateroom and told him, "Get your head up, Disspayne. Shake it off. That one play didn't cost us the game."

"During all the time they were riding high and winning game after game, they never forgot how to lose," McLemore said. "From Coach Neyland down to the last despairing substitute, they took their licking with warming graciousness. They made no excuse, but simply said a great team had beaten them. . . . They lost the game, but not the respect of any who met them or saw them."

CHAPTER 24

War Clouds

1940

The world edged closer to global war in 1940. Germany invaded Norway and Denmark, then swept through the low countries—Holland, Belgium, and Luxembourg. The retreating British army miraculously escaped annihilation at Dunkirk when tiny boats from England rescued it from the beaches on the northern French coast. By late June, France had surrendered to the invading Germans. Hitler was in control of the European continent. In July, German bombers began raining devastation on England, and the air Battle of Britain began.

America watched Hitler's conquests with growing alarm. Congress passed a law inaugurating the first military draft in United States history.

The Rodgers and Hart musical *Pal Joey* opened on Broadway. The film *Pinocchio* featured the song "When You Wish upon a Star." Country music singer Jimmie Davis, later governor of Louisiana, composed "You Are My Sunshine." Henry Fonda starred in *The Grapes of Wrath,* based on John Steinbeck's novel. Trumpeter Harry James left the Benny Goodman orchestra to form his own band and took on a skinny, unknown vocalist, Frank Sinatra.

The task faced by Bob Neyland and his staff in 1940 was replacing three-fourths of the starting backfield (Cafego, Coffman, and Bartholomew), some key linemen (tackles Shires and Boyd Clay, guard Al Thomas, and center Jim Rike), and some key reserves, such as backs Billy Barnes and Joe Wallen. As usual under the Neyland system, however, there were many capable replacements waiting for chances to shine, and the Tennessee juggernaut rolled on, registering 10 more victories in 1940. Johnny Butler again ripped Alabama, scoring one touchdown on a 48-yard punt return and setting up another with a 68-yard run. As he had in previous years, Neyland used many players during the 1940 campaign. Sixteen Vols scored touchdowns.

Tennessee finished the season ranked fourth in the nation and accepted an invitation to play fifth-ranked Boston College in the Sugar Bowl.

Boston College was coached by Frank Leahy, who lettered on Notre Dame's undefeated 1929 team. Although only a reserve tackle, Leahy was an attentive student of the Rockne style of coaching.

In 1939, after years as an assistant coach at Fordham and a high school coach in South Dakota, Leahy succeeded Gil Dobie as head coach at Boston College. In his first season there, the Eagles went 9-2 and were ranked 11th in the nation. The 1940 team was 10-0 going into the Sugar Bowl game with Tennessee.

A few days before the game, Neyland checked the Vols into a downtown New Orleans hotel and allowed his players to enjoy the sights of the famed French Quarter. But Boston College, en route by train to New Orleans, stopped about 60 miles to the east at Bay St. Louis, Mississippi. There, in a secret practice inside the Bay St. Louis High School gymnasium, Leahy installed a special play for the Sugar Bowl game—Neyland's run-pass option.

The game lived up to its advance billing. It was close. The Vols led 7-0 at halftime. But the unexpected happened early in the third quarter; Boston College blocked a Tennessee punt, something the Vols had not allowed in seven years. Henry Woronicz blocked it, and teammate Joe Zabilski recovered at the Vol 17. Boston College quickly tied the score, 7-7. Tennessee scored to take the lead again, but Boston College answered with its own touchdown to knot the score again at 13.

The Vols almost went back ahead when Bob Foxx broke loose into the Eagle secondary. Herman Masin, in his book *Sports Laughs*, tells the story: "Big Chet Gladchuk of BC tore up from behind and nailed Foxx with a tremendous tackle."

"You all certainly thumped me hard that time," Foxx said.

"You all, hell," Gladchuk fired back. "I got you myself."

With six minutes left and backed up on its own 20, Boston College began going to the air game. Tailback Charlie O'Roarke completed three passes to the Tennessee 24. Then, Boston College brought out the "special" it had installed during that secret practice in Bay St. Louis.

Bill Cunningham of the *Boston Post* described how O'Roarke lifted his arm as if to pass, "but instead, he ran straight through the Tennessee right flank, picking his path just inside their right tackle. Knifing through the line of scrimmage, he cut back sharply to his right. With one of the fanciest pieces of broken field running of his career, he traveled virtually untouched through the Tennessee secondary to score the winning touchdown."

Final score: Boston College 19, Tennessee 13. Meeting at midfield a few minutes later, Neyland congratulated the victorious Leahy and complimented him on the execution of the run-pass option that won the game. Neither man at the moment knew what lay in store for them in the coming months. They would certainly take opposite directions—Leahy to Notre Dame, where he would build the magnificent dynasty of the 1940s and win four national championships; Neyland back into the U.S. Army. The world was about to go to war.

1941-1946

PART VI

CHAPTER 25

You're in the Army Now

1941

Franklin D. Roosevelt in 1941 began his record third term in the White House. The hit movies that year included *Citizen Kane* starring Orson Welles, *Sergeant York* with Gary Cooper, and *King's Row* featuring a fellow named Ronald Reagan. The National Gallery of Art in Washington, D.C., was opened. In sports, the Chicago Bears won the National Football League championship, the "Iron Man" of baseball, Lou Gehrig, died, pitcher Lefty Grove won his 300th game, Bob Feller struck out 260 batters, and Joe DiMaggio got base hits in 56 consecutive games, still a major league record.

America listened transfixed, as each night news commentator Edward R. Morrow opened his broadcast: "This is London."

The German military machine swept across North Africa, continued bombing cities in England, and invaded Russia. Most of Europe by mid-1941 was under German control a conquest unequaled since the days of Napoleon.

The United States, shocked out of its isolationism by Hitler's unbridled aggression, sent aid to Great Britain and began preparing for war.

Japanese forces invaded Thailand and the Malay Peninsula and virtually isolated China by cutting the Burma Road, over which supplies had been transported from India to the Chinese army and a group of volunteer American fighter pilots known as the "Flying Tigers."

It was all leading to the morning of Sunday, December 7, and the Japanese attack on Pearl Harbor, the home base of the U.S. Pacific Fleet.

Meanwhile, a football-prominent but militarily obscure retired army major in Knoxville, Tennessee, was the subject of a March 26 memorandum from Major William Bessell, Jr., personnel chief of the Army Corps of Engineers, to the adjutant general of the War Department.

"It is requested that orders be issued calling Major Robert R. Neyland, U.S. Army, Retired, to active duty as District Engineer, Norfolk, Virginia, effective on or about May 10, 1941," the memo said. "Major Neyland has been informed by radio that his orders have been requested."

Bessell said Neyland was being activated "because it was necessary that an officer with his particular qualifications . . . of leadership and aggressiveness" be placed in charge of various projects essential to national defense in the face of impending war.

Clearly, the army was serious. But so was Bob Neyland, head coach of the University of Tennessee football team. And he let the army know it. It was a test of wills—his and the army's.

"In case of war I would welcome recall to active duty," Neyland said to the War Department. "However, I am committed to a signed five-year contract with the University of Tennessee which precludes my concurrence in recall to active duty at the present time under the existing status of the United States as a non-belligerent." In other words, Neyland said, he did not want to be back in the army unless the country was at war. It is easy to understand why Neyland resisted recall to active duty.

The 1938-40 Vols had won 30 consecutive regular season games, and Neyland was having the time of his life. "In early 1941, after we got back from the Sugar Bowl, Neyland told me that he believed he had as many good freshmen moving up to the varsity as he had ever had," said Ed Cifers, starting end on Tennessee's 1939-40 teams. "He was really looking forward to the 1941 season."

Ray Graves, Tennessee's 1941 captain and later head coach at Florida, recalled that Neyland even experimented with the "T-formation" offense during spring practice. "I don't know whether he would have junked the single-wing, but he certainly looked seriously at the 'T' because we installed some 'T' plays that spring." It was an exciting time for Tennessee football.

Anticipating another outstanding football team, Neyland sought military deferment. As had been the case in the late 1920s and early 1930s, every time the army moved to transfer Neyland from Knoxville, the War Department received a flood of appeals from university officials, Tennessee congressmen, and politically influential businessmen. Those appeals, incidentally, always talked about the importance of Neyland to the Tennessee's ROTC program. There was never any mention of Neyland's remarkable football record. And in 1941 the War Department was not impressed with Neyland's "no war" argument or the pressures applied on his behalf, however deceitful. Neyland's job as head coach of the Tennessee Vols football team cannot "be characterized as essential to national defense," Brigadier General Wade Haislip said in a memorandum to his boss, the army chief of staff, General George C. Marshall. "Major Neyland should be called to active duty without his consent," Haislip said. Marshall concurred, and the order recalling Neyland to active duty was signed on May 13.

Rather than resign from the University of Tennessee, as he had done in 1935 when the army sent him to Panama, Neyland obtained a leave of absence—thinking his assignment at Norfolk would last only one year and that he would be coaching again in time for the 1942 season.

Before he left for Norfolk, Knoxville civic leaders threw an appreciation dinner in Neyland's honor. And, although at times embarrassed by it all but retaining his customary equilibrium, Neyland listened for almost two hours as speaker after speaker sang his praises.

"Neyland has no peer in the coaching field, and I am going to miss him more than anyone else," said John Barnhill, the man Neyland designated to be head coach during his absence.

Dr. Nathan W. Dougherty, the dean of engineering and the man responsible for bringing Neyland to the university in 1925, praised Neyland for his abilities as an engineer. "He not only is an expert in football, but an expert in engineering also," Dougherty said. "He ranks among the nation's best in the U.S. Army Engineers." "Uncle Sam was the only one that could get him away from us," said University of Tennessee President James D. Hoskins. Then, he looked at Neyland and said: "You carry with you the respect, love, and admiration of all Tennesseans."

Those who knew Neyland best could sense how deeply affected he was by the honor being accorded him at that moment.

"I have spent the happiest 15 years of my life here in Knoxville," he said. "When I get back next May, and I shall be back unless the war situation becomes much more precarious than at present, only Uncle Sam can get me away again."

Neyland briefly described his duties at Norfolk—building defenses for the Chesapeake Bay area in case of attempted invasion by a foreign power. "I only hope I can make a worthwhile contribution to national defense," he told his well-wishers.

Turning to the subject of football, Neyland urged support of Barnhill.

"John Barnhill's ability cannot be over-emphasized. He will have a staff of experts to help him," Neyland said. "I know of no place which has the spirit of the Tennessee student body. They have shown it in the past, and I believe they will in the future."

Meanwhile, during the days Bob and Peggy Neyland were packing boxes, storing furniture, and preparing to relocate in Norfolk, messages of praise and good wishes poured in from all parts of the football world.

"Bob Neyland is without any question one of the greatest coaches of football history," said Grantland Rice, dean of American sportswriters. "He combines not only a mastery of technique and tactics but is also one of the best when it comes to developing fundamentals. The Major's Tennessee teams have always been perfectly equipped to give the best they had. Not only Tennessee, but all football will miss him during his absence which I hope will be brief."

Jock Sutherland, head coach of the 1937 national champion Pittsburgh Panthers and by 1941 head coach of the pro football Brooklyn Dodgers, spoke publicly to the University of Tennessee about Neyland's recall to the army.

"I think I know how Tennessee feels about losing Bob Neyland," he said. "It's the same feeling Bob has had many times in the past when he has watched his team play its final game and has seen some of its seniors walk off the field to hang up their uniforms. I have had the same experience in my days as a coach—wondering whether the likes of those fine boys would ever come along again. It must be the same when your school loses a man like Bob Neyland."

Sutherland talked about seeing Neyland's Tennessee teams in action. "Their perfection in detail and their spirit, winning or losing, was a perfect tribute to the skill and devotion of their coach. Among other coaches, he is feared on the field, but respected and well-liked personally," Sutherland said. "I'm sorry to see you lose him, but in these times I must admit that it gives me a comfortable feeling to know that we have such men in the army."

On May 26, Major Bob Neyland, Peggy, little Bobby, and Lewis moved to Norfolk, Virginia. Just 195 days later, the Japanese would bomb Pearl Harbor. Bob Neyland the coach would be gone from the University of Tennessee five years—to return after the war a brigadier general.

CHAPTER 26

The Soldier Coach

1942-43

In swift developments during the first six months of 1942, the Japanese seized Burma and cut the Burma Road, and American C-47 transport planes began crossing the "Hump," a series of rugged mountains in northern Burma and southwestern China. The planes would leave air bases in Assam, India, and fly 500 miles across the Hump to the big Chinese-American supply base in Kunming, China. On April 18, flying from the aircraft carrier Hornet, a flight of B-25 bombers commanded by Colonel James Doolittle bombed Tokyo and other Japanese cities. The damage was slight, but the air strike buoyed morale in America.

Bob Neyland, who had taken command of the Norfolk engineering district on June 7, 1941, was promoted to lieutenant colonel seven months later. His responsibilities at Norfolk were staggering. He supervised a $250 million construction program—air bases, depots, ammunition manufacturing and storage facilities, hospitals, and a range of military installations for defense of the Chesapeake Bay area.

Lieutenant General Raymond A. Wheeler said Neyland directed approximately 80 projects, including the $15.6 million Richmond Air Base, the $8 million coastal defense installations to protect massive Norfolk Naval Base and the entrance to Chesapeake Bay, the $11 million Radford Ordnance Works where TNT was produced, and $1.8 million in Air Corps facilities at Langley Field, Virginia. "All of this diversified work was carried out under extreme pressure because of the military situation abroad," Wheeler said after the war. "Consequently, all projects had progress schedules difficult to maintain. That General Neyland maintained the required progress schedules on his jobs, with many of them completed ahead of time, attests to the unusual ability of this officer to cope with engineering problems and to overcome the handicaps of shortages of transportation facilities, machinery, and labor."

Wheeler said Neyland's accomplishments as district engineer at Norfolk were of "inestimable value in preparing the nation for war."

Promotion in rank had come slowly for Neyland since World War I. In fact, his decision to retire from the army in 1936 was predicated partly on the "slow promotion" factor and the frustration he felt when he twice was demoted after "temporary" promotions, even though such demotions were commonplace in the army between the world wars and did not necessarily reflect negatively on an officer's performance.

But in February 1942, Neyland was promoted to lieutenant colonel. After all, he was spending a quarter-billion dollars of government money to build up military installations on the East Coast.

In a fitness report dated June 30, 1942, Neyland was described as "an officer of outstanding all-around ability who performs tasks of any magnitude with judgment, initiative, intelligence, force, and painstaking care." His performance was rated "superior."

Less than a week later, on July 4, Neyland was promoted to full colonel. Also that day he received orders to report to New York on temporary duty "for purpose of consultation regarding public relations." It turned out to be an order with a hidden agenda—one Neyland deeply resented. The War Department wanted him to coach an army all-star football team in three games against teams from the National Football League.

The army felt that the defense projects under way in the Norfolk district were far enough advanced to justify Neyland being diverted for two and a half months to coach a football team. Imagine how he felt. He had not wanted to return to the army in 1941 because the nation still was not at war, and because he wanted to coach the Tennessee Vols that season. Yet, despite his protests, the army reactivated him. Now, a year later, the army wanted him to coach football.

The army also had plans for another officer it had reactivated—Major Wallace Wade, the Duke University coach and Neyland's close friend. Like Neyland, Wade did not want to be coaching an army team. If he were going to coach, he had preferred it to be his Duke Blue Devils. But the army acts in wondrous ways, and Wade too was ordered to "public relations" duty.

"Neither one of us wanted the job," Neyland said. "But when they handed it to us, we went to it with everything we had."

First Lieutenant Robert "Dink" Eldridge, who had been Neyland's team manager at Tennessee in 1939-40, was stationed in Texas when the phone rang that July night.

"Get your ass up to Washington right away," Neyland told Eldridge on the phone. "I've got a job for you."

So Eldridge, acting on orders arranged by Neyland, arrived in Washington. Several days later, he was in an office with Neyland, Wade, and Alexander Surles, the general in charge of staging events to raise money for the Army Emergency Relief Fund. In their temporary assignments, Neyland and Wade were under Surles's command. And Surles wanted the two coaches to divide available army personnel with football experience into two all-star teams—the East and the West—to face the pros.

"I remember walking into some general's [Surles's] office in Washington," Wade recalled. "Bob was a colonel and I was a major. I stood at attention, but Bob sat down and put his feet on the general's desk. I knew right then I was in trouble."

The story of that "draft" in the general's office grew beyond the truth as the years passed. Neyland did not pull rank on Wade, but both men enjoyed telling the story as if that had happened.

"Wallace and I went to Washington to find out what football players there were in the army," Neyland said. "The heat was something awful, but we rolled up our sleeves and went to work. Wallace would take one and then I'd take one, and if it came to a fellow we both wanted, we would toss a coin."

They knew that James Nelson, who had played tailback for Alabama against Neyland's 1939 Tennessee team, was stationed with the army somewhere. They just did not know where, and there were hundreds of James Nelsons on the army personnel roster. "We finally had to call up the boy's parents to find out where he was stationed," Neyland said. Wade took Nelson.

"We sat there off and on for two days in that room, Neyland and Wade alternately picking players for their teams from the available pool," Eldridge recalls. "Neyland picked seven who had played for him at Tennessee, including George Cafego, Sam Bartholomew, Len Coffman, Jim Schwartzinger, Burr West, Abe Shires, and Nick Weber. He also picked Norm Standlee, the great fullback from Stanford and the Chicago Bears."

Next, Neyland summoned former Tennessee associates to form his all-star staff. He got rotund Herman Hickman, his 1929-31 all-American guard, from North Carolina State where he was line coach. He asked for and got First Lieutenant Bob Woodruff, tackle on his 1936-38 Tennessee team. And he called in Captain Bob Brashear, Tennessee's long-time, pre-war team physician. Neyland also brought in Murray Warmath, a tackle on Tennessee's 1932-34 team, and Vol trainer Mickey O'Brien. And he had Eldridge for team manager.

"I was on Allyn McKeen's staff at Mississippi State, but when Neyland called and told me to get up to New Haven, I went," Warmath said. "I never did learn to say 'no' to him. As I recall, I got back to Mississippi State before our first game."

The staff reported immediately to Yale University at New Haven, Connecticut, where Neyland's East All-Stars would prepare for the first of three games—the New York Giants on September 12 at the Polo Grounds in New York City, then the Brooklyn Dodgers and the Chicago Bears.

Eldridge placed an order for 53 complete football uniforms, including shoes and protective pads. "After that last game against the Bears in late September," Eldridge later said, "we left those uniforms on the floor of the dressing room, and I never saw them again."

Neyland's staff quickly installed his Tennessee system. "We have such a short time here [five weeks] that it will be extremely difficult to teach all these men the system which we use," Neyland said.

On the first day of practice at Yale, Neyland told the squad its assignment was to win. "We must carry out successfully the work we have been given. We must win," he said. "Anyone who doesn't want to win can go back at once to the place from which he came. Nothing short of victory is acceptable to the United States Army."

The squad included soldiers with ranks ranging from captain to private, but Neyland made no distinction. "Neyland shouts out instructions without regard to captains, sergeants, corporals, or privates," wrote Stanley Woodward, sports editor of the *New York Herald*. "All he cares about are ends, tackles, guards, centers, and backs."

Neyland's all-star practices were intense, but in the evenings he took Hickman with him to have dinner and do a little drinking. Hickman's presence was a sort of command performance. But after a week, the routine was causing Hickman to drag. So one morning he lumbered into Neyland's office. "Colonel," he said, "I can coach with you, or I can drink with you. But I can't do both."

That Bob Neyland and Wallace Wade were coaching two all-star teams seemed to capture the national fancy. A steady stream of prominent sportswriters visited the training camp at New Haven. One of them was soft-spoken Bob Considine of the *New York Daily Mirror.*

"It gives a guy a clean, optimistic feeling to be around the All-Army football team quartered here under the calculating eye of Colonel Bob Neyland, one of the greatest coaches ever produced," Considine wrote in one of his columns that August.

"You ought to see the American soldiers on this football team," Considine continued. "You never saw such specimens in all your life. Enormous, well-trained, bronzed young men who look good enough right now to whip their weight in wildcats or double their weight in Axis foes. What men they are!"

Neyland said getting the players he had assembled was not easy. "We couldn't get any player who is out of the country, and nobody from officers' candidate school or a point of embarkation post, or air pilots," he said. "I'll say this for the men we did get. They know they're up against a helluva job, playing those pros. But they're as keen as high school kids. Never saw such spirit."

The task of the two all-star teams—Neyland's and Wade's—was seemingly impossible. Neyland's East All-Stars, within the span of nine days, was scheduled to play three National Football League teams—the New York Giants, the Brooklyn Dodgers, and the world champion Chicago Bears. Wade's West All-Stars were to play five NFL teams within 19 days—the Washington Redskins, Chicago Cardinals, Detroit Lions, Green Bay Packers, and New York Giants.

A crowd estimated at 40,000 watched as the Army East All-Stars, in typical Neyland style, limited the New York Giants to only seven first downs, 57 yards rushing, and 74 through the air.

At halftime, with the East All-Stars leading 9-0, General Surles walked into the dressing room and told Neyland that he wanted world heavyweight boxing champion Joe Louis, waiting outside, to address the team.

"Nobody talks to my players but me," Neyland told his commander. Surles insisted, and Neyland stiffened: "General, do you see that door? Go through it and don't come back!" General Surles left, and Neyland years later wondered if that incident was in some way responsible for his promotion to brigadier general being denied three times during the war.

Anyway, Neyland's East All-Stars amassed 224 yards against the Giants, dominated all phases of the game, and won 16-0. One of the big plays was Cafego's 60-yard punt return, setting up a second quarter field goal.

That was on Saturday. Four days later in Baltimore, the East All-Stars found themselves trailing the Brooklyn Dodgers, 7-0, in the fourth quarter. Thinking field position, as he usually did, Neyland called for a quick kick, and Cafego's 56-yard punt left the Dodgers on their own 14. The East All-Stars recovered a fumble at the 19 and scored three plays later. On a subsequent possession, they drove 57 yards and ex-Vol fullback Len Coffman scored. The East All-Stars won 13-7.

Neyland's gridiron soldiers moved on to Fenway Park in Boston for the September 20 showdown with Coach George Halas's world champion Chicago Bears, and Neyland's earlier assessment of his "impossible assignment" proved correct.

After a scoreless first half, the Bears simply overpowered the courageous but battered East All-Stars. The Bears won the game, 14-7, on a 75-yard scoring drive in the fourth quarter. The key plays in that march were pass completions by Bears quarterback Charlie O'Roarke, who had scored the winning touchdown when Boston College beat Neyland's Tennessee team in the 1941 Sugar Bowl.

Neyland told his players how proud he was of their hard work, dedication, and performance. And Wallace Wade praised his West All-Stars, who had beaten the Cardinals and the Lions, and had lost to the Redskins, Packers, and Giants. The players were given 10-day furloughs before reporting to their new assignments. Neyland returned to Norfolk.

On October 13, after completing most of the defense installations he had begun in the Norfolk district, Neyland was reassigned to Dallas, Texas, as division engineer. In that post he was in charge of $1.15 billion in Corps of Engineers projects in Arkansas, Louisiana, New Mexico, Oklahoma, and Texas. The work included construction of military installations, oil pipe lines, and industrial plants vital to the war effort.

Peg and the boys moved with him to Dallas. They rented a home on Princeton Street near the Southern Methodist University campus. When he could find a few uncommitted hours, Neyland would sneak off with former Texas A&M halfback Tyree Bell, a good friend from college days, and go fishing for large-mouth bass.

While carrying out his assignments with usual precision, Neyland despaired somewhat over his state-side post. He read newspaper accounts of Lieutenant General George Patton's successes against the Germans in North Africa and Sicily. He longed for a battle zone command—even more so after learning that his former West Point teammate, General Omar Bradley, had been named commander of U.S. ground forces for the invasion of Europe. And, of course, another West Point teammate, Ike Eisenhower, was supreme commander of Allied forces in Europe.

Then came D-Day, June 6, 1944, the Normandy invasion. Two days later, Colonel Bob Neyland received new orders. Peggy and the boys returned to Knoxville, and Neyland left immediately for a war zone. He had been named commanding officer of the huge American supply base at Kunming, China.

CHAPTER 27

War in China

1944

When Colonel Bob Neyland arrived in Kunming on June 29, 1944, the American war effort there was mired in political infighting and Chinese military inefficiency, and the supply line was in deplorable condition, almost non-existent.

Russia, facing its own menace from the German army on its western front, had quit shipping supplies across the Gobi Desert to China in the summer of 1941. Japanese occupation of Indochina closed the railroad to Yunnan province in southwest China. When the Japanese seized Hong Kong in December 1941 and occupied Burma, the Chinese army and the American Volunteer Group, a band of fighter pilots known as the "Flying Tigers" and commanded by Claire Lee Chennault, became virtually isolated with insufficient munitions to wage a modern war.

The Japanese conquests in December 1941 and January 1942 had spread gloom and despondency in China and had raised fears among the Allies that China might make peace with Japan. Lieutenant General "Vinegar Joe" Stilwell had been sent to China in early 1942 to be chief of staff to Generalissimo Chiang Kai-shek, the supreme commander of Chinese forces. Stilwell's assignment was to reassure Chiang Kai-shek, keep China in the war, and improve the combat efficiency of the Chinese army. But Stilwell's task was complicated by the Japanese seizure of Burma, by Chennault's own needs, and by the independent actions of Chiang Kai-shek.

Into the midst of this procedural and political nightmare flew the master of preparation and organization, Colonel Bob Neyland, who was assigned to the Service of Supply (SOS), that branch of the army which handles distribution of supplies to military units. As commander of Advance Base Section One, he was responsible for receiving supplies from India and distributing them to the American and Chinese ground and air forces operating in China. Chiang and Stilwell each wanted all the tonnage that Neyland received in Kunming.

Neyland was deputy to Major General William E. R. Covell, the SOS commander in the China-Burma-India (CBI) theater of war. As such, he acted on behalf of Covell in meetings with Stilwell, Chennault, and Chiang.

Stilwell had high praise for Neyland's performance in Kunming.

"The Japanese completely surrounded China so that the only line of communication was over the so-called Hump over the Himalaya Mountains, flying supplies from air bases in India and Burma into Yunnan, the southwestern province of China," Stilwell said.

"The capital [of Yunnan] was Kunming, and we had an air base there that was as busy as LaGuardia ever could be, with planes leaving every 90 seconds. There were many demands for supplies being brought across the Hump," Stilwell said. "Bob Neyland had to exercise tact and firmness in allocating the supplies to the ground forces, to the air forces, and to the clandestine forces of OSS [Office of Strategic Services] and Admiral Miles' Navy Group China."

Neyland felt immense admiration for the crews of the cargo planes—usually overloaded, dodging snow-capped mountain peaks, and always under threat of Japanese fighter attack. The flight from Assam to Kunming—across the mountains, then the Mekong and Salween rivers—took three to four hours. As soon as they came within sight of Tali Lake, 175 miles northwest of Kunming, the pilots began to descend.

"The loads . . . packed into those DC-3s would have curdled the blood of the aeronautical engineers who designed the ship," said Brigadier General Robert Lee Scott, who flew the Hump and later commanded Chennault's fighters. "The C-47, or DC-3 . . . was constructed to carry a full load of 24 passengers or 6,000 pounds [of cargo]. The maximum altitude was expected to be about 12,000 feet—but we later went a minimum of 18,000 across the Hump, and sometimes we had to go to 21,500 to miss the storms and ice."

Political historian Theodore H. White, who covered the war in China for Time Incorporated, experienced some of those flights. In his autobiography, *In Search of History*, White recalled: "When one flew the Hump, it was high romance—sorties of blockade runners, little C-47s and later C-46s, ducking Japanese planes by darting into mountain-stuffed clouds, a handful of American boys, itching, scratching, sick, malarial, sometimes cracking under the strain."

The ranking American commanders in China were Lieutenant General Joe Stilwell, commander of U.S. forces in CBI; Major General Claire L. Chennault, Fourteenth Air Force; Major General Curtis E. LeMay, Twentieth Bomber Command; Brigadier General William H. Tunner, Air Transport Command, China Wing; and Colonel Robert R. Neyland, SOS commander, Kunming.

Neyland immediately recognized a deplorable transportation situation in that part of China still unoccupied by the Japanese. There were only 10,000 trucks available to move goods and people, and that number at any one time was limited by poor maintenance and bad fuel. Moreover, the Chinese SOS was not efficient, and consequently troop movements could not be supported by a steady flow of supplies. Even worse, Neyland learned from intelligence reports that unscrupulous Chinese officials sold a variety of commodities, including medicines provided by the Red Cross, to black marketeers in Shanghai and other coastal cities. Also, there was evidence to suggest that some Chinese warlords, acting independently, may have ambushed small American units along the China-Burma border for their weapons and ammunition. In short, corruption was widespread in the Chinese army and government, and both Stilwell and Neyland knew it.

Neyland's duties as SOS deputy commander in China required close liaison with high Chinese officials and frequent, sometimes daily, contact with Chennault. The two American officers had something in common other than China. Both were natives of Hunt County, Texas. The odds must have been a trillion-to-one that two officers, born in the same county on the east Texas plains, would serve in the same high command of a war zone 11,000 miles from home.

Chennault and Neyland had their headquarters in Kunming—Chennault because his biggest fighter base was there, and Neyland because the Kunming airdrome was the only one large enough to handle the high volume of cargo flights. Chennault and Neyland lived in bungalows near the airfield.

Chennault had been born in the town of Commerce, about 15 miles northeast of Greenville, Neyland's birthplace. During infrequent lulls in activity at Kunming, the two of them would talk about Hunt County even though Chennault's family had moved from there when he was a child. Still, they talked about "home."

Neyland eagerly awaited letters from Peggy—filling him in on the progress of Bobby and Lewis in school, the fortunes of the Tennessee Vols, and the latest news about their close friends, such as Knoxville businessman Andy Morton and his wife "Littlely," Hugh and Emily Faust, and Katherine "Kak" Lindsay.

Peggy, however, did not tell her husband about the night oldest son Bobby and some friends broke out 26 street lights in West Knoxville's fashionable Sequoyah Hills. The police apprehended the culprits and called their parents, which meant Peggy got the call about Bobby. The police only threw a scare into the boys and sent them home with their parents.

"I'm not going to tell your father," Peggy told Bobby. "You're going to write and tell him what you did."

Little Bob fretted about that letter, about how he would tell his father he had been caught breaking out street lights. Finally, after agonizing days of procrastination, Bobby wrote the confession letter, telling how he had thrown rocks at 26 street lights but had broken only two.

Six weeks later, a letter arrived from Kunming and Bobby nervously opened it. "Dear Bobby," it began, moving immediately to descriptions of the war in China and the Colonel's experiences there. Then Neyland got to the street lights. "I'm disappointed that a son of mine would get only two out of 26. I'd have gotten that many left-handed."

In mid-August 1944, the ranking commanders in the CBI met at theater headquarters in New Delhi, India. Among the assembled were Stilwell, Neyland, and Stilwell's deputy commander, Major General Dan Sultan. On the way back to Kunming, Neyland stopped at Chabua to confer with his long-time friend, Brigadier General Joe Cranston, the man in charge of SOS bases in Assam, India. Chabua was the site of one of the major air bases from which C-47s crossed the Hump to deliver supplies to Neyland at Kunming.

It was hot and steamy and rainy the day Neyland flew into Chabua to visit Cranston.

"I had spent part of the day slogging through the mud and water with Cranston, inspecting his rail and river points and his 'go-downs,' [warehouses for storing supplies to be shipped to Kunming]," Neyland said. "It was a depressing day."

Their conference completed, Cranston went with Neyland to the airfield where a C-47 was waiting to take Neyland to Kunming. It was late in the afternoon. The C-47 had a large dragon painted on its side, and it was named appropriately "The Assam Dragon."

"Since no co-pilot was available, the pilot asked me to ride in the co-pilot's seat," Neyland said in his memoirs. The story that follows is told in Neyland's words.

"We flew directly into the East, gradually gaining altitude over the low range of hills, which serrated row upon row, higher and higher, rising in gigantic staircase fashion to 'the Hump,' that wild jumble of mountains . . . forming a north-south prong of the Himalayas, the 'Roof of the World.'

"Our payload was two tons of airplane bombs and about one and one-half tons of one hundred octane aviation gasoline which comforted us with the assurance that we would not be crippled in case of a crash, and that we would not put anyone to any undue trouble looking for the pieces.

"Consoled by this thought, we were able to give our full attention to a truly remarkable spectacle. The sky directly in front of us was laced with alternate bands of grey and golden red . . . the full moon, red and bloated like some tropical bloom, soared majestically above the horizon. As it changed gradually from darkest red to golden silver, we reached our safe elevation of 18,000 feet and straightened out in level flight.

"Below us was a solid cloud mass which, as the moon rose higher, took on a brilliant white glow. There was no turbulence in the air, and we seemed to hang motionless in a world of unearthly brilliance and majestic beauty. So bright was the moonlight, reinforced by reflection from the cloud surface, that a newspaper could easily be read with the naked eye.

"It has been said that India is a land of violent contrasts. Surely to be snatched from the mud and sweat of Assam in less than two hours to this eerie world of ineffable beauty is enough to transmute a mood of depression into one of high exaltation."

The 500-mile flight from Chabua to Kunming took the C-47 over Japanese-held territory and within easy range of Japanese fighter planes. Although he was captivated by the beauty surrounding him, the potential danger of the moment did not escape

Neyland's concern. And his quiet meditation was interrupted by the pilot.

"Would you mind keeping a close watch to your right and above," the pilot said. "I'll watch to the front and the left. This is a fine night for Zeros."

"Zeros?" Neyland asked, suddenly aware that Japanese fighter planes could attack at any moment.

"Oh, yes," the pilot explained, "on clear moonlight nights like this they fly north from Burma bases, hunting cargo planes like this one. They got a C-46 night before last."

Neyland groped for reassurance: "But all you'd have to do would be to duck down into those clouds perhaps a thousand feet below us, and you could elude a Zero easily, could you not?"

"Shucks," the pilot replied, "a Zero could fly around us three times before we got our nose down good, and I hate to think what an incendiary bullet would do to our temperamental cargo."

Neyland instantly and somewhat obediently shifted his concentration from the surrounding beauty to an intense but fortunately fruitless search for possible intruders.

"We flew into the Kunming air base without untoward incident, and I proceeded to bed and a sound sleep," Neyland said.

During the summer of 1944, British and Indian forces turned back the Japanese thrust into India, and Chinese troops captured the air base at Myitkyina in northeast Burma. But the Japanese were having successes elsewhere in the CBI theater. They had begun advancing toward American air bases and Chinese ground units in east China. And to make matters worse, the feuding between Stilwell and Chennault had escalated.

The air base at "Kweilin was blown up by order of Stilwell and over the protests of Chennault at midnight, September 15, 1944," Brigadier General Robert Lee Scott said in his book *Flying Tiger.*

"Liuchow, the very last of the eastern bases, held out until November 7. Instead of the 90-day blitz the Japanese had predicted for the securing of a path through China from the Yellow River south to Indochina, they were forced by Chennault to take six months."

Neyland had allocated to Stilwell a large stockpile of emergency fuel and other supplies. And, in an attempt to slow the Japanese offensive from the air, Chennault borrowed heavily from the theater reserves.

Stilwell "ordered Chennault to pay back all the aviation gasoline he had borrowed from theater reserves," Scott wrote. "Thus Chennault was forced to curb his offensive operations [in east China] drastically to comply with such a directive."

The deteriorating situation in China came to a head in October 1944. Because of his outspoken criticism of corruption among Chinese officials and his sharp disagreements with Chiang Kai-shek and Chennault, Stilwell was recalled to Washington. But before he left, he recommended Neyland for promotion to brigadier general.

CHAPTER 28

Calcutta

1944-46

With "Vinegar Joe" Stilwell out of the picture, China-Burma-India was divided into two theaters. Lieutenant General Dan Sultan, who had been Stilwell's deputy theater commander, became commander of the India-Burma Theater, and Lieutenant General Albert Wedemeyer was named Generalissimo Chiang Kai-shek's chief of staff and commander of American forces in China.

At the time of Wedemeyer's arrival on October 31, 1944, the Japanese had advanced to within several hundred miles of Kunming, and there was concern that the Japanese might attack Kunming in a northward thrust from Indo-China. The 69th Composite Wing of the 14th Air Force, headquartered at Kunming, shifted its attention from the campaign in Burma to the defense of Kunming.

Wedemeyer inherited a contingent of 27,739 American troops, 2,400 of them under Neyland's command, when he arrived in China. But Wedemeyer wanted his own staff and moved quickly to replace key members of Stilwell's staff. One of the casualties was Colonel Bob Neyland.

On November 10, Wedemeyer named Major General Gilbert X. Cheves the SOS commander at Kunming, replacing Neyland, who became the commanding officer of the port of Calcutta, known as Base Section Two.

The following day Neyland was promoted to brigadier general.

In his new assignment, Neyland reported to General Sultan, whose job as India-Burma Theater commander was to supply Wedemeyer's theater, to command U.S. and Chinese combat troops operating against the Japanese in Burma, to supply British, Indian, and Chinese divisions in Burma, and to build the Ledo Road. To carry out his assignment, Sultan in November 1944 had a U.S. force of 183,900 troops, many times the size of Wedemeyer's.

Neyland's assignment was to operate the port of Calcutta, unload supply ships, and move those supplies to depots at Chabua and Ledo, both in Assam, for transport to appropriate field commands in China and Burma. Like other SOS commanders, he was responsible for all installations in his area.

Calcutta, the heart of Base Section Number Two, was the principal seaport in the India-Burma Theater. The port at Karachi, on the other side of the Indian continent, was too far from the front and received very few cargo ships. At the time Neyland assumed command at Calcutta, the port there was handling a fraction of its capacity.

Neyland immediately went to work on the problem. He implemented some labor-saving devices, began an intensive training program for the Indian dock workers, and set some ambitious but achievable goals for unloading cargo ships. He believed the principles of football and military command were essentially the same.

"Your men must be in good physical condition. They must have technical ability. And they must have high morale," he said. "It was tough at first to use these rules in Calcutta, but in the end they prevailed. India was a land of the underprivileged with the heat and rains making cholera, dysentery, and bubonic plague commonplace."

Neyland organized a gigantic sports program that played a significant role in raising morale among his troops and the native workers. Newspaper columnist Bob Considine saw it in action when he visited Neyland in Calcutta.

"Neyland had turned the unromantic task of unloading ships into a huge game," Considine said. "He had hundreds of teams engaged in baseball, basketball, softball, tennis, swimming, track, boxing, and just about every sport known. He built 'Monsoon Square Garden' to permit sports during the rainy season."

Not only had Neyland developed an expansive sports program to boost morale of his own troops, but he made athletic facilities and personnel within his command available to all troops of the Burma-India Theater. Lieutenant Colonel Paul Zimmerman, former sports editor of the *Los Angeles Times*, was one of those who spread the word about Neyland's accomplishments. He had help from Neyland's public information officer, Walter Stewart, who after the war would return to the *Memphis Commercial Appeal* as sports editor.

Fred Beene, from Decherd, Tennessee, remembers seeing Neyland at Tinsukia, the site of fuel depots in eastern Assam, in the fall of 1944. Beene was a sergeant assigned to a railroad battalion at Tinsukia.

"They were having a football game that day, and I recognized General Neyland when two jeeps of officers arrived at the field," Beene said. "There were no bleachers, just an open field, but some of the troops placed wooden planks on two 55-gallon drums for General Neyland and his staff to sit on." Beene did not talk to Neyland that day and never has. "I was just a lowly sergeant, and you don't walk up and start talking to a general. But I knew who he was."

Neyland caused a furor in late 1944 when he inadvertently authorized the location of some recreational and rest facilities in a section of Calcutta he had already declared out of bounds to American troops. That particular section of the city contained a number of brothels, and it was not too long before Neyland's medical staff noticed an alarming increase in venereal disease. Following an official inquiry, the rest camp was relocated to a more appropriate section of the city, and the venereal disease rate dropped sharply in the next two months. The furor was forgotten.

By early 1945, supplies were flowing in large volume to the depots and tank farms in Assam, from which they would be flown or piped to China. By now, the Burma Road was reopened and a pipeline laid beside it into China. But, although operational, the Burma Road still could not handle the volume of supplies needed in China, and therefore Neyland relied on planes flying the Hump. He expedited the movement of troops, weapons, ammunition, food, medicine, and clothing by train or truck to the airfields around Chabua. He piped fuel to the tank farms at Tinsukia.

During the period from March 15 to March 27, 1945, about 114,000 tons were unloaded at Calcutta. At the end of March only 889 tons remained in transit sheds on the docks. Calcutta, once a bottleneck in the CBI Theatre, had become free-flowing under Neyland. His troops could unload a ship in record time, 44 hours. Within two months after taking command at Calcutta, the monthly average of tonnage unloaded from supply ships increased from 75,143 long tons to 134,960 long tons.

In April 1945, General Sultan wrote to Neyland: "Dear Bob. You are breaking more records at Calcutta than did [your] Tennessee football team. Keep up the good work."

Calcutta (Base Section Two) now was handling virtually all of the supplies and personnel moving through India to China or Burma. So the army deactivated the port at Karachi (Base Section One), and Neyland was handed more responsibility. General Sultan explained in a directive to all commanders in his theater: "At midnight, 20-21 May 1945, the activities of the SOS were consolidated with those of the Theater Headquarters. General Neyland is now serving as the Commanding General, Base Section, India-Burma Theater." That meant all military supplies flowing into or out of the two theaters, India-Burma and China, were Neyland's responsibility.

In May, General Covell, the SOS commander in India-Burma, recommended Neyland for promotion to major general. "Practically all supplies for the India-Burma Theater and the China Theater move through this [Neyland's] port," Covell said in the recommendation. "This port has established world records in the discharge of cargo and turnaround time of ships, which accomplishments have made it possible to expedite supplies to the forward areas in support of the American and Chinese combat forces." But the close of the war did not render enough time to process such a promotion, and Neyland never became a major general.

As summer approached, the war was nearing an end. Hitler had committed suicide, and Germany had surrendered. The Japanese were in full retreat in southeast Asia and in the Pacific.

In June, the India-Burma Theater commander, General Sultan, was recalled to Washington to become chief of the Army Corps of Engineers. In a letter to Neyland, Sultan said "the success of this theater was made possible in large measure by the very efficient operation of the port of Calcutta."

A month later, Lieutenant General George E. Stratemeyer became the commanding general of U.S. air forces in China. He had been the U.S. air commander in the CBI and then the IB Theater. In a letter to Neyland, Stratemeyer said: "I would like to tell you . . . how much I appreciate the help you have been to us ever since you assumed command. There has never been a moment when you were not ready and anxious to help the A.A.F. [Army Air Force] in any way which was in your power. You have made the solution of our many supply problems infinitely simpler."

Then Stratemeyer wrote a letter about Neyland to Lieutenant General Raymond A. Wheeler, new commanding general of U.S. forces in India-Burma. "I should call to your attention the very superior manner in which Bob Neyland has handled this Calcutta job. He has done it without any fanfare and in spite of the fact that many of his key personnel were sent to China. My contact has been so close with Neyland's activities that I feel it incumbent on me to submit to you a strong recommendation for his promotion," Stratemeyer said. "Not only has Bob done an outstanding job both under Covell and now directly under your headquarters, but his relationship here with the British and the top Indian officials is excellent."

The accolades kept arriving. "With the closing of our headquarters in India, I would like at this time to express our gratitude and appreciation for the assistance rendered the XX Bomber Command during the period of our operations in the India-Burma and China Theaters," wrote Brigadier General Joseph Smith.

The world was stunned on August 6 when a U.S. B-29, "Enola Gay," dropped the first atomic bomb and virtually destroyed the city of Hiroshima, Japan. President Truman ordered a second A-bomb to be dropped on Nagasaki three days later. On September 2, aboard the battleship Missouri in Tokyo Bay, Japan formally surrendered and World War II ended.

Neyland figured that he had done his part and that it was time to go home, to return to his family and coaching the University of Tennessee football team.

"I have enjoyed my work here and really hate to leave. However, it is imperative that I return to the University of Tennessee somewhere around the first of the year," Neyland said in a letter to Major General T. A. Terry, the new theater SOS commander. "I must either return to the University of Tennessee (where my contract has five more years to run) by the first of 1946 or lose a whole year. All of the coaches' contracts expire December 31."

Neyland said assistant coaches' contracts, alumni activities, scholarships, recruiting, scheduling, and other matters demanded his attention. "They may not be delayed without serious damage ensuing." But General Terry was not impressed. The army needed Neyland as much in the post-war months as they did while the fighting continued. He had to ship back to the States much of the supplies that had flowed through the port of Calcutta to the combat troops.

So, Terry denied the request for deactivation, but a month later, he recommended Neyland for promotion to major general. Surprisingly, however, in January 1946 Neyland's wish was granted. He was being relieved of command in Calcutta and discharged from military duty.

"Prior to your departure from this theater, I want to express to you my appreciation of the distinguished services you have rendered as commanding general of the Base Section," Terry said in a personal letter to Neyland. "Your command has been just as busy since V-J Day as it was during the war, and certainly the problems have been more difficult because of the tremendous turnover in personnel and the increasing perplexities of the shipping situation. . . . Your earnest attention to the health, discipline, comfort, and welfare of your troops was a substantial contribution to your overall accomplishment."

In five years of service, involving major commands at Norfolk, Dallas, Kunming, and Calcutta, Neyland had been decorated by the U.S., British, and Chinese governments. He was awarded the Legion of Merit, the Distinguished Service Medal, the Chinese Order of the Cloud and Banner, and the Knight Commander, Order of the British Empire.

As he stepped aboard a C-54 transport plane in Calcutta, Neyland paused and turned for one last look. Calcutta had been an important command. By increasing the flow of supplies to American fighting forces in China, he had helped win the war against Japan.

The flight from Calcutta, across southeast Asia and the Pacific Ocean gave Neyland time to reflect on his 20 months in China and India and to contemplate a return to his family and college football.

John Barnhill, his long-time assistant, had compiled an admirable won-lost record as head coach of the Tennessee Vols during Neyland's absence. Barnhill's four Tennessee teams (1941-42, 1944-45) had won 32 games, lost five, and tied two and had played in the Sugar and Rose bowls. (Tennessee did not field a team in 1943 because of the war.) Barnhill liked being a head coach, and, knowing Neyland would be returning in time for the 1946 season, he accepted an offer to become head coach and athletics director at the University of Arkansas.

During a brief stopover in Honolulu, reporters bombarded the general with questions about Tennessee's upcoming season. Would the Vols be as good as his teams of 1938-40?

"About all I know about my team is what I've read in the papers," Neyland responded. He declined to comment further.

The plane landed at Travis Air Force Base near San Francisco on January 31, and Neyland grabbed a newspaper. Associated Press football editor Harold "Spike" Claassen reported the end of the war had triggered 37 head coaching changes in major college football. Wallace Wade returned to Duke. Don Faurot was back from the navy and headed for Missouri. Jim Tatum, who had coached with Faurot at Iowa Navy Pre-Flight School, went to Oklahoma. And a young man named Paul Bryant, who had been discharged from the navy in time to coach Maryland in 1945, moved to Kentucky in 1946.

After the refueling layover at Travis AFB, during which Neyland phoned Peggy, the plane lifted off the runway, its nose pointed eastward. And Robert R. Neyland, who five years earlier had left as a major, was coming home to Knoxville a brigadier general. Home to Peggy, little Bob, and Lewis, to the University of Tennessee, and to thousands of Vol football fans who eagerly awaited a fresh taste of gridiron glory.

CHAPTER 29

Heroes Return

1946

The door of the C-54 opened at 7 a.m., Friday, January 31, and Brigadier General Robert R. Neyland walked down the steps and back into the world of college football. Flashbulbs illuminated the descending figure. The general smiled and waved to the welcoming delegation of university officials and close personal friends. He hugged and kissed Peggy.

The general and Peggy drove directly to their home at 1442 Agawela Drive. Following in a second car were three members of his Calcutta staff—Colonel H. W. Langley, his executive officer; Lieutenant Colonel N. Y. Marsilius, the ordinance officer; and Captain W. R. Blackwell, Neyland's aide-de-camp. Soon, they returned to the airport to resume their homeward journeys. And Bob Neyland was alone with Peggy.

Later in the day, the general went to his office on the university campus. He walked quietly, reflectively, on Shields-Watkins Field, where Tennessee played its home games. He met the players returning from the 1945 team—there were only eight.

Neyland that day met for the first time with his coaching staff—Ike Peel, John Mauer (who also coached basketball), Murray Warmath, Harvey Robinson, and trainer Mickey O'Brien. Peel and Mauer were holdovers from Barnhill's staff. Warmath came from Mississippi State, where he had been a wartime assistant. Robinson, a 1930-32 Vol tailback, left Knoxville Central High where he had compiled an 85-5-5 record. Ray Graves, a Barnhill assistant in 1945 and years later head coach at Florida, had gone to rejoin the Philadelphia Eagles as a player. Colonel Bill Britton was returning from the air force.

Lindsey Nelson, who had served under General George Patton in Europe, was assigned by the *Knoxville Journal* to cover Neyland's first day home.

"I can't seem to get used to this strange thing of driving on the right-hand side of the road," Neyland said, explaining that traffic drove on the left in both China and India. "See what I mean?" Neyland said as he swerved to the right to evade an approaching car.

"I was able to keep up fairly well with football," the General told Nelson. "My wife sent along clippings, and occasionally I was able to pick up a delayed broadcast. Then, too, I got into occasional sessions with former footballers whom I chanced to meet. Charlie Marr, the old Alabama guard, and I did quite a bit of rehashing."

The Neylands' sons, Bobby and Lewis, were not at the airport when their father arrived from China. They were students at Baylor School in Chattanooga, and Peggy did not want to disrupt their routines, even for their father's return. Bobby was a sophomore and Lewis a seventh-grader.

"Several days after he returned from China, he came down to Baylor to see us," Bobby said. "I remember Dad coming to the school, still in his uniform. We were proud and overjoyed, and naturally his visit was exciting for the other Baylor cadets."

Before General Neyland could throw himself whole-heartedly into building a football team for 1946, he faced the formality of separation from the army. Part of the routine was an exit physical examination, which threw a scare into the General. The electrocardiogram suggested a partial blockage in his heart, and army physicians at Fort Oglethorpe, Georgia, recommended that he be hospitalized for further evaluation. But a short stay at the hospital in Fort Knox, Kentucky, revealed no serious problem, and Neyland retired from the army.

Slowly, one by one, Vol lettermen who had served in the military during the war began returning to campus. They were eligible for the GI Bill, a scholarship fund to help World War II servicemen pay for college educations.

Among the early arrivals was Walter Slater, a star tailback for the Vols in 1941-42. Walter was the navigator on a B-24 bomber that flew numerous missions over Germany. Others were fullback Bill Gold, a B-29 bomber pilot, and tackle Dick Huffman, a marine who had been wounded in the bloody landing on the Japanese-held island of Saipan in the Pacific. The list of returning vets who had lettered at Tennessee before the war also included guards Jim Myers, Ray Drost, and Royal Price, center Clay Stapleton, tackles Denver Crawford and John Francis, ends Bud Hubbell and Dick Jordan, and wingback Bill Hillman.

Myers years later would become head coach at Texas A&M and then chief assistant to Tom Landry of the Dallas Cowboys. Stapleton became head coach at Iowa State. Crawford was Warmath's chief assistant at Minnesota when the Golden Gophers won the 1960 national championship. Slater, after a stint on Beattie Feathers's staff at North Carolina State, became a successful high school coach in Florida.

Four ex-Vols did not come home. Rudy Klarer, Willis Tucker, Bill Nowling, and Clyde Fuson were killed in the war. Their Tennessee jersey numbers have been retired, and plaques commemorating their lives are on display in the football Hall of Fame room on campus.

The most notable Vol returnee from the war was Huffman, a speedy, 225-pound star tackle on the 1942 team. Huffman and Neyland also had another sport in common—boxing. Huffman had fought as an amateur heavyweight back in his hometown of Charleston, West Virginia, and almost turned professional before deciding on football at Tennessee. He was undefeated in five fights as a marine heavyweight. Because of boxing, Neyland related to Huffman much as he had identified with two other Vols who also were boxers, Ed Molinski and Abe Shires.

As spring practice got under way, the personnel situation was unstable. War vets were still arriving, and five of the players who started in the spring game did not return in September. To accommodate the late arrivals from the war, Neyland held additional drills in late summer.

One of the freshmen candidates was walk-on tailback Charles A. "Gus" Manning, an ex-marine. "It didn't take me long to see my situation," Manning said. "Neyland had a bunch of fine tailbacks—Slater, Bob Lund, Hal Littleford, Hubert Becker, and J. B. Proctor. So I quit football and began helping with publicity." After graduation in 1950, Manning became Tennessee's sports information director and ultimately the senior associate athletics director.

Slater had been offered a pro football contract with the Philadelphia Eagles in 1946, and, although he still had football in his blood, a college degree was his top priority. He recalled moments of conflict between Neyland and the players who had fought in the war.

"We were older, some of us battle-hardened, most of us married, and some with kids," Slater said. "And Neyland hadn't changed. He was the same in 1946 as he had been before the war—tough, inflexible, and demanding. But I decided to stay at Tennessee and play my senior year of eligibility."

When fall practice began the day after Labor Day, Neyland greeted a squad of 21 war veterans with previous varsity experience, 45 freshmen, and eight lettermen from the 1945 team.

Neyland traditionally had scheduled a breather for Tennessee's opening game, but Barnhill had lined up Georgia Tech and Duke as the Vols' first two games of 1946. A four-game Tech-Tennessee series (1946-49) captured the imagination of the sportswriters—Neyland the conservative teacher against Bobby Dodd the dare-devil student, for the first time.

"Neyland was proud of Dodd as his most celebrated pupil," Tim Cohane wrote in *Look* magazine. "But the general was not one to dilute his pride in the pupil with any willingness to lose to him. Dodd was not only a formidable foe, he had also become in Neyland's mind a bit of a technical renegade by switching to the 'T,' the then new and, to a pure single-wing man, rather frivolous formation."

"I was supposed to be his star pupil, and I was coaching against him," Dodd recalled in his autobiography. "I knew what he was gonna do. With Neyland, there was nothing fancy—just sound, fundamental football. Intercept passes, play the kicking game, sound defense, field position."

Georgia Tech outplayed Tennessee that day, but lost on two pass interceptions that led to touchdowns. George Balitsaris returned one 55 yards for the game-winning TD. But the game-saving play was executed by Slater. Nursing a 13-7 lead with time running out, the Vols were backed against their own goal with three consecutive penalties. After three plays into the line, Slater took the snap from center and began evading Tech tacklers in the end zone. Finally, he stepped out of the end zone for a two-point safety. Tennessee got a free kick from its own 20, and Tech had time for only three plays—two incomplete passes and a completion to the Vol 35 as time expired. The Vols won 13-9. Ironically, in that four-year series, Tennessee won two games in Atlanta and Georgia Tech won two in Knoxville.

In Tennessee's second game of 1946, at Duke, Slater threw touchdown passes to Hillman and Hubbell for a 12-7 victory in the resumption of the Neyland-Wade rivalry. The biggest drama that day, however, occurred off the field. Actually, in a taxicab. Four Vols—Huffman, Jordan, Partin, and Jack Armstrong—caught a cab from the Washington Duke Hotel. The driver thought Tennessee was playing North Carolina and took them to Chapel Hill, 15 miles from Duke Stadium in Durham. Racing frantically back to Durham, the cabbie got them back to the stadium just in time for the game.

Tennessee and Alabama, as usual, were undefeated when they met in Knoxville for their traditional "third Saturday in October" game. Alabama's sophomore all-American tailback, Harry Gilmer, completed 16 of 28 passes against the Vols even though he was smashed to the ground time after time by Dick Huffman. Near the end of the game, as Gilmer limped to the sidelines and collapsed in exhaustion, Tennessee fans gave him a standing ovation.

"I doubt that football has or ever will see his equal," Neyland said of Gilmer's performance that day. "Gilmer is all they said he was and more. Don't let anybody tell you any different."

The Vols defeated Alabama, 12-0, on two touchdown passes by Bob Lund, the flashy sophomore understudy to Slater. The loss ended Alabama's 14-game winning streak and the rivalry between Neyland and 'Bama coach Frank Thomas, who had decided to retire because of poor health.

Disaster struck Tennessee the next Saturday. "I don't know what happened," Slater said. "We just weren't ready to play Wake Forest, and they had a much better team than we had expected."Wake Forest had an outstanding backfield—Nick Ognovich at quarterback, Rock Brinkley at fullback, and twin halfbacks, Nick and Bo Sacrinty. In the third quarter, Nick Sacrinty threw a touchdown pass, and Brinkley scored from the four after a 32-yard run by Bo Sacrinty. Wake Forest won 19-6. In his ledger, Neyland scribbled: "WF sound on fundamentals . . . good passing . . . good protection and kicking . . . defense very good . . . MADE NO MISTAKES."

Lindsey Nelson remembered a photograph in the Sunday paper showing a Vol fan sitting alone in the stadium after the game. The caption said, "Don't Worry, the General Will Think of Something." And he did. The Vols defeated North Carolina the following week and rolled to four more victories for a 9-1 regular season record.

The Vols were trailing North Carolina, 14-13, in the third quarter when Slater fielded a punt by Tar Heel tailback Charlie "Choo Choo" Justice, a freshman whom Neyland had tried to recruit out of Asheville, North Carolina. Slater slipped through two waves of Carolina tacklers and was racing down the left sideline. The only man between him and a touchdown was Justice, closing fast.

"I knew he was going to get me unless I could throw off his timing," Slater said. "Dick Jordan was trailing behind me to my right."

"Slater faked a lateral to Jordan, I took the fake, and Slater went in for the touchdown," said Justice. "Tennessee beat us 20-14 on that play, and I believe Neyland had my picture on Tennessee season tickets the next year."

No Vol had ever thrown three touchdown passes in a single game—until the afternoon of November 9 in Memphis. J. B. Proctor connected with Jim Powell three times in the second half to give the Vols a come-from-behind victory over Ole Miss.

"We had provided Jim with all the medication prescribed for a bad case of diarrhea," Vol trainer Mickey O'Brien said. "It was late in the fourth period [Ole Miss was leading 14-12 with 30 seconds left] when we took a time out and I ran to the dressing room to see if Powell was able to get back into the game. He barely got to the field in time for the play."

Powell caught his third touchdown pass of the day from Proctor with less than 30 seconds left in the game. Powell "laid the ball down in the end zone and returned to his sickness in the dressing room," O'Brien said.

The Vols beat Mississippi, 18-14, but Tennessee's aerial bombardment that day was a contradiction of the Neyland philosophy. "When you put the ball in the air, three things can happen—and two of them are bad," Neyland often said, referring to incomplete passes and interceptions.

The Vols played at Boston College a week after the Mississippi game and found themselves trailing 13-7 at the half, but Neyland did not seem concerned. Before the game he had told his team: "They're bigger and slower than you are, and they'll tire in the first half. We may be behind two touchdowns at the half, but we'll win."

As the first half ended, Neyland jumped off the bench and gave a blood-curdling yell. "Warmath," he shouted, "yell and run toward the tunnel." The Tennessee squad followed, and Boston College players watched in astonishment as the Vols dashed past them. "You should have seen the looks on their faces," Warmath said of the BC players.

Slater was startled by what happened just before the start of the second half. "As we started onto the field, Neyland began running ahead of the squad, yelling," Slater said. "I had never seen him run like that. And I think it inspired us. We won 33-13."

Tackle Al Rotella, one of the war vets, remembered helping his teammates give Neyland a "victory ride" to the middle of the field. "Years later," Rotella said, "Neyland himself told the story of two old ladies overheard saying in Boston: 'Wasn't it a shame about Neyland. He was so drunk after the BC game that the boys had to carry him off the field.'"

Slater's 54-yard punt return beat Kentucky, 7-0, and Charlie Mitchell's extra point provided the margin of victory, 7-6, over Vanderbilt.

Then came an invitation for the Vols, ranked seventh in the nation, to play tenth-ranked Rice Institute in the Orange Bowl. Neyland asked for a team vote, and, on the first ballot, the war vets prevailed.

"All of us veterans were married and some had kids, and we didn't want to go to the Orange Bowl," Slater said. "Most of us had been to a bowl game before the war, and we wanted to work for the Post Office during the Christmas holidays and earn some money. But the Bull [Neyland] wanted to go, so he and some of the assistant coaches talked to the younger players. Neyland called for another vote, and that time the majority voted to go."

Neyland soon regretted his referendum victory. The Vols did not have their hearts in the trip, and it showed in the game. The veterans wanted to take their wives and kids on the trip, and they wanted free time in Miami. So they sent Slater, the team captain, to see the General.

"Every time I mentioned a demand, the Bull told me that was an administrative matter," Slater said. "I went back to the team and told them 'no soap.' What really made us mad after we got to Miami was that [Jess] Neely, the Rice coach, had allowed his war veterans to bring their wives and families to Miami."

Neyland housed the team in the Venetian Hotel where his 1938 Vols had stayed for their memorable game against Oklahoma. He scrimmaged the team during hard two-a-day practices. The vets did not like it.

Sportswriters who were there called it one of the dullest bowl games in history. Rice scored a touchdown and a safety in the first quarter. The safety resulted from something unprecedented in Neyland's coaching career—two consecutive blocked punts. Tennessee's only chance to score came when Rice fumbled the second half kickoff. The Vols recovered at the 18 but could not score, and Rice won 8-0. Neyland's summation was terse: "We were out-run, out-blocked, out-tackled, out-played."

1946-1952

PART VII

CHAPTER 30

Friendly Fire

1947-49

In the spring of 1947, the University of Tennessee approved a new five-year contract for Neyland to expire January 1, 1951. His salary under the old contract was believed to be $18,500, and reporters speculated that the new figure was at least $20,000, which is approximately what he had been offered by the University of Southern California after the 1946 season.

The college football landscape that spring looked like a Neyland finishing school. Many of his former players were college head coaches—Dodd at Georgia Tech, Bowden Wyatt at Wyoming, Bob Woodruff at Baylor, Beattie Feathers at North Carolina State, John Barnhill at Arkansas, Allyn McKeen at Mississippi State, and Ralph Hatley at Memphis State. Dozens of others were college assistants or high school head coaches.

The expectations of Vol football fans were extremely high in the spring of 1947, but Neyland knew the score. "It will take us five years to rebuild," he had confided to friends shortly after returning from the war in 1946. He was talking about replenishing the roster with quality players fresh out of high school, but his stubborn streak probably was the biggest factor contributing to Tennessee's disastrous seasons in 1947 and 1948. The college football rules committee in 1941 had liberalized substitution, enabling coaches to move entire offensive and defensive units onto and off the field. They called it two-platoon football. But Neyland believed football was meant to be played both ways, and he refused to join the pack. Moreover, Tennessee had lost its starting backfield (Slater, Bill Gold, Mitchell, and Partin), ends Hubbell and Jordan, and tackle Dick Huffman, who had relinquished his final year of eligibility to sign with the Los Angeles team in the NFL.

Georgia Tech and Duke were Tennessee's first two opponents again in 1947, and both beat the Vols easily. Dodd's Yellow Jackets became the first team ever to score four touchdowns in one game on a Neyland team. The final score was 27-0.

"One of the greatest games ever played," a jubilant Dodd said. "Everything we did was right. We just killed Neyland's team. I called 'em off."

Memphis Commercial Appeal sports editor Walter Stewart, Neyland's close friend, described Tech's assault on Tennessee as "delicately balanced and deadly as a guillotine."

Atlanta writer F. M. Williams, later with the *Nashville Tennessean*, was more succinct: "The pupil taught the teacher a thing or two about football."

Ralph McGill of the *Atlanta Constitution* watched Dodd's expression during the final minutes of the game: "The smile on his face was such as the angels have when they look over the rim of Heaven and see a sinner saved."

"That was a big game to me," Dodd said. "I'd beaten my coach, who'd beaten me the year before, and I'd beaten him decisively . . . and he didn't like it a damn bit."

Nor did Tennessee fans. The grumbling began in Atlanta, minutes after the game. Walter Stewart overheard some vicious comments during an elevator ride at the Biltmore Hotel. "Those bums are terrible," said one critic. "I threw my Tennessee colors away before the end of the third quarter," said another. "I'll never pay to see that mob get beaten again."

Indeed, it was the first time a Neyland team had lost by a margin of 27 points. He could not have dreamed an even worse fate would befall the hapless 1947 Vols six weeks later at Memphis, a 43-13 loss to Mississippi, whose first-year head coach was John Vaught. Charlie Conerly, the Mississippi quarterback, passed for four touchdowns and ran for two more that day. Neyland was furious. "They put Conerly back in the game with only a few minutes remaining," he said. "I never tried to humiliate any coach, but I'll tell you one thing. My teams will get every point they can score against any Vaught team." (Neyland lost to Vaught again the next year, then beat Mississippi, 35-7, 35-0, and 46-21.)

Two weeks after losing to Mississippi, the Vols defeated Kentucky in Lexington. Thrilled by the victory over Kentucky, a University of Tennessee trustee patted Neyland on the back and said, "You're the greatest coach in the world." To which Neyland replied: "That's not what you sons-of-bitches said two weeks ago."

Team captain Denver Crawford and sophomore tailback Hal Littleford provided the heroics in the last two games. Littleford's 20-yard touchdown run in the fourth quarter beat Kentucky, 13-6, and Crawford threw a block that destroyed Vanderbilt, 12-7. "We were behind 7-6 when Vanderbilt punted to me on our side of the 50," Littleford recalled. "I started up field, then cut to the right, trying to reach the wall [of Tennessee blockers]. All of a sudden I saw three or four black jerseys closing in on me. I thought they were going to knock me up into the stadium seats."

"I was the off-side tackle on the punt rush, and it was my job to be the last man on the return wall," Crawford said. "But I got there early and saw these three Vanderbilt players getting ready to crunch Hal. So I just laid out a body block on the first one, and he fell into a second Vandy player—and Hal sailed on by for the winning touchdown."

Littleford could not believe it when he turned his head at about the Vandy 20 and looked back upfield. "I didn't see anybody for a good 30 yards," he said. "Denver had mowed 'em all down. And I was so surprised, I guess I'm just lucky I didn't fall flat on my face."

That play was one of the few times in Neyland's coaching career that he became demonstratively excited on the sidelines. He jumped up and down, screaming, "Atta boy, Crawford. Atta boy, Crawford." Years later, Neyland still called it "the greatest block I've ever seen."

The Vols finished the season with five wins and five losses, and the critics were howling for a change. They said that Neyland's offense, the single-wing, was antiquated and that his refusal to switch to the split-T was going to be the demise of Tennessee football. But Neyland was thick skinned. He knew the fans, and some university officials, wanted him fired, but he did not let it bother him.

Denver Crawford had planned throughout his college career to become a coach, but he was bothered deeply by the treatment Neyland was receiving. He went to Neyland.

"You've had such a great coaching career and done so much for Tennessee," Crawford told his coach. "And the way they're treatin' you now, I don't know if I want to get into this coaching business."

"Crawford," Neyland said firmly, placing a hand on Denver's shoulder, "I don't care what you go into. You can't live on your clippings. You've got to produce."

So Denver Crawford became a college coach and in 1960 helped Murray Warmath build a national championship team at Minnesota. Neyland ignored his critics, even turned down another West Coast coaching offer, and kept his mind's eye on 1950, the year he had predicted would be Tennessee's return to the top.

But 1948 was no better than 1947. The Vols finished 4-4-2.

In May of that year, the Neylands had bought two lots on St. Armands Key near Sarasota, Florida. Peggy begged the general to quit coaching and retire to Florida, but he refused. He knew that Tennessee's 1948 freshman class was loaded with outstanding talent. He was especially intrigued by the potential of fellows named Hank Lauricella, Harold Payne, Bert Rechichar, Andy Kozar, Jimmy Hahn, Jim Haslam, Bob Davis, Ted Daffer, and Bill Jasper.

Tensions were running high in Tuscaloosa and Knoxville as the Alabama Crimson Tide and the Vols prepared for their mid-October encounter. Both teams had 1-1-1 records, and their fans were restless. Alabama was in its second year under Harold "Red" Drew, who had succeeded Thomas as head coach in 1947.

Alyce Walker, writing in the *Birmingham News* about the wives of Neyland and Drew, said "If you think it's easy to sit in the stands and watch a green quarterback run the wrong way with your husband's job, think again." The Vols managed to beat Alabama, 21-6, but neither team distinguished itself the rest of the season.

Meanwhile, Neyland was seething about two-platoon football, and he articulated his views in an October issue of *PIC* magazine.

"I am completely opposed to the free substitution rule," Neyland said. "It has seriously damaged the game of football for the spectators, the players, and the coaches. This rule, which was perpetrated upon the United States in a period of mental blackout, has de-emphasized antecedent requirements for sound coaching theory, . . . has tended to eliminate certain character-building aspects of football and, finally, has largely negated the delirious claims of proponents who believed that their new rule would aid the smaller schools against the large universities."

Under the free substitution rule, Neyland said, the coaches got away from teaching the fundamentals of football and started trying to outwit each other.

"The game has gotten out of all bounds as a spectator sport," he wrote in the magazine article. "Yesterday's football not only required players to be able to block and tackle—to be adequate in all phases of the game—but it also required them to attain and maintain the highest pitch of physical condition." In the late stages of a game, he said, invariably the key factors were brains, conditioning, and resolution.

"I am quite aware that certain cynics are prone to laugh up their sleeves and into their typewriters when character-building and football are mentioned in the same conversation," Neyland said. "A sneer at this juncture is looked upon as the height of sophistication. But I honestly believe that lessons learned upon the football field are carried usefully from the field into life."

Then, Neyland the soldier took over from Neyland the coach.

"I believe that the record of football players in the recent war will support these claims. They were fine soldiers, not merely because they were tough-fibered and powerful men, but because they had learned to pay a bitter price and continue the action. It has been said that there is guts at both ends of a bayonet. Well, there is guts, too, on both ends of a tackle," Neyland said.

"The tired and battered boy who schools himself to throw a shoulder at the thrashing knees of a fullback learns something which must necessarily remain foreign to the player who sits upon the bench for 58 minutes and trots out to lift a long punt, to the tall pass defender who sees service only when the opposition is in the throwing zone."

Neyland concluded: "I sincerely believe that unlimited or 'liberal' substitution has robbed football of 75 percent of its basic values and will, if continued, ruin the game completely."

In early 1949, Neyland called in Lindsey Nelson, who had been the play-by-play announcer of Tennessee's 1948 games on radio station WKGN. Neyland asked Nelson to set up a statewide radio network for Tennessee's games.

Nelson, in his autobiography, recalled the following conversation.

"General, I have a great name for our network," Nelson said. "Let's call it the Volunteer Network."

"Let's call it the Vol Network," Neyland retorted.

"Yes, sir, let's call it the Vol Network," Nelson quickly agreed.

Neyland told Nelson he could select the announcer, and so Lindsey selected himself. "I think the announcer should get at least a hundred dollars [per game]," Nelson told the General.

"Well, let's see," Neyland responded. "The referee gets a hundred dollars a game. Do you work as hard as the referee?"

"Harder," Lindsey answered.

"Okay," Neyland said, "you'll get a hundred dollars a game."

The 1949 opener against Mississippi State was a Bert Rechichar spectacular. The sophomore wingback and safetyman scored all of Tennessee's points in a 10-0 victory over Mississippi State. He caught a seven-yard touchdown pass from Littleford, kicked the extra point, and then kicked a 24-yard field goal. The Vols rolled easily over seven opponents, tied Alabama, and lost to Duke and Georgia Tech.

Neyland and Tech's Bobby Dodd never again opposed each other as head coaches. Each had won two games from the other. Neyland retired long before Dodd, but Dodd always used the basics he had learned from Neyland at Tennessee. "Axioms, he called 'em," Dodd said. "I didn't know what that meant, but I knew what he was talking about. The team that makes the fewest mistakes wins. If the game is close, the kicking game will determine the outcome."

The 1949 Vols beat Kentucky, coached by Bear Bryant, 6-0. That loss nagged Bryant for years, as did all of his games against Neyland-coached teams. Bryant never beat Neyland.

"Every time we played I went out there like a wild man and changed everything around," Bryant confessed in his autobiography. "One year [1949] we painted all the dummies orange, then took the team out to a horse farm, and brought the clergy in, and had everybody so tight they could barely move. Next day we lost 6-0. We had a lot of gimmicks, and I threw out all the things we could do, the good plays, and put in something new. For Neyland."

Trying to beat Neyland became an obsession with Bryant.

"They used to kid me around the office that anytime Tennessee was mentioned during a coffee break, I had to excuse myself and be sick," Bryant said. "They weren't far wrong. I lost my breakfast regularly before the Tennessee game. Everybody thought Neyland had a jinx on us. It was no jinx. He was a better coach, and he had better football players—and I couldn't stand it."

The season finale, a 26-20 conquest of Vanderbilt, was a game of intense emotion—so much so that fights erupted on the field at the end, and Vanderbilt head coach Bill Edwards had to be restrained by police.

Referees had nullified two Vanderbilt touchdowns and had failed to call an interference penalty when Vandy's Lee Nalley, waiting to field a punt, was bumped before the ball arrived. Nalley fumbled, Tennessee's Charles "Chaddy" Baker recovered, and Lauricella threw a touchdown pass to Charles Cummins to win the game.

"We were leading 19-0 in the first quarter but hadn't made a single first down," Lauricella recalled. "Bud Sherrod had intercepted a pass and returned it 37 yards for a touchdown. John Gruble returned a blocked punt 20 yards for a touchdown. And I threw a touchdown pass to Rechichar."

Lauricella said the Vols won that Vanderbilt game, as they did most games, on defensive fundamentals. "We may have scored 26 points, but they were all made possible by the defensive effort," Lauricella said.

The stage was set for the 1950 season and one of the greatest teams in Tennessee history.

CHAPTER 31

The Cotton Bowl

1950

Although he despised two-platoon football, Neyland adopted it at Tennessee in the spring of 1950. He suspected his team was about to blossom into a championship contender, but reality dictated that he give his players the rest and opportunity at specialization that their opponents would have.

In his private notebook, Neyland listed the squad's depth by positions after spring practice:

Tailbacks—Lauricella, Payne, Cooper, Ellis, Shires.

Fullbacks—Polofsky, Ernsberger, Kozar, Pruett, Moeller, Sizemore.

Blockingbacks—Hahn, Meyer, Hill, Maiure, Twitty, Kyker.

Wingbacks—Rechichar, Sherrill, Markloff, Rotroff, Morgan, Drake.

Strong ends—Sherrod, Carter, Atkins, Gruble, Stupar.

Strong tackles—Stroud, Boring, Pearman, Eschenbach, Myers.

Strong guards—Jumper, Markelonis, Laughlin, Gentry.

Centers—Davis, Jasper, Ford, Felty, Morris, Vest.

Left guards—Daffer, Michels, Malach, Campbell.

Left tackles—Haslam, Smith, Donahue, Holohan, Lughes, Stokes.

Left ends—Kaseta, Alexander, Trubits, Flora.

Defensively, Neyland already had his eye on 6-foot-8, 260-pound sophomore Doug Atkins at end, sophomore Francis Holohan at tackle, junior Ted Daffer at guard, and Gordon Polofsky, Bill Jasper, and Gene Moeller at linebacker.

"It seems we have the following men adequate to play in this league," Neyland wrote in his journal.

"Offense: Hank Lauricella, Herky Payne, W. C. Cooper, Gordon Polofsky, Dick Ernsberger, Andy Kozar, Andy Myers, Jimmy Hahn, Jimmy Hill, Joe Maiure,

Bud Sherrill, Bert Rechichar, Bud Sherrod, David Carter, Jack Stroud, Tom Jumper, Jerry Malach, Bob Davis, John Michels, Ted Daffer, Earl Campbell, Vince Kaseta, Frank Alexander.

"Defense: Lauricella, Polofsky, Hill, Sherrill, John Gruble, Stroud, Jim Markelonis, Dan Laughlin, Bill Jasper, Gene Moeller, Ken Pruett, Roy Smith, Doug Atkins. Possibilities for safetyman—Rechichar, Hill, Sherrill." When the season began five months later, those three were the starting defensive backs—Rechichar at safety, Hill and Sherrill at the halfbacks.

Neyland, as late at September 6, still anticipated using Gruble, Stroud, and Rechichar offensively and defensively. "Rechichar has no adequate replacement," he reminded himself in his notebook. On the next page, he noted: "Bring Kozar up to par on blocking . . . get an adequate performance out of Michels on offense . . . make Morgan block and Rotroff run reverses . . . drill Atkins on defense."

The Vols opened the 1950 season by crushing Mississippi Southern, 56-0, but came back to earth the next week at Starkville, Mississippi, where they lost to Mississippi State, 7-0. It was on the flight back to Knoxville that Neyland challenged the squad: "You think they love you in Knoxville? Look around you, at your teammates. They're the only friends you have in the world."

"We were simply overconfident," Lauricella said. "We grew up that day; the defeat actually helped us."

Neyland analyzed the loss to Mississippi State before Monday's practice. "Our team nervous and jittery, very little poise," he said. "Team leadership is colorless. Our kicking game was pitiful and our passing poor." But the Vols recovered quickly and posted easy victories over Duke and Chattanooga, then tangled with Alabama. In fact, after the loss to Mississippi State, it would be two years and 22 games before the Vols would lose again.

"The boys seem to be interested in this game," Neyland said on the eve of the Alabama game. Trailing 9-7 in the fourth quarter, tailback Herky Payne engineered a long scoring drive, and Kozar banged across for the winning touchdown with 62 seconds left.

The next game—against underdog Washington and Lee—was almost a nightmare for Tennessee. Rechichar returned a punt 100 yards and scored a second touchdown on a 50-yard interception return, and Jimmy Hahn scored on an 82-yard kickoff return. But Washington and Lee refused to fold, scored two touchdowns in the fourth quarter, and threatened to tie the game in the final seconds. The Vols held on four downs inside the five-yard line and won 27-20. Neyland said Tennessee was lucky that day.

A fight erupted during that goal-line stand, and one of the referees ordered Polofsky and mammoth Doug Atkins out of the game. "I think probably I'm the only player ever to be kicked out of a Tennessee football game twice in the same game," Polofsky said. "As soon as he threw me out, something else happened and the ref didn't walk me to the sidelines. I moved to the back of the crowd, out of sight. Then, he saw me again and once more told me to get out of the game. I walked to the sidelines."

"They kicked Doug out of the game, and that's what all the commotion was about. That's why they left Gordon in there," Payne said. "Doug was angry and wouldn't leave the field. You can imagine a 6-8, 260-pound kid who was mad and wouldn't leave the field. Well, the official walked over to Neyland and said, 'General, get number 91 out of here or I'm going to forfeit the game.' And the General replied: "YOU kicked him out; YOU get him off the field."

"On the Friday before the Washington and Lee game, we walked through game situations and then were told to go to our rooms in East Stadium and rest," tackle Bill Pearman remembered. "Instead, a bunch of us went to the Sigma Chi Derby. Bud Sherrod climbed on somebody's shoulders and suddenly spotted Neyland sitting in a car. We got the hell out of there."

Neyland did not say anything that night or on game day. "But in the locker room after we almost lost the game, he told us to report to the stadium at six o'clock Sunday morning.

"Give me a hundred [laps]," Neyland said as the squad arrived at dawn.

"He sat there and counted every lap. I got through about 11 o'clock," Pearman said. "The next year we beat Washington and Lee, 60-14."

The 1950 W&L game showed that Neyland—the hardened army general—could succumb to moments of depression. His notes told the story: "Personnel problems are serious . . . Carter, Jumper, Michels, Davis have been weak blockers . . . Stroud, Haslam barely adequate . . . Rechichar not as good as last year . . . Kozar and Drake are terrible blockers . . . Cooper can't do it . . . Hill and Sherrill are liabilities . . . Polofsky not as good as last year . . . Jasper has deteriorated badly . . . Sherrod makes too many mistakes . . . Atkins is reading his clippings and is hard to coach."

But it did not take long for Neyland to see the bright side again. Those players about whom he had been concerned after the W&L game bounced back in the weeks ahead as the Vols racked up five more victories, including shutouts against Mississippi, Kentucky, and Vanderbilt to end the season.

The Kentucky game occupied the national spotlight. Kentucky, ranked third in the nation, was a seven-point favorite over the ninth-ranked Vols. Both were bound for bowls—Kentucky to play top-ranked Oklahoma in the Sugar Bowl, and Tennessee matched against third-ranked Texas in the Cotton Bowl. A storm dumped 14 inches of snow on Knoxville the day before the game. At kickoff, the temperature was 10 degrees above zero, and Shields-Watkins Field was frozen.

Kentucky coach Bear Bryant had built his game plan around his all-American quarterback, Vito "Babe" Parilli, a masterful passer. Parilli filled the air with passes that day, including three to a tackle who became eligible when the team shifted its alignment. "We ran it three times and made a mile," Bryant said, "and instead of giving it to us they brought it back and penalized us every time."

Kentucky fumbled eight times, and the Vols limited the Wildcats to 36 yards rushing. "It was the greatest defensive line play I've ever seen," Neyland said.

In his post-game notes, Neyland observed that Kentucky had no confidence in its running attack.

"Pass, pass, pass," Neyland wrote. "The spread type of passing attack was not effective. The making of a tackle eligible was momentarily successful, but did not justify the time they [Kentucky] must have spent on it."

Neyland underlined each word of the next sentence: "Bryant does not know the percentages!" He may not have understood them that day, but obviously he later learned, because Bear Bryant, in 38 seasons (1945-82), won 323 games to become the winningest head coach in college football history. "I never did beat Neyland," Bryant later told Gus Manning, "but I learned a lot of football from playing him."

The 10-1 record had earned the Vols an invitation to play Texas in the Cotton Bowl, and Neyland was thrilled at the thought of taking his team "back home"—to within 40 miles of his birthplace.

"I'll never forget the General's pre-game optimism," tailback Hank Lauricella said. "The Texas band was outside our dressing room playing 'The Eyes of Texas Are upon You.'"

"When this game's over with," Neyland said, "they'll be playing the 'Tennessee Waltz.'" Assistant coach Hugh Faust remembered Neyland cupping a hand behind his ear, listening to the band outside, then starting to waltz with an imaginary partner. "He was waltzing the Tennessee Waltz, and the players looked at him in amazement. Then they broke into great laughter," Faust said. "It was just enough to relax the boys—before time to get serious about the game."

In his brief pre-game talk, Neyland repeated what he had told an earlier group of Vols before the 1946 Boston College game: "Texas is a physically stronger team than we are, but they aren't in as good condition. They'll probably lead us at halftime by one or two touchdowns, but don't be discouraged. Keep plugging. Keep your poise. We'll wear 'em down and win in the fourth quarter."

A dazzling 75-yard serpentine run by Lauricella early in the game set up the first touchdown. On the play, Texas end Don Menasco said he was blocked four times. A tired Lauricella was finally brought down at the five-yard-line, so Neyland took him out and sent in Payne.

"Neyland knew that Texas knew Payne could not pass as well as Lauricella and therefore would run," Knoxville sports columnist Tom Siler said years later. "So what did they do? Neyland had Payne pass to John Gruble for a touchdown. But Texas scored twice in the second quarter and went to the halftime locker room leading 14-7."

A misting rain had been falling most of the game, and the turf was becoming slippery. Andy Kozar and Jimmy Hill recalled Neyland's halftime reminder: "You've got 'em right where you want 'em. It's wet out there, and they want to pass. You'll intercept a pass and maybe recover a fumble, and you'll win the game in the fourth quarter."

The Vols drove 83 yards and scored a touchdown early in the fourth quarter, but tailback Pat Shires missed the extra point attempt and returned dejectedly to the sidelines. "Neyland met me coming off the field and said, 'Don't worry about that, son. We didn't come down here to tie.'"

With the Vols trailing 14-13 late in the game, Hill recovered a Texas fumble at the Longhorn 43. Two carries by Lauricella and Kozar and a pass by Lauricella to Rechichar advanced the ball to the Texas one, where Kozar dived into the end zone for the winning touchdown. "It happened just like the General said it would," said Kozar, named the most valuable player of the game.

Vol captain Jack Stroud had played the game even though his broken jaw was wired and the only food he had was what his wife fed him through a straw four times a day for a week.

The Tennessee locker room was bedlam—the players caked with mud, but joyous and festive. In one of those rare moments when he seemed overwhelmed with joy and almost unable to contain himself, Neyland climbed onto a small table and screamed, "I love every one of you sons-of-bitches." "I think it was the happiest I ever saw him in my four years at Tennessee," center Bob Davis said. Other seniors agreed.

The final Associated Press poll, before the bowl games, ranked Oklahoma first, followed in order by Army, Texas, and Tennessee. If a poll had been taken after the bowls, as is done now, the Vols would have won the national championship. Oklahoma had been beaten by Kentucky in the Sugar Bowl, Army fell to Navy, and Tennessee beat Texas in the Cotton Bowl. In fact, one mathematical rating service, the Dunkel System, ranked the Vols number one after the Cotton Bowl.

Neyland and the team flew back to Knoxville wearing 10-gallon cowboy hats, and those players who would return the next fall began thinking about 1951—the year that would bring the Tennessee Vols the AP and UPI national championships.

CHAPTER 32

The National Championship

1951

The loss of 15 lettermen from the 1950 team concerned Neyland. Eight were starters. But his first two offensive backfields and the entire offensive line, except for tackle Jack Stroud, returned for the 1951 season. On defense, he lost only four starters—and one of those was defensive end Atkins, whom the General did not intend to lose.

"Doug already was on scholarship probation for rowdy conduct in the athletics dorm, and he got in deeper trouble when we had a wreck," tailback Pat Shires recalled. Neyland had a strict no-car rule.

So Neyland kicked Atkins off the squad and took away his scholarship. Gus Manning, then the sports information director, picked up the story: "Old Doug left with big tears in his eyes, and the General called me aside and said, 'Gus, you make damned sure that Breezy [Wynn] has got Atkins a summer job so we can have him back next fall.'"

Wynn, who had starred for Neyland in the early 1930s, had become a wealthy Knoxville industrialist and made himself and his money available whenever the General called. And sure enough, Atkins was back in a Vol uniform in the fall of 1952 and made all-American. Atkins became an all-NFL defensive end and was named the Player of the Quarter Century(1950-74) for the Southeastern Conference.

"Our 1951 team will be far below the average in weight, much smaller than most teams we will meet," Neyland said. "Last year's team went much beyond our expectations, and the big factors were spirit and incentive. Having gone through a successful season last year and having played in the Cotton Bowl and won, that fine edge of ambition is certain to be dulled."

Neyland worried about losing his secondary—Hill, Sherrill, and W. C. Cooper, who had alternated with Rechichar at safety in 1950. He knew that sophomores and freshmen would have to fill the gaps left by graduation.

"The very achievement of our success last season will make the 1951 season immeasurably more difficult," Neyland said. "Last year's team was the underdog in key games against Duke, Alabama, and Texas in the Cotton Bowl. That [underdog] position always carries with it a certain definite psychological advantage that we will miss during the 1951 season."

The uncertainties faded quickly when the season began. The Vols disposed easily of Mississippi State, 14-0, Duke, 26-0, and Chattanooga, 42-13. Then came Alabama, which uncharacteristically had three losses going into the Tennessee game. For the first and only time in 1951, the Vols found themselves behind. Bobby Marlow, Alabama's great running back, had scored an early touchdown and the Tide led 7-0.

"They came out with a wing-T and demoralized our defense," Neyland said. "Our tackling was as bad as a Tennessee team has ever shown." And even though the Vol offense rolled up 390 yards, Neyland said it "sputtered and fizzed." Still, the Vols won 27-13 on the passing of Lauricella and Payne. And on the following Tuesday, the Vols were ranked first in the nation by the Associated Press.

The next five games were no contest. The Vols rolled over Tennessee Tech, 68-0, North Carolina, 27-0, Washington and Lee, 60-14, Mississippi, 46-21, and Kentucky, 28-0.

Some years later, after Paul Dietzel had become head coach at LSU, he visited General Neyland in Knoxville. Young Bob Neyland was there and overheard their conversation. Dietzel, who had been an assistant to Bear Bryant at Kentucky, told about the year Bryant instructed him to dress the scout team in orange and run Tennessee's offense and defense week after week in preparation for the annual Vol-Wildcat game. "We'll beat 'em good now," Bryant told Dietzel. That was in 1951, and Tennessee beat Kentucky, 28-0.

The 1951 Vols were so hot that the media, and even fans, were calling the Neyland home at all hours of the night. "We had to have our phone number unlisted [for the first time in years] to get any rest," Peg said. "The fans usually wanted one of three things. They wondered about Tennessee's chances of winning the upcoming game. They wanted to tell Bob they had bet on Tennessee and wondered if they had given too many points. And they wanted football tickets. I never did hear him predict victory."

Peg said even her friends wanted "inside" information.

"'Peg,' they'd ask, 'are we going to win this one? What does the General tell you privately?' "I always told them I was just his guinea pig and he never really told me anything," Peg said. "I always told them . . . if my husband had *me* just about three jumps ahead of the running and barking fits on the day before the game, I figured the *team* would be ready."

Between the end of the 1951 season and the bowl game with Maryland, Peg granted her first newspaper interview. The reporter asked her what Neyland was like on game day, if he was a worrier. "He doesn't pace the floor or tear his hair. Sometimes I wish he would let off steam. But I can tell when he's worried," she replied. "I never make any engagements for him the day before a game or the night after. He gets so tense during a game that when it's over, he's exhausted and just wants to go home and rest. Sometimes it takes him 24 hours to get the tension unwound."

After each game, Neyland entered detailed analysis in his ledger. What worked. What didn't. Where certain phases of the game broke down. He overlooked nothing. And not all of his evaluations concerned the games. At the bottom of his 1951 North Carolina game notes, for example, he wrote:

"Washington Duke [Hotel in Durham] unsatisfactory. Food not good. Elevators and phone service inexcusable. Might try Sir Walter in Raleigh in 1953. Or a tourist court if good one can be found."

Vanderbilt had beaten Tennessee only once (1948) in their last 11 games, and the Commodores with good reason believed 1951 might be their year to upset the Vols. Vandy had a great passer, quarterback Bill Wade, who could thread a needle 50 yards away. Wade made all-SEC in 1951 and 12 years later quarterbacked the Chicago Bears to the NFL championship.

Against the Vols in the 1951 game, Wade was sensational. Neyland, in his pregame notes, had said the Vols "must stop Wade, stop his passes." For a while, the Vols did neutralize Wade's passing and built a 21-0 lead. During the games, Peggy would not allow any celebrating by those seated around her until the Vols had scored at least three touchdowns. With the Vols ahead 21-0, a friend asked: "Peg, can we have some fun now?" With the game seemingly under control, Peg consented, but Wade engineered four second-half touchdown drives and pulled the Commodores to within one point, 28-27, of the Vols. Tennessee regrouped, however, and behind the running of Kozar and Payne, went on to defeat Vandy, 35-27.

It was Tennessee's first undefeated regular season since 1940. The Vols had averaged 37 points a game, Lauricella had rushed for a school-record 881 yards and had averaged 7.9 yards per carry, and Payne had led the Southeastern Conference in scoring (84 points). A statistical footnote: the third-team wingback who averaged 14 yards on three carries was a sophomore named Bob Neyland—the General's son.

When the final wire service polls were released on December 4, Tennessee was ranked number one, followed in order by Michigan State and Maryland, two other unbeaten teams. The Vols were national champions.

The Sugar Bowl drooled at the prospect of matching top-ranked Tennessee and third-ranked Maryland, coached by Jim Tatum. Aside from the fact that both teams were unbeaten, the Sugar Bowl folks knew the drawing power of Tennessee's all-American tailback, Hank Lauricella, the Heisman Trophy runnerup to Princeton's Dick Kazmaier. Lauricella was a native of New Orleans. And so the deal was done—Tennessee and Maryland in the Sugar Bowl.

A lot of factors figured in the outcome of the bowl game, not the least of which was the strength of Maryland's football team. But some of the other nuances are worth mentioning.

First, Neyland and Tatum were good friends. "Among football coaches," said Lewis Neyland, the General's youngest son, "Jim Tatum was my father's closest friend." Tatum had visited Neyland's spring practice in 1950. And that summer, Tatum had invited Neyland to join him in Minnesota for some serious fishing. Just the two of them. And for Neyland, the consummate fisherman, it was an offer he could not turn down.

So there they were—Neyland the single-wing man and Tatum the split-T man—sharing a boat on an isolated lake somewhere in the wilds of Minnesota. On the first day out, Tatum was handling the boat and Neyland was seriously engaging the walleyes. While they fished, they talked football. After an hour or so, Tatum asked Neyland a question about defenses, and Neyland, turning around to answer, saw Tatum writing in a notebook. "You son-of-a-bitch," Neyland exclaimed, laughing, "you invited me out here to pick my brain." It was an incident they both laughed about many times afterward.

The holiday experience of defensive guard Francis Holohan foreshadowed what lay ahead for the Vols in the Sugar Bowl. The Vols were to assemble in Knoxville the day after Christmas and fly to New Orleans, but shortly before take-off Neyland received a telegram: "General Neyland . . . Snowed in . . . Advise." It was signed "Holohan."

By return wire, Neyland said: "Francis Holohan, Niagara Falls, New York. Start walking." The storm stranded several other Tennessee players from New York, but Neyland made special arrangements to fly all of them, including Holohan, to New Orleans.

The Sugar Bowl adventure turned into a nightmare. Maryland led 21-0 just one minute into the second quarter. Vol defensive tackle Bill Pearman remembered an ominous early sign when Maryland fumbled on the third play of the game, but Bob Shermonski recovered for the Terrapins 10 yards downfield. "Normally, we got all the fumbles," Pearman lamented.

Tatum had devised a defense, an eight-man line led by tackle Dick Modzelewski, which stifled Tennessee's offense. Lauricella gained only one yard in seven carries and had three passes intercepted.

"I don't feel half as bad over what happened to us [as a team] as I do over what happened to Hank," Neyland said.

"Maryland came up with a defense we had never seen," Lauricella said. "It was a version of a four-man line, and we were late adjusting to it. That year we enjoyed so much success running, we didn't have to throw the ball much. In the Sugar Bowl, when we had to reach back to our passing game to try to get back into the game, we wound up doing things out of our normal sequence. Things simply didn't go as planned."

Dick Modzelewski's brother, Ed, ripped Tennessee's defense for 153 yards, just three short of Tennessee's total offense for the day. The final score was 28-13, Maryland.

"We had something to prove," Tatum said afterward. "Our boys were busting with eagerness. They just soaked up coaching. I've got no greater friend in coaching than General Bob Neyland. It was my greatest thrill to beat his team. There is no greater honor than to have won from the greatest coach in the country."

In his ledger, Neyland questioned himself about the loss to Maryland:

"Our team flat. Why? Could we have done any better with a 'hate Maryland' approach?"

Then he observed: "Three fumbles and four interceptions spelled our doom."

As spring arrived, Neyland realized the end of his coaching career was approaching rapidly—1952 would be his last team.

CHAPTER 33

Neyland's Last Team

1952

Graduation had taken a heavy toll on the Tennessee football team in the spring of 1952. Gone were two three-year starters—center Bob Davis and end Vince Kaseta. Fullback Andy Kozar was the only returning backfield starter. The 1952 Vols would be extremely short on experience.

"I will consider the 1952 team fortunate if it wins half the games on its schedule," Neyland said. "Offensively the team looks as bad as 1948." Not counting two "breathers," the 1948 Vols had scored only 73 points.

The biggest problem of all, going into the 1952 season, was finding tailbacks to replace Lauricella and Payne, who together had gained 1,447 of Tennessee's 3,068 rushing yards in 1951. Counting their passing, the two senior tailbacks had been responsible for 53.6 percent of Tennessee's total offense.

"We have three inexperienced tailbacks coming back, therefore our offensive team will be much weaker than the offensive teams of the past two years," the General said.

"Defensively the team doesn't look too bad," he said. "[Doug] Atkins and [Darris] McCord look good at tackles. [Roger] Rotroff a good pass rusher." The gaps created by the departure of safetyman Bert Rechichar, linebackers Gordon Polofsky and Bill Jasper, and defensive linemen Ted Daffer and Bill Pearman were major concerns. Surprisingly, Neyland emerged from spring practice rather optimistic about the Vol defense. "We hope to be stronger defensively than we were last year," he said.

In addition to adjusting to new personnel, the biggest factor that could affect the 1952 season was Tennessee's schedule. Four of the Vols' opponents were expected to be very strong and proved to be just that. Duke finished 1952 with an

8-2 record. Alabama was 10-2 and ranked ninth in the nation. Florida ranked 15th and Kentucky 20th.

The buildup to the annual Tennessee-Alabama game was extraordinary for two reasons—the media hype, and something Neyland did on the night before the big game. Alabama was unbeaten in four games, and Tennessee had a 2-1 record, its loss a 7-0 struggle with Duke.

The Tennessee student body held a huge pep rally the night before the big game. Hal Ernest, a student leader whose father owned the Ellis and Ernest Drug Store on the edge of the campus, was in charge of organizing the rally. Chancing that his father's relationship with Neyland might open a door, young Ernest invited the General to speak at the pep rally.

"It'll be the biggest pep rally in the school's history, and the students want to show you how much they support the team," Ernest told Neyland.

"I'm not going to do it," Neyland said emphatically. "I'm too busy. I've got a ball game to prepare for. I'm not going to do it."

Ernest knew of Neyland's shyness and was aware the General rarely made public speeches, except for his annual pre-season scouting report on the Vols to the Knoxville Rotary Club. Nonetheless, Ernest spread the word throughout Knoxville that Neyland would attend the rally that night.

As the pep rally fire was beginning to fade and the students were preparing to leave, Ernest saw a "long, black Cadillac drive through the gate. It was Neyland." He mounted the platform and told Ernest, "I'm only going to say a word or two."

"He talked for 20 minutes," Ernest said. "He must have rehashed every Tennessee-Alabama game since McEver's run in 1928. When he finished, I turned to the students and led them in cheering Neyland. A few seconds later, I turned around to thank him—and he was gone. Vanished."

The next day, Jimmy Wade, a slender sophomore tailback from Lynchburg, Virginia, stole the show for Tennessee. Heavily taped because of a leg injury, Wade ripped through the Alabama defense 18 times for 153 yards, 24 more than Alabama's total offense. Kozar gained 124 yards through the middle, and Pat Shires added 48. Wade scored one touchdown and set up a second, and the Vols won 20-0.

As he usually did against so-called "breathers," Neyland played his reserves the next week in a 50-0 cakewalk over Wofford. He was using three tailbacks almost equally—junior Pat Shires and sophomores Pat Oleksiak and Jimmy Wade.

Next, the Vols cut down North Carolina, 41-14, LSU, 22-3, and Florida, 26-12. But the Florida game was costly for Tennessee. Kozar, the Vols' star fullback, suffered a lower vertebrae injury that ended his college football career. The Florida Gators—coached by ex-Vol Bob Woodruff and quarterbacked by Doug Dickey, who years later would be Tennessee's head coach and athletics director—went on to beat Tulsa in the Gator Bowl.

As November 22 approached, Bear Bryant's Kentucky Wildcats were celebrating their fourth straight year in the AP's Top 20. Bryant's won-lost record, going into the 1952 Tennessee game, was 59-22-4. His Wildcats had played in four bowl games and, in 1950, had won the SEC championship and finished the season ranked seventh in the nation. But, in spite of those successes, Bryant was unfulfilled. As a coach he had never beaten Neyland. In the six previous games, the General had beaten Bryant five times, and one game had been a tie.

With less than three minutes remaining in the 1952 game in Knoxville, the Vols were leading 14-0 and it appeared Bryant would lose again to Neyland. But Kentucky quarterback Herb Hunt had other ideas. He directed a 62-yard touchdown drive, and Bryant immediately called for an on-sides kick that Kentucky recovered. Seconds later, Hunt threw a touchdown pass to Jim Proffitt. Bob Bassitt's second extra point tied the score, 14-14, and that is how it ended. The jubilant Kentucky players gave Bryant a "victory ride" to meet Neyland at the middle of the field.

"All credit must be given Kentucky for such a determined comeback," Neyland said in the silent Tennessee dressing room.

Bryant was ecstatic. "I have never seen greater courage any time than that displayed by those boys of mine," he said. Bryant did not know he would never again have the chance to beat Neyland.

The following week at Nashville, sophomore Pat Oleksiak had a "dream" game against Vanderbilt. It was one of the best performances ever by a Tennessee tailback. Oleksiak, who ran with power and threw well, reminded old-timers of ex-Vol all-American George Cafego. Against Vanderbilt that day, he ran for three touchdowns and passed for two in a 46-0 romp.

"Our defensive team set up the chances for us," Oleksiak said modestly. "They had the most to do with winning the game."

"We could have beaten any team in the nation today," said Vol linebacker Moose Barbish. "It was by far our best game."

And so Neyland's last team compiled an 8-2-1 record and accepted an invitation to play Texas in the Cotton Bowl. Texas had revenge on its mind.

Neyland physically had not felt good since before the season began, and there had been rumors that 1952 would be his last season. Yet, fans and friends and university officials were not ready for the announcement made on Christmas eve, just before the football team was to fly to Dallas for the Cotton Bowl game. The General was ill.

Dr. C. E. Brehm, president of the University of Tennessee, broke the news: "General Robert R. Neyland's physicians have advised him that, on account of his health at the present time, he should not participate in coaching activities preliminary to the post-season game in the Cotton Bowl." Acting on Neyland's recommendation, Brehm named offensive coordinator Harvey Robinson acting head coach "pending the recovery of General Neyland." Only hours before the team was to depart for Dallas, Robinson had inherited sole responsibility for preparing the Vols for the Cotton Bowl game with Texas.

Tennessee football fans were stunned—primarily because the tone of the announcement clearly indicated Neyland's illness was serious. Even Neyland was not ready to step aside.

"My plans had been to leave Florida Christmas afternoon [Thursday] so that I would be in Knoxville for the practice sessions Friday and Saturday, but the doctors objected," Neyland said at the time. "They have taken several tests. Apparently I have a low white corpuscle count. This is not a normal condition."

Unable to be involved personally in preparing the team for the Cotton Bowl, Neyland waited until two days before the game to fly to Dallas.

After pre-game warmups, Neyland met with the Vols in their dressing room and wished them luck. He then rejoined the official university party and watched the game as a spectator.

It was a Texas ambush. Tennessee ran only two offensive plays in the first quarter. On second down, Vol tailback Dave Griffith lined up to punt from the end zone, but he fumbled the snap and was tackled for a safety. The Vols fumbled the next time they had the ball, and Texas recovered and drove to a touchdown. The Longhorns scored again in the fourth quarter, and the final score was 16-0.

Texas had used the same defensive scheme Duke used earlier in the season to beat the Vols, 7-0. The Longhorns held the Vols to a net loss of 14 yards rushing and only 46 through the air. Pat Shires, trying to establish a passing game, was sacked for losses totaling 36 yards. The Vols lost three fumbles, but Neyland said Texas would have won without them.

"We have no excuses, no alibis," Neyland said. "We got beat badly by a great Texas football team, one of the finest I've ever seen." With that, he and Peggy returned to their new home in Florida. The General needed time to rest and recuperate.

Seven weeks later—on February 17—General Robert R. Neyland asked to be relieved of his head coaching duties for the 1953 season. The request was couched in an implication that he might resume coaching in 1954.

1953-1962

PART VIII

CHAPTER 34

Retirement Years

1953-54

Peggy Neyland had watched her husband's health decline steadily during the fall of 1952. What bothered her most was that the problem had not been diagnosed. At first, doctors thought his teeth might be causing infection. Then, after further tests, they diagnosed cirrhosis of the liver. Moreover, Neyland was told, the "fever of unknown origin" diagnosed by army doctors when he got sick in China in 1944 likely was infectious hepatitis and was now complicating his condition. The doctors and Peggy together convinced the General, now 61 years old, that he needed to take a rest—a long rest.

So in mid-February, Neyland met in Knoxville with Dr. N. W. Dougherty, dean of the athletic board, and requested a leave of absence for the 1953 football season. President Brehm and the university trustees quickly granted his wish and named Harvey Robinson head coach. Neyland remained athletics director.

"I have a definite understanding with the athletic board and trustees that when I get ready to quit active coaching, I will stay on here as athletic director during the remainder of my athletic career," Neyland said.

In late February, Neyland entered the Walter Reed Army Hospital in Washington, D.C. An exhaustive series of tests confirmed the earlier diagnosis—cirrhosis of the liver. Neyland needed rest, and Peggy intended to see he got it. She packed their bags for a long stay at their home in Sarasota. The irony of Neyland not coaching in 1953 was that college football was returning to single-platoon football, for which he had fought so hard.

The NCAA rules committee in 1941 had legalized free-substitution because so many players were going into the military. Coaches said they needed unlimited substitution to maintain a respectable game. Free-substitution, they said, would enable them to use players with limited ability in the most productive way.

By 1949, most major college teams employed the two-platoon system, separate units specializing in offense and defense. Some coaches even had special kicking teams. As a member of the rules committee, Neyland led the movement against two-platoon football and got it abolished in 1953.

The liver ailment had scared Neyland, so he followed doctors' orders—and Peggy's orders. He soaked up the Florida sun, fished almost daily, puttered in the yard with flowers and shrubs, and regained some strength.

By late summer, he was ready to return to Knoxville. Pre-season football practice would soon be starting, and the General did not want to be too far from that, even though he was not coaching the team. So he and Peggy packed their bags, climbed into the car, and headed north.

On the night of August 18, at Cherokee Country Club, where he had spent thousands of hours playing bridge, General Neyland was the guest of honor at a testimonial dinner attended by his former players, university officials, college and high school coaches, sportswriters, and broadcasters. The dignitary list included Tennessee Governor Frank Clement, U.S. Senators Estes Kefauver and Albert Gore, Sr., and Congressman Howard H. Baker, Sr. Georgia Tech's Bobby Dodd, whose methods and discipline as a coach and player were practically opposite Neyland's, had conceived the idea for the dinner. He was joined by head coaches Bowden Wyatt of Arkansas, Murray Warmath of Mississippi State, DeWitt Weaver of Texas Tech, Bob Woodruff of Florida, Phil Dickens of Wyoming, Bill Meek of Kansas State, Harvey Robinson of Tennessee, and Arkansas athletics director John Barnhill—all Neyland pupils. And there were dozens more.

They presented the General with keys to a new Cadillac, but the keys were only symbolic—the car had not arrived from Detroit.

Kentucky coach Bear Bryant, winless against Neyland in seven tries, came to pay tribute. Dodd heard Bryant mutter that night: "Thank God the old guy finally quit."

Neyland was presented with a padded guest book in which each former player wrote his old coach a brief message of appreciation. Harry "Hobo" Thayer wrote about how Neyland had been a friend to the players and ended by saying simply: "I love you, General Neyland." Herman Hickman wrote: "Thanks for everything." Bud Sherrod said: "Thanks for everything you have taught me both in football and in life."

There were dozens of entries in the book, the last one by reserve center Gene Felty, class of 1951: "You have been like a father to so many of us all these number of years. Words cannot express the sentiment we have toward you. You have taught us the way to accept life both on the field and in everyday happenings. We shall never forget you and all you have done for us. Thanks for everything, and may God bless and keep you."

And then there was the letter from an old West Point teammate: "May the memories of your distinguished career as an officer of the army and as an outstanding football coach and athletic director—and the knowledge of the inspiration you have imparted to the countless young men with whom you have worked—bring you enduring satisfaction through all the years ahead." It was from President Dwight Eisenhower.

Finally, it was Neyland's turn, and he asked his former players to stand. "To you boys who played for me," he said, "I want to express my unbounded esteem, admiration, and affection. To me, you are and always will be the best."

In the fall of 1953, Tennessee's new head coach—scholarly, soft-spoken Harvey Robinson—walked into an almost no-win situation. Following Neyland as head coach was bad enough, but Robby found it difficult to convert "specialists" to single-platoon football—to teach them to play offense and defense. And the 1953 results did not please Tennessee fans. The Vols finished 6-4-1, not good by Neyland standards.

Neyland watched the 1953 campaign from the press box on game days and from the sidelines during practices. He resisted the temptation to "counsel" with Robinson that season. But on one occasion he did engage George Gardner, the head of SEC officials."George," Neyland said, with some humor seeping into his tone of voice, "I want you to know that I'm not complaining about the officials. But Mamma [Peggy] is sore at the boys who worked the Vanderbilt game."

"I'm burned up because they called back a Tennessee touchdown," Peggy said. "It was on a pass, and we had an ineligible man downfield."

"What Mamma is sore about," Neyland explained to Gardner, "is that the officials took away the only touchdown her boy [Bob] ever scored."

The Neyland sons, Bob and Lewis, were good athletes. Lewis lettered three years at the University of Tennessee in basketball and tennis (1954-56), was a starting forward his junior and senior years, the tennis captain as a junior, and a golf letterman as a senior. Bob played three years for the General (1951-53), earned two football letters (1952-53), and was captain of the 1953 Vol swimming team. He was a third team wingback behind Bert Rechichar and Ed Morgan on the 1951 national championship team and was the number one backup to Morgan and Jerry Hyde in his junior and senior years. Bob averaged 6.3 yards per carry during his career.

"The boys lived in the stadium dorm, and the General would walk in unannounced and check Lewis's room," Gus Manning said. "As a matter of fact, Lewis's room was the only one he ever checked in the athletes' dorm. He'd jump all over Lewis about not keeping his room straight." The General found pleasure in watching his sons compete athletically, but he seldom displayed any emotion related to their performances—especially when it came to Bob and football. "The General sure didn't make it any easier on Bobby," former Vol center Bob Davis (1949-51) said. "The General was tough on Bobby Neyland on the practice field."

Basketball was another matter, however, especially at the SEC tournament if the General had downed a drink or two. "If the Vols did something exciting, he'd do his Tarzan yell up in the stands," Gus Manning said. "And when Lewis did something really good, the General would let go with a big one."

"He could make the damnedest Tarzan yell you ever heard," writer Ben Byrd said. "It was almost frightening."

After the 1953 football season, Neyland decided to make his retirement permanent. The liver ailment was still a problem, and Peggy wanted him free of the tensions of coaching football. So Robinson remained Tennessee's head coach.

"Dad really loved football, and I believe he would have continued coaching if he had felt his health permitted it," son Lewis said years later.

In early April 1954, the telephone rang in the Neyland home. Norman Downey, a family friend and one of Neyland's players in the mid-1930s, was in the room and could hear only Neyland's half of the conversation. "You do me a great honor, Ike," Neyland said, "but I'd do you irreparable harm because I believe half those sons-of-bitches over there are communists." Neyland told Downey that President Eisenhower had just asked if he would accept the chairmanship of the Tennessee Valley Authority.

During his military and coaching careers, together spanning 40 years, Neyland developed some strong convictions but kept them to himself, except when Roosevelt challenged him in the 1930s. In his memoirs he reaffirmed his earlier feelings about the New Deal politics of FDR and his previously unspoken attitude toward President Truman.

"I do not have any politics now, and haven't had for 30 years. I am an 'Aginner.'" he said.

"I am 'agin' presidents who run for a second term on the slogan 'He kept us out of war,' while at the same time he had our destroyers battling German submarines and our transports carrying British troops in violation of all neutrality laws.

"I am 'agin' a president who said 'I have said before, and I will say it again and again and again that I will never send your sons to fight in a foreign land,' meanwhile giving the British 50 destroyers, convoying their ships, and issuing an ultimatum to Japan which definitely assured we would get into World War II.

"I am 'agin' a president who, without the approval of Congress, sent our soldiers into a 'police action' in Korea which resulted in one of the bloodiest and most costly wars we ever fought; who also, having sent our troops into Korea, denied the greatest general and probably the greatest man this country has produced in the last hundred years [reference to Douglas MacArthur] the permission to use his air superiority in order to gain the victory.

"There are other similar things I'm 'agin,' but you have the dope now. If you must say I have political leanings, place me as follows: Well to the Right of the Far Right."

1954

The 1954 Tennessee team was loaded with talent, but it was heavily dependent on sophomores—guys like Buddy Cruze, Edd Cantrell, and Roger Urbano (ends), John Gordy and Charles Rader (tackles), Bruce Burnham (guard), Bob Hibbard (wingback), and Johnny Majors (tailback). As seniors, two years down the road, they would win 10 games. The juniors included guard Charles Coffey, wingback

Terry Sweeney, and tailback Pat Oleksiak. Among the seniors were linemen Darris McCord and Lamar Leachman, wingbacks Hugh Garner and Terry Sweeney, fullback Tom Tracy, and tailbacks Jimmy Wade and Bobby Brengle.

The 1954 squad had all the earmarks of a winner, but something happened. Tailbacks Majors and Wade missed key games because of injuries. The Vols lost their last four games of the season, including a 26-0 shutout by Vanderbilt, the worst beating by Vandy since 1925. The Vols finished with a 4-6 record, Tennessee's first losing season since 1935, the year Neyland was in Panama.

Two days before the Kentucky game, Robinson walked into Neyland's office, closed the door, and said he wanted to talk confidentially. Because of the team's record (4-4) and friction on his staff, Robby was considering firing three, possibly four, assistant coaches.

"I told him that now was not the time to bring this subject up, that his whole concentration should be put on making as good a showing as possible in the last two ball games," Neyland wrote in a memorandum to himself. The General noted that he was disturbed by the prospect of firing assistant coaches because of what it would do to their wives and children.

"The cold-bloodedness of this procedure has never appealed to me," Neyland wrote. "I have never fired a football coach in all my years of coaching. Actually, I have not the heart to fire anybody. . . . My wife has to fire all the household servants."

Then, in the privacy of his own thoughts, an option Neyland had been considering for several weeks was revealed in the phrase ". . . regardless of whether we replace Robinson. . . ."

Four days after the season-ending loss to Vanderbilt dropped Tennessee's record to 4-6, Neyland dismissed Robinson and his entire staff. "It was the hardest thing I ever had to do," he said. "They were all my boys."

CHAPTER 35

The Final Years

1955-62

Bowden Wyatt, the captain of Bob Neyland's 1938 undefeated team, had rebuilt football programs at Wyoming and Arkansas. And that is who Neyland wanted to be Tennessee's new head coach.

Although there was much newspaper speculation that Wyatt would leave Arkansas for Tennessee, Wyatt refused to answer reporters' questions about the matter until after the Cotton Bowl, in which his Arkansas team lost to Georgia Tech, 14-6. Prior to the bowl game, Wyatt never confirmed he had been offered the Tennessee job, nor did he deny it.

But on January 8, 1955, after a meeting with Neyland at the National Collegiate Athletic Association convention in New York, the university announced that Wyatt was "coming home" to be Tennessee's new head coach. He signed a five-year contract for "the job I've always wanted."

Wyatt's first two appearances in Knoxville as Vol head coach were at a student rally in his honor and the football banquet. Neyland proudly introduced Wyatt at the rally outside the student center. Then, as Wyatt talked to the crowd about the future, Neyland sat in a chair, his eyes riveted on the young coach.

At the banquet, Wyatt pulled from his pocket and presented to captain-elect Jim Beutel a silver dollar that Wyatt said he had carried for 17 years. "I won this silver dollar in a coin toss in one of the 1938 games, and I decided to keep it to give to my first captain if I ever became coach at Tennessee," he said. Wyatt's 1955 team, after losing its first two games, won six of the next eight and finished 6-3-1. Neyland praised the Wyatt staff and promised even better things the next year.

Indeed, the next year brought much better things to the Vol football program and to Neyland personally. He was elected to the college football Hall of Fame, joining ex-Vols Gene McEver and Beattie Feathers, who had been elected in previous years.

Although he maintained an office schedule from mid-summer through the football season, Neyland's health continued to decline noticeably. "He'd sit in a chair on the sidelines and watch practice without comment," Gus Manning said. "He'd usually have that stop-watch with him, timing the passers and punters. But it was apparent at times that he didn't feel good."

As Lindsey Nelson said in his autobiography, Neyland found himself in competition with his own legend.

"If a man survives to become contemporary with his legend, the legend always overshadows and sometimes smothers the man," Lindsey said. "The legend is immortal, unchanging, etched forever in stone, unassailable, a source of inspiration for others, but not for him."

But, Lindsey asked, what about the man who is human and therefore heir to human frailties?

"No living man has ever escaped them," Nelson said. "The legendary Neyland discipline that had inspired and sustained so many, became unavailable to Neyland, unattainable to its creator. The lean, ramrod-straight military figure grew overweight and out of shape, which he despised and was powerless to control. The closing years were filled with frustration."

Then one morning in the mail, Neyland received a letter he cherished the remaining years of his life. It was a personal letter from retired General Albert C. Wedemeyer, under whom Neyland had served briefly 15 years earlier in China.

Wedemeyer had brought in his own man to replace Neyland as commander of the supply base at Kunming. From there, Neyland had become commander of the huge port and supply center at Calcutta, but he had resented being relieved of command in Kunming.

"An officer in China told me, General Neyland, that you were drinking to such a degree that it was militating against the performance of your duties [in Kunming]," Wedemeyer wrote.

"I made many changes—one which involved you and which, I must tell you now, in retrospect and in all sincerity I deeply regret, for I found that I had made a gross mistake," Wedemeyer said in an extraordinary admission.

"You were sent to Calcutta . . . a real mistake or error in judgment on my part," Wedemeyer continued. "Incidentally, it would please you to know as time went on in the China Theater and I became acquainted with Chinese and Americans who knew you there, uniformly their reaction to your name was very favorable. This only, of course, increased my feeling of stupidity."

Wedemeyer's letter profoundly affected Neyland. But Neyland was doubly moved the following year when he received in the mail a copy of the official history of the China-Burma-India Theater published by the army. Neyland was prominently mentioned. Wedemeyer wrote the following to Neyland on the first page: "Because of my sincere admiration of your own outstanding service in that theater of war and of your attributes of leadership which are in keeping with the finest traditions of West Point, I want to express my appreciation and good wishes."

Neyland also was deeply moved in 1957 when his older son, Bob, was hospitalized at Johns Hopkins Hospital in Baltimore, Maryland, for severe depression.

"When Bob went in that hospital, it hit Dad like a ton of bricks. He and Mother felt like they had failed miserably as parents," the General's younger son Lewis recalled.

"My father came to the hospital and spent seven straight days with me in that room. He slept on a cot by my bed, just letting me know he was there," Bob remembered. "Lewis and I knew he loved us, but I didn't know until that week just how much he loved us, how much he really cared."

Bob recovered, and after that it seemed as if the boys and their dad were much closer than they had ever been.

"Dad was mellowing in those years after he quit coaching, and he was trying to be more of a parent," Lewis said. "About a year after I had a serious traffic accident in Georgia, Dad and I had an argument about something. I think I questioned his concern about me, and he reminded me he was the first one there when I was in trouble."

Peggy confided to Lewis's wife, Libby, some feelings of guilt about the type of parents she and the General had been. "Granny said that, as a mother, she hadn't been with the boys as much as she should have," Libby said. "Granny said she often chose to go with Papa, rather than being with the boys. And Papa's career was a lifestyle of travel and mixing with adults."

Even though his days of coaching were behind him, Neyland remained close to the game—sitting on his little wooden folding chair near the practice field sidelines, watching the games from the press box, writing notes to himself, notes he sometimes shared with the head coach.

When Bowden Wyatt came on board as head coach, Neyland continued attending practice almost every day, just as he had during Robinson's tenure, and he was in the press box on game day, surveying the action below with his binoculars, watching analytically and scribbling notes. Notes which ultimately wound up on Wyatt's desk.

Wyatt's line coach, Dick Hitt, once told sportswriter Tom Siler that Neyland never imposed his will on the coaching staff. "He'd sit quietly and listen to all of the discussions, the pros and cons, what we planned to do. He'd sit and say nothing," Hitt said. "When the talk was all over, he'd pull out a little piece of paper and recite to us a few things he had observed in practice, or an idea or two that might have occurred to him. That was the extent of it. Sometimes, as we walked down the hall, he'd say, 'I wish you'd talk to Bowden and get him to do so and so."

"The General taught me this game," Wyatt said. "I would be crazy not to listen to him."

"I never butt into his business," Neyland said. "Of course, I don't suppose I'll live long enough to get over the urge to coach, to run the team. But that's his business now." And Bowden was doing his business pretty well.

The 1956 Vols went undefeated in 10 regular season games and were ranked second in the nation. Senior tailback Johnny Majors won all-American honors and was runner-up for the Heisman Trophy. And Wyatt was named national "Coach of the Year" by the American Football Coaches Association. The Vols were back on top.

One of those 1956 victories was a classic confrontation of defenses, and Neyland loved every minute of it. It was a chess game between Wyatt and Georgia Tech's Bobby Dodd. More than that, said Tom Siler in his book *Football's Greatest Dynasty*, it was Neyland versus Neyland. It was the movement of battlefield troops into positions of geographical advantage. It was punting and field position. Majors quick-kicked 68 yards, and Vol tailback Bobby Gordon, Majors's understudy, outdid him with a 72-yarder.

In the third quarter, Majors and Buddy Cruze connected on a 45-yard pass play to the Tech one. Bronson scored on the next play, and that is how it ended.

"The greatest football game I have ever seen—Tennessee 6, Georgia Tech 0—has been over 15 minutes now," the *Knoxville Journal*'s Ben Byrd said in the lead of his game story. "The slate gray horseshoe stadium is almost cleared of fans now, except for a bright orange patch across the field in the east stands."

The 1956 seniors were the last class recruited while Bob Neyland was still head coach. John Majors, who years later would become Tennessee's head coach, said Wyatt and all Neyland-trained coaches adhered to the General's conservative principles: "Make it sound, make it simple, and keep it consistent."

During his first decade at Tennessee, Neyland had the quarterback (later called a blockingback) decide in the huddle which plays to call. Tailback Babe Wood says that changed after the Vol quarterback had Babe carry the ball nine straight times in a game in 1937. Babe was exhausted and went to Neyland. "If I'm gonna have to carry the ball nine times in a row, I want to be calling the plays," an exhausted Wood told Neyland. Thereafter, Tennessee tailbacks called the plays in huddle.

Majors, of course, was a tailback. In his autobiography, *You Can Go Home Again*, Majors told about the last thing Wyatt would say to him at the pre-game meal: "If you can't think of anything else to call, kick the damned ball."

That was Neyland's philosophy. He loved to surprise the opponent by quick-kicking on first or second down, sometimes even from near the 50-yard line.

"We weren't nearly as interested in who had the football, as in where it was on the field," Majors said. "If we got it inside the 25-yard line on our end of the field, we were apt to punt on third down rather than risk a turnover close to our own goal."

Inevitably Wyatt's 1956 team would be compared with Neyland's great teams of 1928-30, 1938-40, and 1950-52. But those comparisons were made by fans or occasionally a sportswriter, never by Neyland. He refused to be drawn into that debate.

Although no team of his had ever beaten a Neyland team, Bear Bryant enjoyed Neyland's company. Bryant felt he was learning from Neyland whenever they were together. In 1958, Bryant's first year at Alabama, Neyland got sick during the spring SEC meeting in Florida and was hospitalized. Gus Manning was there.

"Bowden and Molly, Margaret and I, Bear and Mary Harmon, and Carney Laslie stayed there, visiting with Neyland during the day and going out to dinner at night," Manning said. "Bryant thought so much of Neyland."

Years later, after Bryant's Alabama teams had won five national championships, Bryant told Manning: "Everybody thinks I'm the greatest damned coach in the world, but you worked for the guy who taught me everything I know."

Neyland was spending more and more time in Florida. He and Peggy loved it there, and they were constantly entertaining friends and former football associates at their home in Sarasota. He did some recruiting of high school players along the Gulf Coast of Florida, and he made a number of fishing trips in Mexican waters.

Bowden and Molly Wyatt visited Bob and Peggy in Sarasota every chance they got. "The General treated me like a daughter," Molly said. "The four of us would go dancing. The General was a marvelous dancer. He knew all the steps."

The General enjoyed his grandchildren during the last few years of his life. Ironically, the man who had difficulty relating to his own children during their early years took delight in their children. Reese and Blake were the sons of Bob and Anne. Reese, the oldest of the grandchildren and the General's namesake, was born in 1955 and was old enough for the General to enjoy playing with. Blake, born in 1960, was too young to remember much about his grandfather in later years, as were Lewis's children, Lewis Fitch, Jr. (Lee), and Kim.

When they were in Knoxville for the football season or special occasions, Bob and Peggy lived in a motel owned by a friend. The General's health was not good, but physicians had not diagnosed the problem. He continued to do the things he enjoyed—fishing, playing bridge, working with his flowers and shrubs. But Peggy became concerned that Bob might die suddenly, and she wanted the matter of a burial plot settled well in advance. Young Bob's wife, Anne, remembered the episode.

"My Bob and Granny [Peggy Neyland] began conferring with cemetery people behind Papa's back," Anne said. "Then one day, someone from the cemetery called on the phone for Bob and Granny, but got Papa by mistake. He instantly assumed he was dying and that Bob and Granny were keeping it from him. Papa had a fit—he was dying and nobody was telling him. Papa finally calmed down when Bob and Granny explained what had happened."

The General, mellowing in retirement, began attending the kind of public and private functions he would never have considered during his coaching years. And, of course, he was always ready for reunions at West Point, the University of Tennessee, or in Greenville.

He attended the 50th reunion of his high school graduating class at Greenville in 1960. Naturally, on that occasion, the Greenville newspaper was filled with feature stories and columns about Bob Neyland.

"Bob was always a great competitor and a perfectionist," recalled W. Walworth Harrison, a Greenville civic leader and Neyland's boyhood friend. "He never gave up and was the spark that kept alive teams that were apparently hopelessly behind, and ultimately lead them to victory. He really got the foundation for all of his athletic stamina by following a greyhound all day on Saturdays, chasing rabbits. Ready almost to drop by nightfall, he never quit, and that spirit made him the nationally known champion that he is."

Neyland served as chairman of the rules committee of the National Collegiate Athletic Association from the mid-1950s until his death. He had successfully led the fight for return to limited substitution, single-platoon football in 1953 and steadfastly resisted repeated attempts by other coaches to restore two-platoon.

"Although he could not vote except in case of a tie, he could as chairman control discussion to some extent," wrote Edwin Pope of the *Miami Herald*. "And no one denies that the General is tremendously influential in the formation of rules. Wielding the hand of control is old stuff to Neyland."

Toward the end of one rules committee meeting, Coach Ray Eliot of Illinois rose and addressed the chair: "General Neyland, there are a lot of coaches in this game and a lot of people in this room, a lot of rules-committee members, who would like to move to return to two-platoon."

There was a pause as Neyland silently surveyed the room. Then he spoke: "I don't see any people who want to return to two-platoon. All in favor of the present rules say 'aye.'"

Lindsey Nelson's book relates what happened next. Neyland quickly raised his own hand and that of committee secretary Dave Nelson of Delaware and roared: "Aye. Opposed no. The ayes have it—and we won't have any chickenshit football this season."

A few days later, as they lounged at the Monte Carlo, Neyland asked Pope: "Did you hear what Ray Graves said the other night? Graves said college football would never return to unlimited substitution as long as I was head of the rules committee."

"Is that true?" someone asked.

"No comment," Neyland said with a chuckle. "But I'm flattered that Graves thinks I'm so powerful."

Powerful or not, college football did not return to two-platoon football until after Neyland died.

The General's health was fading rapidly in the fall of 1961, but he actively directed the planning for the addition of an upper deck on the west side of the football stadium. The stadium had 3,200 seats when Neyland arrived at Tennessee in 1925. He oversaw five expansions to a capacity of 46,390. Using Neyland's grand design, athletics directors Bob Woodruff and Doug Dickey eventually enlarged the stadium to accommodate 96,000 fans. The General's ultimate plan, a double-decked bowl, called for 103,000 seats.

On January 14, 1962, Neyland entered the Ochsner Foundation Hospital in New Orleans for tests and treatment. He was very sick. His kidneys and liver were failing, and he knew the end was near.

Peggy was at the General's bedside constantly during the next few weeks. Norman Downey, who had been a member of Tennessee's teams in the mid-1930s and who loved Neyland like a brother, left his work in Birmingham to be with the General and provide Peggy with moral support. Bowden Wyatt and Gus Manning visited the General frequently.

Bobby had just started a new job with a bank in Bristol, Tennessee, when his father entered the hospital, "but they told me at the bank to take as much time as I needed." Lewis, a businessman in Baltimore, took time off from his work and joined brother Bob and their mother in New Orleans.

"We knew he was getting worse, but everybody there, including Dad, kept things upbeat. We kept his spirits up," Lewis said. "He was still telling tall tales and joking with us like he always did. Toward the end, I shaved him every day. And he'd tell me, 'You missed a spot.' He was still coaching."

In February, as Neyland observed his 70th birthday from that hospital bed in New Orleans, the University of Tennessee trustees voted to give the football stadium his name. It was a gesture that pleased him.

Wyatt and Manning now were making frequent trips to New Orleans. "Bowden went to see the General almost every weekend," Bowden's wife, Molly, said. "It was true devotion. You could see the worry and grief in Bowden's eyes as the General got worse. Their relationship was very special—almost like a father and son. They loved each other."

DeWitt Weaver, who had been one of Neyland's players and had been head coach at Texas Tech, drove in from Texas to be with the General and Peggy.

Neyland lapsed into a coma the night of March 27 and died at 11:30 a.m. the following day. Peggy, the boys, and Norman Downey were with him at the end. Reflecting on that moment 28 years later, tears came to Lewis's eyes as he remembered thinking, "There goes a hell of a man." Lewis said he felt overwhelming pride at that moment, "pride of being General Neyland's son."

An autopsy, requested by Ochsner Hospital and authorized by Peggy, revealed cancer of the liver.

When the news of Neyland's death reached Bowden Wyatt back in Knoxville, he was swept with a feeling of emptiness. Then, collecting himself but fighting back the tears, Wyatt issued a statement: "General Robert Reese Neyland now becomes a legend."

CHAPTER 36

The Neyland Legacy

In the simple dignity that so characterized his life, General Robert Reese Neyland was buried in the U.S. military cemetery at Knoxville on March 30, 1962. "Just as he had dominated college football," wrote F. M. Williams of the *Nashville Tennessean*, "Neyland dominated the final rites said for him. He ordered that 'as little commotion' as possible be made when he died."

Peggy Neyland and sons, Bob and Lewis, rode with the casket on the flight from New Orleans to Knoxville aboard a four-engine military plane.

Neyland wanted his funeral held in a small sanctuary so his many friends would not feel obligated to attend. It was held in a 400-seat chapel.

Neyland wanted to be dressed in a gray, double-breasted suit—the kind he had worn on the sidelines. And he was.

He asked that the casket not be opened. And it was not.

The casket was draped with an American flag and encircled by floral arrangements, including a wreath from the West Point class of 1916. Other flowers came from Notre Dame, Duke, Georgia Tech, and many other universities.

The Reverend David E. Babin, curate of St. John's Episcopal Church in Knoxville, performed a simple service as Neyland had ordered. The Reverend Babin read two Psalms, one verse of Romans, and the 14th chapter of St. John. Then he and the audience recited the Lord's Prayer. The service took just 10 minutes.

As sad as the occasion was, General Neyland's funeral was a celebration. Thousands of people who had known him through the years paid their respects to the family. They came from New York, California, Florida, and points between. Former players, former members of his staff, and coaches he had opposed assembled in clusters, quietly recalling the magic he had brought to college football—the punting duels, the close games decided by a single play, and always the defense. Always the General sitting in his chair, his arms folded across his chest, or his thumb and first finger cradling his chin signaling deep thought.

The sky had been overcast during the morning, and rain began falling just as the graveside service ended. An army major presented the folded American flag to Peggy Neyland, and the service was over.

Paul "Bear" Bryant, whose Alabama team had just won the national championship, stood silently in the mist—a parting tribute to the man he had never defeated as a coach.

General Herbert Vogel, chairman of the Tennessee Valley Authority, was there. So were Bernie Moore, commissioner of the Southeastern Conference, and air force Lieutenant Colonel Mayo Neyland, the General's nephew.

"It was the way the General would have wanted it," wrote Scripps-Howard's Powell Lindsay the next day. "Neat and simple. General Robert Reese Neyland, a football immortal, was laid to rest . . . as scores of men he made great watched silently."

Gene McEver, once described by Neyland as the "greatest football player" he ever coached, said simply: "Football has lost a really great man."

Beattie Feathers, one of Neyland's favorite and best tailbacks: "Nobody ever wanted to win a football game more than the General, and nobody knew more about how to do it than he did. Playing for him was the greatest honor of my life."

Bob Foxx, wingback on Neyland's 1938-40 teams: "General Neyland was a father to me. He had a tremendous effect on my life."

Murray Warmath, Minnesota head coach: "Neyland was loved by everyone that played under him. His friendship and counsel meant everything to me. He contributed more to defensive football than any other man ever in the game."

Bobby Dodd, Georgia Tech head coach: "The General's defensive principles changed college football forever. We all learned from him, and coaches a hundred years from now will still be using his defensive theories. He was the greatest coach of modern football."

Bob Woodruff, former Neyland player who became Tennessee's athletics director after Neyland died: "The General's record as a coach speaks for itself. Somehow I know when we stop to listen, he will be around all of us in the coaching profession."

Jimmy Elmore, who scored the first touchdown of Neyland's coaching career at Tennessee and who became mayor of Knoxville: "To my way of thinking [Neyland] was successful because of his attention to detail and timing."

Hugh Faust, who played for, coached under, and roomed with Neyland on road trips: "There was no one like him. I loved him."

Sam Bartholomew, blockingback on Neyland's 1937-39 teams: "I never knew of a boy on any of his teams he wouldn't go to bat for."

Jim Haslam, president of Pilot Oil Company and 1952 Vol captain: "When I was captain, General Neyland would talk to me about what it means to be a leader, about the importance of being poised and confident, and learning to rise above adversity."

Jack Armstrong, 1946-48 Vol blockingback and successful high school coach: "He was always willing to help any of his boys. A fellow could lean on the General's shoulder. He'd never let you down."

Phil Dickens, Indiana head coach: "Psychologically, no one could touch him as a football coach."

Bert Rechichar, starting wingback and safetyman in 1950-51 and 1951 Vol captain: "Whenever General Neyland told you something, he meant it. He was fair. He'd never do you wrong. He was like a father to me."

Allyn McKeen, a Neyland player in 1926-27 and later head coach at Mississippi State: "He was a master of the punting game, a great psychologist, a great coach, and a great man."

Ray Graves, Florida head coach and 1941 Vol captain: "Any boy who had an opportunity to play under him couldn't help but gain confidence and acquire a solid background in football."

Hank Lauricella, tailback on the 1951 national championship team: "General Neyland put the best players on defense. To him, defense and the kicking game were most important. He coached the coaches. He prepared his teams Monday through Friday and, on Saturdays, he let the players play the game."

Billy Barnes, UCLA head coach: "General Neyland was a great teacher and leader of men. He demanded perfection in the fundamentals of the game. His theories on defense, kicking, and quarterbacking are the Bible of sound football."

Bowden Wyatt, Tennessee head coach and 1938 Vol captain: "He was a man of great personal dignity and quiet strength whose devotion to duty and dedication to high ideals were a constant inspiration. The precepts of honesty and integrity which he instilled in the minds and hearts of countless young men who came under his exacting tutelage will live on and on."

The people General Neyland hired to work for him at Tennessee held him in high esteem. He was demanding, but fair.

John P. "Deanie" Hoskins, Neyland's stadium and practice field groundskeeper for 35 years, was one of the few people at the university who ever argued successfully with the general. "Is the field going to be ready for the opening game?" Neyland would ask Deanie. "It'll be a lot more ready than your football team will be," Deanie would fire back. "OK," Neyland would say. When the General died, Deanie put it simply: "Never did have any trouble from him. He was a mighty good old man."

Dr. Robert Brashear, Tennessee team physician for four decades: "I admired General Neyland. As a coach, his first concern always was the welfare of his players." John Mauer, Tennessee basketball coach (1939-47) and assistant football coach: "All the football I know was learned under him. He was wonderful to me."

Emmett Lowery, Vol basketball coach (1948-59) and assistant football coach: "Neyland was ideal to work for."

Harvey Robinson, Vol head coach whom Neyland fired: "General Neyland was the greatest mind in modern football, a meticulous organizer and an inspirational leader to everyone who was fortunate enough to work for him."

George Mooney, Vol Network announcer when Neyland retired from coaching, said part of the General's "rich, full life" was helping others. "Neyland was about 30 years ahead of his time in thoughts and ideas pertaining to athletics, the military, and business," Mooney said.

Some who knew him best say it is a wonder that Neyland remained at the University of Tennessee. He was a magnetic personality, and his gridiron successes were the envy of major universities from coast to coast. Fordham University wanted him desperately and did not get him. Southern Cal thought it had him and did not.

"I thought he was going to Fordham because of the money situation at Tennessee during our early years there," Peggy said. "He was concerned about the lack of money for recruiting and facilities and scholarships, but he liked Tennessee and got some financial help."

In 1925, Neyland's "assistant coach" year at Tennessee, the athletics department had a net profit of $55.85. He organized the finances of the department, inspired outsiders to contribute money, and systematically enlarged the stadium.

A single sheet of brittle, brown stationery inserted in his private notebook reveals Neyland's early solicitation of contributions, ranging from $25 to $250 a year per gift. Neyland himself gave $250. The money was doled out to players on the basis of financial need, and during the Depression many players would not have had enough change for a glass of milk at the campus hangout, the Ellis and Ernest Drug Store, if it had not been for Neyland's "scholarship" fund.

Of all the men who have been college head football coaches for 20 years or more, Tennessee's Bob Neyland had the best won-lost percentage—82.9 percent. His teams through 21 seasons won 173 games, lost only 31, and tied 12. During the 12 years he coached after the Associated Press began its poll, Neyland's Vols finished eighth or higher seven times, and they won the AP national championship in 1951.

But the measure of Neyland's greatness and his contribution to the game extends far beyond his won-lost record at Tennessee. He was an innovator—movies of games and practices, press box-to-sideline telephones, better protective equipment for players, protective covering for the football field, detailed scouting reports, tear-away jerseys, low-cut shoes.

Most important, however, were his rules of life and his football theories. He constantly reminded himself and others around him: "The first rule of life is 'Don't kid yourself.'"

Neyland believed that repetition resulted in preparedness, that preparedness produced self-confidence, and that self-confidence translated into victories.

"To defeat a weak opponent is not the problem," he said. "The problem is to win when he is as good or better than you."

Neyland preached readiness. "Almost all close games are lost by the losers, not won by the winners," he maintained. "Football is composed of nothing but accidents. The great art is to profit from such accidents. It follows that all plans must be made to minimize our own mistakes and to magnify the effect of the opponents' mistakes."

Although Neyland strived for perfection, he knew it was only a goal.

"I expected my players to understand the nature of this game," Neyland said. "There is no such thing as a perfect play. Football is a game of mistakes. You must understand that. You're going to make mistakes. You must be prepared to adjust when you make the mistakes. Don't let them upset you, and be ready to be tougher than ever when you see the mistakes. Once you understand this, you can get ready to play football."

Neyland stressed physical conditioning. He said the team that is still energetic and aggressive in the fourth quarter has the advantage in a close game. "When we went onto the field, we believed we were better conditioned and better prepared mentally than the other team," 1950-52 Vol linebacker Gene Moeller said.

Neyland's constant companion in practice and during games was a stopwatch. He clocked his punters, insisting they kick the ball within two seconds of the snap from center. He stressed the importance of "hang time" on a punt. "It's essential that our players rushing downfield converge on the punt returner just as he's receiving the ball," he said.

"The General exploited the quick kick, punting when he thought the opposing team least expected it," Hank Lauricella said. "He added up the punting yardage of the two teams. To him, the difference in net punting yardage was just as important as a long drive with the ball."

George Halas, owner-coach of the Chicago Bears, called Neyland "a great tactician." To Lou Little, Neyland was "one of the great masterminds" of football. Paul Brown, then coach of the Cleveland Browns, called Neyland a "pillar" of the football world. Notre Dame's Knute Rockne had said Neyland was the "greatest defensive coach." And Oklahoma coach Bud Wilkinson called Neyland a "defensive genius."

Neyland's defensive theories were magnificent, Wallace Wade said. Magnificent, yet uncomplicated. "Keep the opponent's play contained inside the ends, do not allow pass completions, surround the football with orange jerseys, gang tackle, exploit the kicking game," Neyland preached.

The soundness of his defensive theories can be seen in the NCAA record book (through 1989):

- Most consecutive regular season shutouts (17 in 1938-40).
- Most consecutive regular season quarters holding opponents scoreless (71 in 1938-40).
- Fewest points allowed in a single season (none in 1939-shared with others).
- The last team to hold opposition scoreless during regular season.

Furthermore, Tennessee's opponents were held scoreless 106 times in the 173 games Neyland's teams won. And eight of his 21 teams were undefeated.

Neyland's passion for the kicking game, both coverage and returns, was perhaps best exemplified by the 1950-51 teams. Neyland devoted hour after hour of practice time to the long kick return. In 1950, Bert Rechichar returned punts of 72 yards against Southern Mississippi and of 100 yards against Washington and Lee. In 1951, Billy Blackstock led the nation in punt return average (25.9 yards per kick), still the NCAA major college record in 1990.

Neyland preached blocking and tackling—and execution. And Tennessee's current head coach, John Majors, says those underlying basics are still the foundation of the game, even with the multiple offenses and complex defensive schemes of today.

"I still use those old maxims I learned at Tennessee as a player, starting with 'The team that makes the fewest mistakes usually wins.'" Majors said in his autobiography. "The things that were true in General Neyland's time are just as true today." "His monuments are everywhere," sportscaster Lindsey Nelson said. "Bob Neyland was football's greatest coach. His impact on the game was the most widely felt and the least publicized of all who have contributed to it. Thousands of players and coaches, unaware of Bob Neyland, have exploited his theories and practices on defense. His positive philosophy has been adopted and passed on by the scores of men who have sought and succeeded in making a life's work of teaching others what they were taught by General Neyland."

Colonel Earl "Red" Blaik, coach of Army's national championship teams in 1944-45, considered Neyland one of the three best coaches in football history. "General Neyland ranks with two other great fundamentalists in football—Jock Sutherland and Gil Dobie," Blaik said. "His legacy to the game is to be found in the number of fine coaches in high school and college football who played under him. From the day he became a head coach, he became a force for a better college game."

One of Neyland's greatest admirers was Fritz Crisler, the great Michigan coach whose 18-year record (1930-47) was 116-32-9. They were contemporaries and served together on the NCAA football rules committee. Crisler called Neyland one of the "great soldiers" of football.

Ara Parseghian, who coached Notre Dame to two national championships, said Neyland's field position philosophy became a key element in football tactics. "He brought a military presence to the game with his theories about field position," Parseghian said. "In other words, where you are on the field has much to do with play selection. Field position and the [defensive] tactics that are employed by most coaches today are those taught by Neyland."

Carl Snavely, the former North Carolina coach whose teams had faced Tennessee many times, said Neyland was "a leader of unsurpassed stature . . . a cherished and respected friend."

Dick Hitt, a Tennessee assistant coach in the mid-1950s and later manager of Memorial Stadium in Jackson, Mississippi, said Neyland knew more football than any other coach who ever lived. "General Neyland was America's greatest scholar of football."

A few months before his death, Neyland had approached University of Tennessee administrators about establishing a program to attract outstanding scholars.

"Neyland was an outstanding student at West Point, and he believed in scholarship. He believed in doing what was right," said university trustee Tom Elam, a lawyer and retired army colonel who had been one of Neyland's student team managers in the early 1930s.

"General Neyland came to [President] Andy Holt and Harold Read, our vice president for finance, about using athletic department funds or soliciting contributions to set up the scholarship endowment," said Dr. Edward J. Boling, then the vice president for development and later the president of the university.

"It was his dream that the university offer four-year academic scholarships to students with outstanding academic and leadership qualities," Boling said. "He really wanted to do something for academics, to demonstrate the athletic department's interest in academics."

Neyland suggested that football and basketball players not be eligible for the new scholarships, but that participants in other sports be eligible if they had outstanding academic records. In his mind, the parameters were logical. The football and basketball players were receiving full scholarships anyway, but many of the athletes in the non-revenue sports were not. Most importantly, however, Neyland wanted the athletics department to help academically outstanding students who were not participating in athletics for the university.

"I had the impression from talking with him that he simply wanted to help students other than athletes," Boling said.

Responsibility for implementing Neyland's wishes fell to Boling and his top development officer, Charles Brakebill. Among those who served on the national advisory committee for the Neyland Scholarship Fund were General Douglas MacArthur, motion picture producer Clarence Brown, Dallas journalist Felix McKnight, *Look* magazine sports editor Tim Cohane, Stokely-Van Camp president William B. Stokely, Jr., Knoxville industrialist Herman "Breezy" Wynn, and coaches Bear Bryant of Alabama, Bud Wilkinson of Oklahoma, Fritz Crisler of Michigan, Wally Butts of Georgia, and Dana Bible of Texas, and, of course, Neyland's dear friend, Wallace Wade of Duke. "I am honored to serve . . . in memory of a great man," Wade told UT President Andy Holt.

The campaign to raise the Neyland endowment fund began on October 20, 1962, the day of the Alabama game, when the stadium, recently named Neyland Stadium, was dedicated in a pre-game ceremony.

The first Neyland scholarships were awarded in 1963 to Ann Baker (Furrow) of Maryville, Tennessee, who later served on the board of trustees for the university, and Robert English Allen of Columbia, Tennessee. Each year since then, the university has awarded four Neyland scholarships, provided by funds from the athletics department as Neyland intended.

The late U.S. District Judge William E. Miller, a member of the University of Tennessee board of trustees, greatly admired Neyland the scholar, Neyland the soldier, and Neyland the coach. "I regard him as one of the greatest influences that has ever been brought to bear on the affairs of the University of Tennessee," Miller said.

"No man ever carved his name deeper into the football history of a university than Bob Neyland did at Tennessee," said Nashville's Fred Russell. "He was a person of action and discipline."

"Tennessee and the nation will never again see a Bob Neyland," wrote Austin White of the *Chattanooga News-Free Press.* "His record as a military leader, an engineer, and a coach reflect the personal philosophy of a man who did not come here to tie. He played to win."

"He'd win," said Duke's Wallace Wade, two decades after Neyland's death. "He'd adapt to the game of football as it is played today. He'd win today, just like he always did."

The Neyland Scrapbook

PART IX

Andy Kozar, a star fullback on the last three teams Neyland coached(1950-52), remembered the attention he received from Neyland after suffering a broken collar bone as a freshman. Kozar, from the coal-mining town of St. Michael, Pennsylvania, was one of seven children whose father died when Andy was 12. Andy's two oldest brothers worked in the mines so he could get an education. Kozar escaped death from spinal meningitis in 1945 and was told he would never play football again, but he did—the next fall.

Following his freshman year injury at Tennessee, Kozar began to hear from coaches at other schools—telling him that he would not play at Tennessee and that they would like for him to transfer to their schools.

"I was in the little student infirmary there on campus when General Neyland walked in," Kozar said. "He told me that, even though I might never play a single minute for Tennessee, he wanted me to get well and remain at Tennessee. He said I would have a scholarship as long as I remained there, and to go ahead and get my degree."

Kozar recovered, helped Neyland's teams win 29 games in 1950-52, and went on to earn a Ph.D. at the University of Michigan. He returned to the University of Tennessee and, for many years conducted research, taught, and served as an administrative assistant to the president of the university.

Neyland was all business on the day of a game, and several people tell about a confrontation between Neyland and CBS sportscaster Ted Husing immediately prior to the 1939 Tennessee-Alabama game.

Ted Husing interviews Neyland on radio in 1939.

George Mooney, the last Vol Network "Voice of the Vols" in the Neyland era, says he heard the story from Neyland himself in the mid-1950s.

Neyland, of course, hated to waste time with reporters who asked irrelevant questions. He was not fond of spending much time with reporters under any circumstances, although a few reporters were his close friends. At any rate, shortly before the kickoff, Husing sent an emissary down to the field to talk to Neyland.

"Mr. Husing wants you to come up to the broadcast booth for a pregame interview on the air," the emissary said.

Neyland responded that he was about

to take his team back into the dressing room and did not have time to go up to the press box.

"But Mr. Neyland," the aide is said to have protested, "Mr. Husing is about to go on the air. He needs you now."

To which Neyland answered: "Tell Mr. Husing to kiss my ass. I have a game to coach."

The same story is told by author Tim Cohane in his book *Great CollegeFootball Coaches of the Twenties and Thirties.* The only difference in the two accounts is the quote attributed to Neyland. In Cohane's version, Neyland is quoted: "Tell Ted Husing to go to hell."

Neyland and Major Jack Dempsey in Calcutta, 1945.

During World War II, when Neyland was commanding general of the port of Calcutta, former world heavyweight boxing champion Jack Dempsey, an army major, paid him a visit. Dempsey had been champ in 1919-26.

"I honestly believe I could have beaten Jack Dempsey for the championship," Neyland told Ed Harris and SEC commissioner Bernie Moore one night in Lexington, Kentucky. "I would have fought him like [Gene] Tunney did in later years and won the title at Chicago. It would be a jab, jab affair and keeping out of reach from Dempsey's dynamite." Dempsey and Neyland became friends during World War II. And after the war, whenever Neyland was in New York City, the two would visit at Dempsey's restaurant in midtown Manhattan.

Atlanta columnist Furman Bisher, after Neyland's return from the war, wrote about Neyland's ability to build winning football teams with Tennessee-bred players. "Tennessee loves its Neyland because he's shown the football world that a coach could thrive on home-grown talent," Bisher wrote.

"Year after year he's taken boys out of the hills around Knoxville and made the rest of the country say 'uncle.' An occasional carpet-bagger will drift in, settle down and make a name for himself, but as a whole Tennessee is kept pure for Tennesseans."

Neyland and A. C. "Scrappy" Moore were long-time friends—from the late 1920s when Scrappy was an assistant to head coach Frank Thomas at the University of Chattanooga. Thomas had played for Knute Rockne at Notre Dame and therefore, as expected, used Rockne's Notre Dame box formation. Red Drew, who succeeded Thomas at Chattanooga, and ultimately Moore, who took over for Drew, also used the Notre Dame box. For 15 seasons, from 1939 through 1957, Tennessee's schedule had Chattanooga the week before the Alabama game. Neyland had thought it a good idea to play Chattanooga, which used the Notre Dame box, a week before playing Alabama, which also used the Notre Dame box.

But Thomas retired after the 1946 season, and his successor at Alabama, Red Drew, installed the T-formation in 1947.

Lindsey Nelson related the following story about Neyland's phone call to Scrappy Moore at Chattanooga after Drew installed the "T."

"Scrappy, do you like playing us the second Saturday in October?" Neyland asked.

"Hell, yes," Scrappy replied. "It makes our budget."

After a long pause, Neyland spoke again: "Scrappy, did you ever consider switching to the T-formation?"

The next season, Scrappy Moore's Chattanooga Moccasins ran the T-formation offense the week before Tennessee faced it against Alabama.

Neyland and Lindsey Nelson, 1950.

Andy Kozar, Bert Rechichar, Jack Stroud, Hank Lauricella, and Herky Payne on the sideline with Neyland in 1950.

Neyland insisted that his players remain seated on sideline benches during the game. "The only players who stood were those called to the general's side or those being sent into the game," ex-Vol Bob Davis said.

"He sat there in his little straight chair, watching the game, andeverybody was behind him," Lauricella said. "The offensive players were seated on one side of the 50, the defensive players on the other. The general knew exactly where to find any player he wanted."

Jim Haslam, the captain of Neyland's last team, remembered how calm the general was during the game. "I remember a New York writer asking him how he could remain so calm during a close game," Haslam said. "And General Neyland replied, 'I have prepared my team for any eventuality. There is nothing for me to do now except sit back and watch them execute.

Gus Manning, Tennessee's sports information director during the latter part of Neyland's career, recalled that the general was not above using some timely gamesmanship to gain an edge.

Adolph Rupp, Kentucky's legendary basketball coach, and Neyland were good friends.

"On the week of a Tennessee-Kentucky game, when Bear Bryant was up there [at Kentucky], Neyland would call Adolph and say, 'With all that material, Bryant ought to beat us two or three touchdowns,'" Manning said. "Neyland knew Adolph would run to the media because Adolph couldn't stand Bryant anyway. The media would print that, and it'd make Bryant so damned mad."

Peggy and Bob Neyland loved the game of bridge. It tested their intelligence. The Neylands frequently invited another couple, sometimes three other couples, to their home for an evening of dinner and bridge.

Peggy and the General at their home in Sarasota,

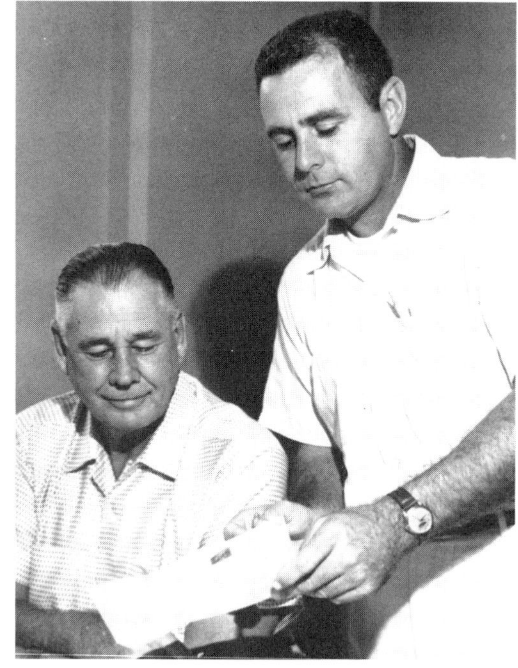

General Neyland and sports information director Gus Manning, about 1956.

Lewis Neyland remembered one episode that clearly illustrated his mother was a fierce competitor too.

"They both were excellent bridge players, but Dad would always tell Mother to bid correctly and let him do the 'fooling around' to get to the final contract," Lewis said.

Then, after the war, Peggy began going to New York City once or twice a year—to shop for clothes and see old friends she had known when she worked for a publishing company before she and Bob met.

"On one of those trips, some friends introduced her to the Cavendish Club where all the great bridge pros—Jacoby, Goren, Culbertson—played," Lewis said.

The Cavendish Club members instantly liked Peggy and her spunkiness, and they recognized her talent for the game. So her trips to New York, for a while, became a little more frequent. And on each occasion she played at the table with Goren or Jacoby or other Cavendish Club members. They welcomed her with open arms.

One night back in Knoxville, as a bridge game was about to begin, Neyland gave Peggy her usual instructions—to bid normally and let him take the bidding risks. But Peggy startled everybody.

"Now, let me tell you something, Mr. Neyland," she said firmly. "The days of me playing the straight hand and you messing around are all over. I'd prefer that you play the straight hand and let me do the fooling around."

And that is how they played thereafter. "Mother and Dad were very competitive, and she didn't like to take a back seat to him on anything."

Coming out of the shower room one day after practice, Neyland summoned defensive tackle Bill "Pug" Pearman who was still soapy. "You know, Pug, I was a heavyweight champ at West Point. Let me show you," Neyland said. "Brace yourself."

With that, Neyland delivered a straight left jab to Pearman's shoulder. But Pug's shoulder was slick with soap, and Neyland's punch slipped off the shoulder, caught Pearman on the chin, and decked him.

Shortly after Neyland's retirement from coaching, some members of the university faculty openly criticized the academic performance of the school's athletes. The faculty spoke of a double standard, poor scholarship and lack of progress toward a degree. Neyland responded: "The athletic department cheerfully and proudly admits a 'double standard' in its own operations. We say to our scholarship men: 'You must behave yourself as students and athletes should; you must attend classes and make satisfactory marks; you must strive diligently and loyally to carry out instructions from the university.'"

Heavyweight boxing champion at West Point, 1914, 1915, and 1916.

Then Neyland went to the heart of the double standard issue.

"You can be a good student and a poor athlete and remain in good grace; you can be a poor but passing student and a good athlete and stay on a probationary status; but you can't be a poor student and a poor athlete and get by. This is a double standard because our judgments on 'poor' and 'good' remain elastic and are tailored to fit the individuals concerned. This, however, is done by every other department in the university," he said.

"We want all our boys to graduate. But . . . are not former students but not graduates such as Wyatt, Wynn, Hickman, Dodd, McEver, Feathers, et al, men who have brought national fame to the school?

"We feel that the athletic department is far tougher on its athletes than any other department, or the university as a whole.

Memories of great players from the early teams. Clockwise from upper left: Bobby Dodd, Herman Hickman, Beattie Feathers, and Gene McEver.

Our standard of behavior, of diligence, of loyalty, of discipline and, in most cases, of scholarship are higher and more strictly enforced. In the nature of things, we HAVE to know our athletes infinitely better than any other department head could possibly know the great numbers of students with whom he has to deal.

"There are certain elements in our faculty that approach this question in the light of a battle between the 'lowbrow professional athlete' and the 'educational' faculty. This approach is truly hysterical; in most cases this group is in ignorance of the facts cited above; in other cases some of its members are blindly convinced that grades constitute a true index of student ability. . . .

"Everyone should know that one instructor will give a 'D' where another would give a 'C' or even a 'B.' Also that a 'B' at Mississippi could easily be an 'F' at West Point or MIT. This element also loses sight of, or chooses to ignore, the indisputable fact that coaching athletes is just as much an educational process as teaching sociology."

Robert Reese Neyland III, born February 17, 1892.

Neyland home, Greenville, Texas, circa 1900.

Young Robert Neyland, sitting on the steps on the far left, graduated from Greenville High School in 1910. Photograph taken about 1906.

Texas A&M baseball team, 1911. Neyland is on the far right.

1914 Army football squad; First Row: Hodgson, Coffin, Prichard (Capt.), Benedict, Hobbs. Second Row: Britton, Van Fleet, Bradley, Parker, Ford, Neyland, Goodman, Harmon. Third Row: Merillat, Larkin, McEwan, Weyand, Butler, Kelly, Woodruff. Back Row: Pendleton (Mgr.), Hess, O'Hare, Meacham, Herrick, Timberlake, Tully, Crane (Asst. Mgr.)

Corporal Robert R. Neyland, 1915, United States Military Academy.

Ripley cartoon, 1915.

Bob Neyland, Army end, 1915.

On the mound for Army, 1915.

Cartoon from the Washington Star, 1915.

Neyland, beaned early in the 1916 game, recovered to pitch the Cadets to victory over Navy for the fourth time in as many years.

Bill Britton, Omar Bradley, Bob Neyland, 1916.

Neyland back at West Point, second from left in second row, 1921.

Ada Fitch "Peggy" Neyland, photograph circa 1922.

1925 University of Tennessee coaching staff: Neyland, second from left, assistant to M. B. Banks, far right.

Neyland's first staff at Tennessee, 1926: Bob Neyland, with assistants Paul Parker, Lenox Baker, and Bill Britton.

Still an athlete, 1928.

Little Bob, 1930.

Paul Parker and Bob Neyland on the sidelines about 1934.

Neyland (in white) reviewing troops at the farewell ceremony for his departure from Panama, 1935.

Knoxville News-Sentinel cartoon celebrates Major Neyland's return to coaching.

Neyland observing punting practice, 1936 or 1937.

Pursuing favorite pastime, mid 1930s.

On the sidelines during the 20-7 victory over Clemson, 1938.

George Cafego, Neyland, and Babe Wood, 1938.

At the pre-game festivities for the 1940 Rose Bowl: producer-director Clarence Brown, Neyland, actress Florence Rice, and her father, renowned sportswriter Grantland Rice.

Lewis and Bobby Neyland and their dad, 1939.

1940 coaching staff, First Row: Hugh Faust, Bob Woodruff; Second Row: John Barnhill, John Mauer, Bill Murrell, Bill Britton, Neyland.

Lewis and Bobby wait with Peggy, while the Colonel serves his country.

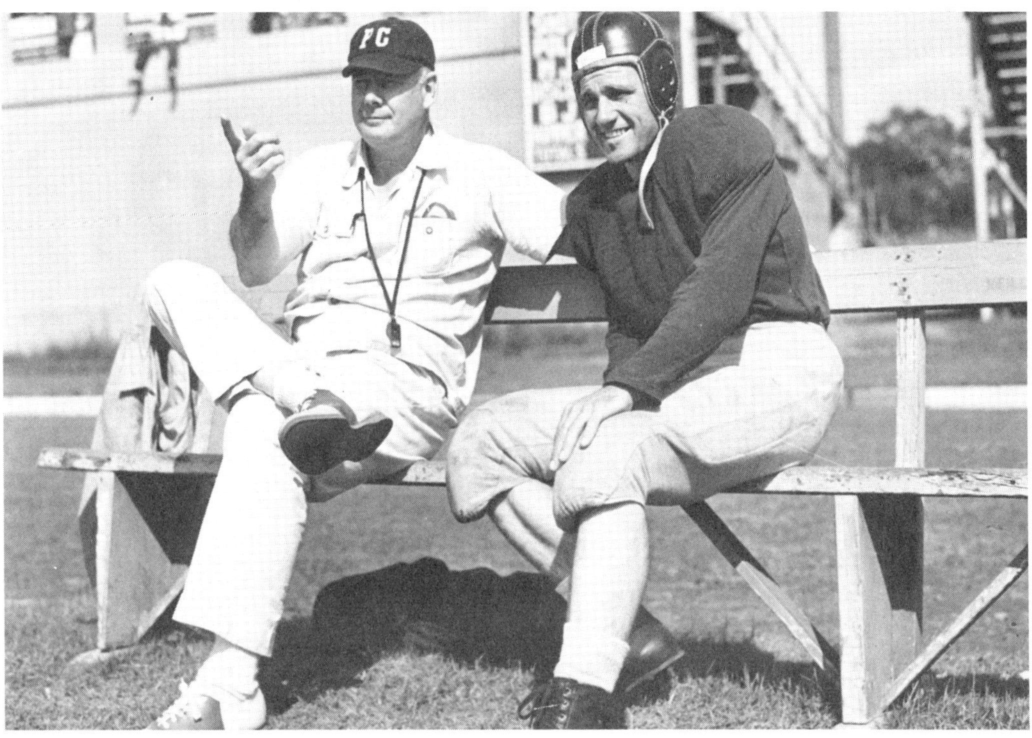

Lieutenant Colonel Neyland coaching the East All-Stars for the army in 1942.

Neyland and his army assistant coaches: Dr. Robert Brashear, Herman Hickman, Neyland, Mickey O'Brien, and Murray Warmath, 1942.

Brigadier General Neyland saying goodbye to Lieutenant General Dan Sultan at Dum Dum Airport, near Calcutta, 1945.

Neyland, second from right, and army brass relaxing in India.

The General draws a humorous parallel between gridiron and battlefield strategies.

Reconnoitering near Calcutta in 1944.

Returning from the war, 1946.

The victorious Vols carry Neyland from the field after downing Kentucky, 13-6, in 1947.

General Neyland pauses during a 1947 practice to pose with Denver Crawford's son Ronnie.

An uncharacteristically animated Neyland entertains his team after defeating Alabama, 21-6, in 1948.

1950 coaching staff; Front row: Al Hust, L. B. "Farmer" Johnson, Neyland, Harvey Robinson, Ike Peel; Back Row: Ralph Chancey, Bill Hildebrand, Mickey O'Brien, Burr West, Chan Caldwell, Emmett Lowery.

Bob and his dad pause at practice in 1951.

On the sideline with Hank Lauricella and Jim Haslam in 1951.

General Neyland observes calisthenics during preparation for the 1951 Cotton Bowl.

The General and his troops celebrate their 20-14 victory over Texas in the 1951 Cotton Bowl.

Neyland and university president C. E. Brehm, left, receive the J. Hugh O'Donnell award, symbolic of the 1951 collegiate national championship, from J. Frank Miles of Notre Dame.

Gene McEver, Quinn Decker, Bobby Dodd, and Buddy Hackman, the stars of the 1928 backfield, flank the General at the 1953 celebration commemorating his retirement.

Bill Rives presents the distinguished service award to General Neyland from the Football Writers Association.

Athletics director Neyland in his office, circa 1955.

General Neyland congratulates sons Bob (receiving his law degree) and Lewis on graduation day, 1956.

Classmates and teammates, colleagues and friends: Bill Britton, Bob Neyland, and Paul Parker.

Tennessee Governor Frank Clements presents the Helms Hall of Fame Citation in 1953.

Reminiscing with former player and Tennessee coach Bowden Wyatt, 1960.

Florida fishing, around 1960.

"General Robert Reese Neyland now becomes a legend." Lewis and Peggy Neyland, and the General's nephew, Lieutenant Colonel Mayo Neyland, Jr., at the funeral.

Alabama assistant coach Carney Laslie, former Wake Forest coach D. C. "Peahead" Walker, and Paul "Bear" Bryant pay their respects.

1921.

1956.

1989.

Growing with success. Of all the measures of General Robert R. Neyland's legacy, there is none more visible than the extraordinary expansion of the Tennessee football stadium.

General Bob Neyland's football principles:

•The head coach must remain a little aloof from the players and, to a certain extent, from the coaches.

•The first qualification of a head coach is to possess a cool head so that he may see things in their true perspective. There are things in football of which the head coach alone can comprehend the importance.

•His first principle must be to calculate what he must do to win, and see if he has the necessary means to surmount the obstacles with which the enemy will oppose him. Once the decision is made, see that all do their respective parts to earn the victory.

•Football is composed of nothing but accidents. The great art is to profit from such accidents. This is the mark of genius.

•It follows that all plans must be made to minimize our own mistakes and to magnify the effect of the opponents' mistakes.

•Nature of the struggle between equal teams. The difference: never physical, but invariably mental.

•Important to keep the squad eternally aware of the very nature of football and so not dismayed when things are going wrong.

•To defeat a weak opponent is not the problem. The problem is to win when he is as good or better than you.

•Almost all close games are lost by the losers, not won by the winners.

•Proper mental stance on game day stems almost entirely from attitudes built up over a considerable period of time. Pre-game harangues, as a rule, do more harm than good. Inspiration at zero hour is a poor thing to rely on.

Before a game, Neyland wrote a few of his "maxims," or rules, on the blackboard for the Tennessee players to see as they left the locker room to begin the game. Some of his favorites were:

1. The team that makes the fewest mistakes will win.

2. Play for and make the breaks, and when one comes your way—score!

3. If at first the game, or breaks, go against you, don't let up. Put on more steam.

4. Protect our kickers, our QB, our lead, and our ball game.

5. Ball, oskie, cover, block, cut and slice, pursue and gang tackle . . . for this is the winning edge. (Neyland introduced Tennessee players to "oskie" the first day of practice. "When the other team puts the ball in the air with a pass, it belongs to us. It's ours, and we go get it," he said. "And when you intercept it, yell 'oskie-wow-wow' and that'll let your teammates know we've got the ball. They'll pick out a man and block him.")

6. Press the kicking game. Here is where the breaks are made.

7. Carry the fight to our opponent and keep it there for 60 minutes.

In the ledger book where he kept private notes to himself, Neyland listed his 10 most intense memories at Tennessee:

1928—Tennessee 16, Alabama 13. Gene McEver returned the opening kickoff 98 yards for a touchdown.

1928—Tennessee 13, Florida 12. Bobby Dodd deflected an extra point pass that would have tied the game in the fourth quarter.

1930—Tennessee 13, Vanderbilt 0. Dodd's touchdown pass to BuddyHackman from the Vol end zone. The play covered 78 yards from scrimmage.

1932—Tennessee 16, Duke 13. Herman "Breezy" Wynn kicked the game-winning 28-yard field goal late in the game. The snap from center was mishandled, and the ball was laying on its side when Wynn kicked it.

1932—Tennessee 0, Vanderbilt 0. On a play beginning at Tennessee's 28-yard line, Vol tailback Beattie Feathers caught a pass from Pug Vaughan and scored a touchdown, but referee Battle Begley ruled that Feathers had stepped out of bounds near the 50 and nullified the score.

1936—Tennessee 7, Kentucky 6. Phil Dickens's 70-yard punt return to the 2 set up a Vol touchdown, and Dick Porter's extra point won the game.

1936—Tennessee 0, Alabama 0. Marion Perkins's goal-line tackle kept Alabama from scoring late in the first half.

1938—Tennessee 17, Oklahoma 0 in the Orange Bowl. Tennessee pre-vailed in a game marred by frequent fights.

1957— Tennessee 3, Texas A&M 0. Bobby Gordon's bone-jarring tackle that stopped touchdown-bound John David Crow.

1959—Tennessee 14, LSU 13. Bill Majors, Charlie Severance, Wayne Grubb, and Joe Schaffer stopped LSU all-American Billy Cannon's run for a two-point extra point.

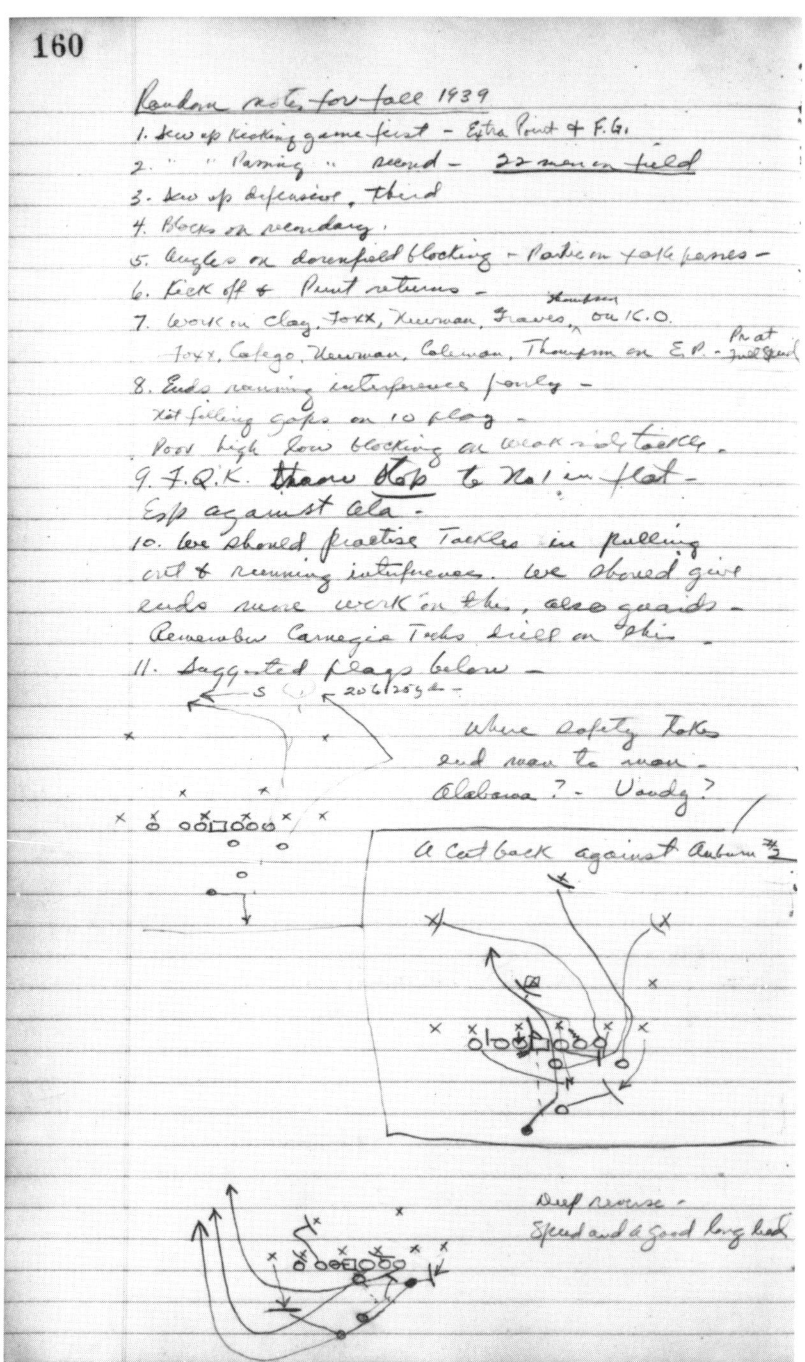

160

Random notes for fall 1939

1. Sew up kicking game first – Extra Point & F.G.
2. " " Passing " second – 22 men on field
3. Sew up defensive, third
4. Blocks on secondary.
5. Angles on downfield blocking – Particular on forward passes –
6. Kick off & Punt returns –
7. Work on Clay, Foxx, Newman, Graves, Thompson on K.O.
   Foxx, Cafego, Newman, Coleman, Thompson on E.P. – Pr at full speed
8. Ends running interference poorly –
   Not filling gaps on 10 play –
   Poor high low blocking on weak side tackle.
9. F.Q.K. throw flop to No 1 in flat –
   Esp against Ala.
10. We should practice Tackles in pulling out & running interference. We should give ends more work on this, also guards –
    Remember Carnegie Tech's drill on this –
11. Suggested plays below –

Where safety takes end man to man. Alabama? – Vandy?

A Cutback against Auburn #2

Deep reverse – Speed and a good long lead

The Neyland ledger, 1939.

The tailback run-pass option was a staple of Bob Neyland's playbook throughout his head coaching career. He introduced it in his first year at Tennessee, and it produced at least 50 touchdowns—sometimes on the run, sometimes the pass.

The 1939 game with Auburn was scoreless in the fourth quarter when Vol tailback Johnny Butler called the run-pass option. He took the snap from center, started left at full speed, faked a cut inside the end, then swung outside. He picked up an escort of blockers. At midfield, he was hit and knocked off balance, but he recovered

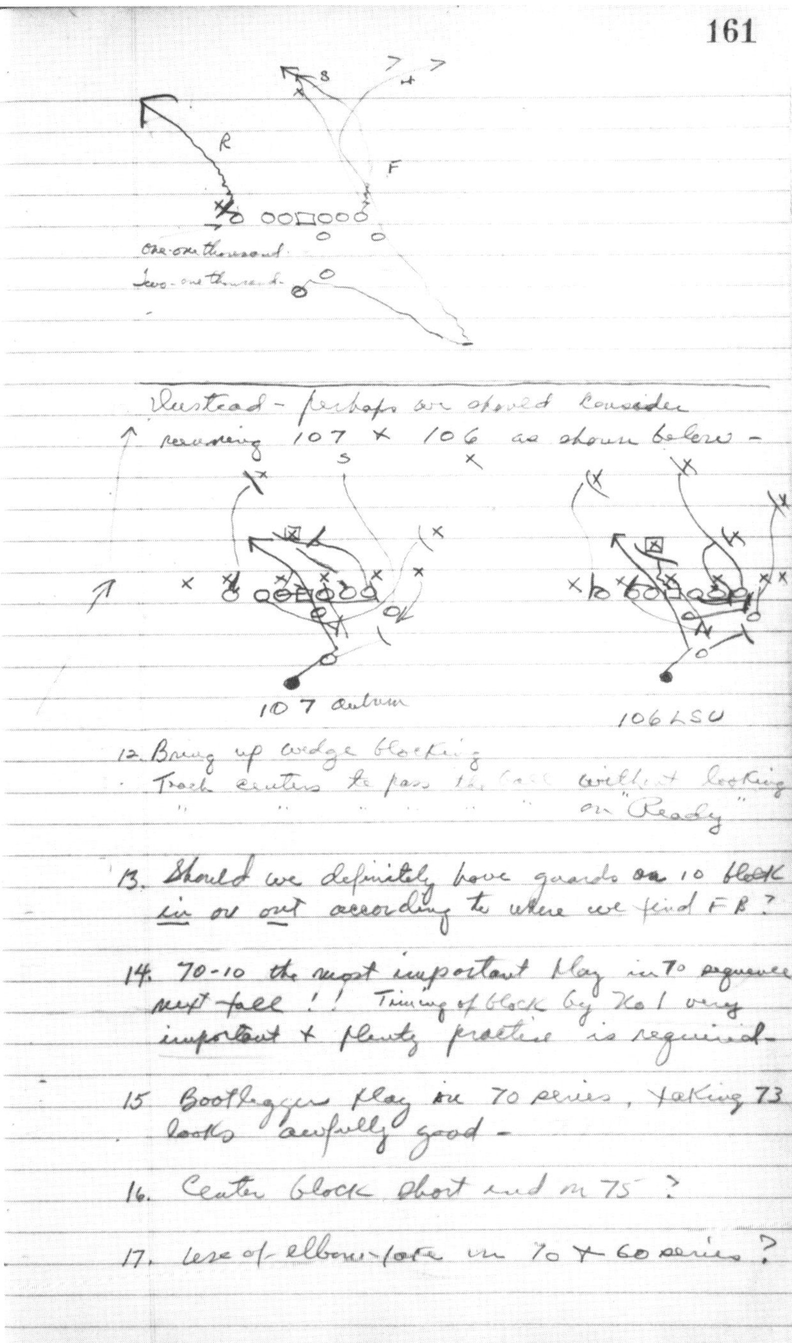
161

One-one thousand
Two-one thousand

Instead – perhaps we should consider reversing 107 & 106 as shown below –

107 Auburn

106 LSU

12. Bring up wedge blocking
Teach centers to pass the ball without looking
" " " " " " on "Ready"

13. Should we definitely have guards on 10 block in or out according to where we find FB?

14. 70-10 the most important play in 70 sequence next fall!! Timing of block by No 1 very important & plenty practice is required.

15. Bootlegger play on 70 series, taking 73 looks awfully good –

16. Center block short end on 75?

17. Use of elbow-lock in 70 & 60 series?

and actually ran about five yards backwards. Retaining his balance, he found he had a clear field and reached the end zone to give Tennessee a 7-0 victory and an invitation to the Rose Bowl.

On the same play in 1930, Bobby Dodd threw to Buddy Hackman for the first touchdown of a 13-6 victory over Florida. In 1946, Walter Slater passed to Bill Hillman for the winning touchdown against Duke. And in 1947 against Kentucky, Hubert Becker passed to Alan Fielden for the winning touchdown, again off the run-pass option.

Before cinematography became practical for recording game action, Neyland used still photographs to analyze team and individual performance. The above pictures, with Neyland's handwritten notes, are from the 1928 and 1929 seasons.

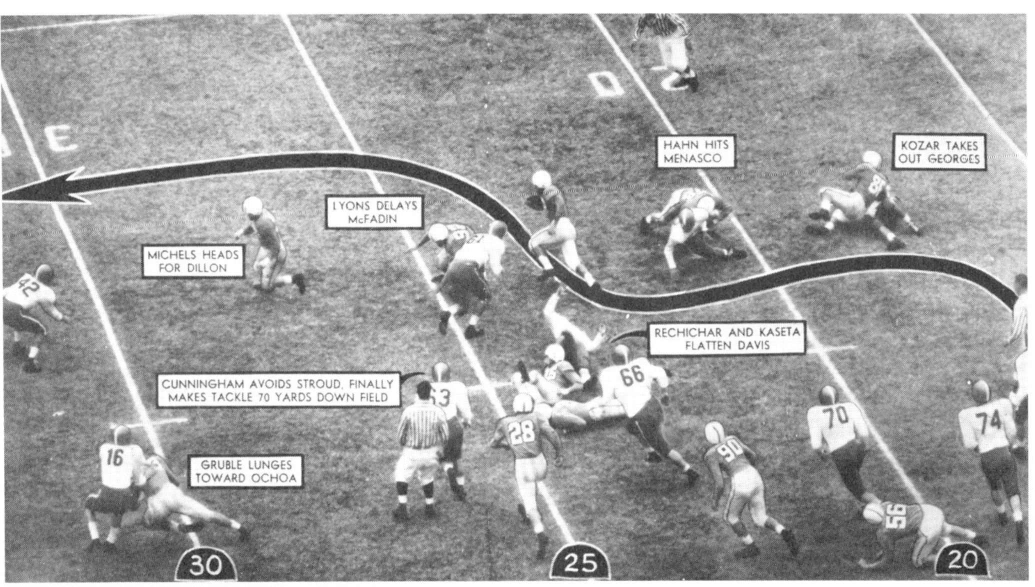

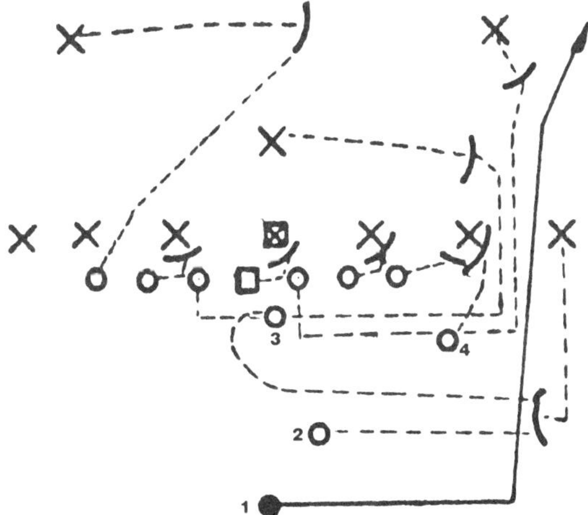

RUNNER GOES INSIDE END

In the old single-wing, which bears striking resemblance to the still-popular pro-style "shotgun" formation, the backfield was made up of 1.) a tailback, 2.) a fullback, 3.) a quarterback, or blockingback, and 4.) a wingback. Neyland's play #10, illustrated here from the 1928 play chart on the following pages, was the bread and butter of his precise single-wing attack for decades. Considered a relative dinosaur by proponents of the more modern T and split-T formations, the single-wing nevertheless suited options he needed to wage battle with opposing defenses. One of those options was the fake quick-kick, which Hank Lauricella turned into a 75-yard gain to set up Tennessee's first touchdown in the 1951 Cotton Bowl victory over Texas. Note the textbook line-of-scrimmage and downfield blocking, a trademark of Neyland teams.

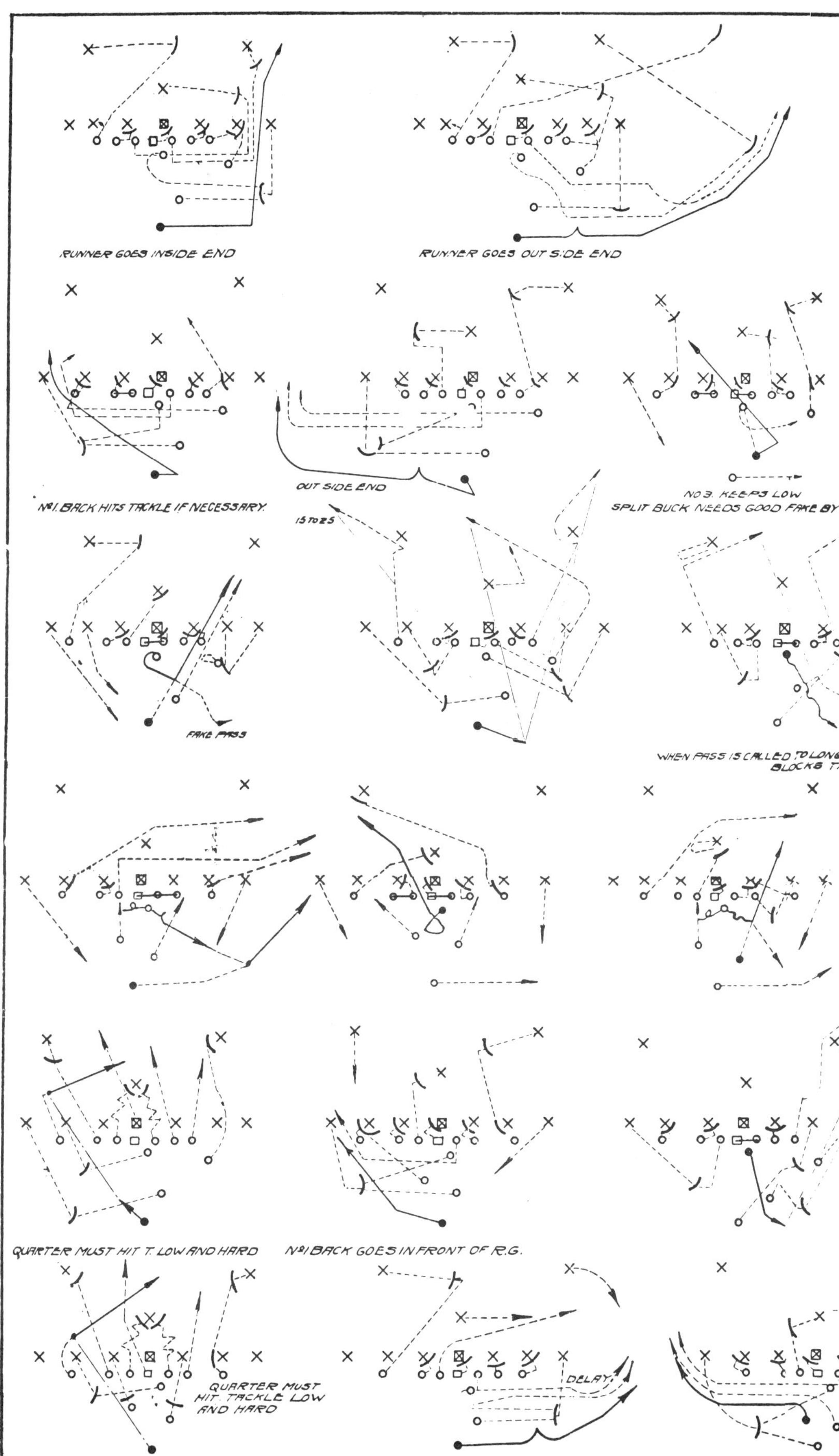
RUNNER GOES INSIDE END
RUNNER GOES OUT SIDE END
OUT SIDE END
NO 3. KEEPS LOW
SPLIT BUCK NEEDS GOOD FAKE BY N
Nº1. BACK HITS TACKLE IF NECESSARY.
15 TO 25
FAKE PASS
WHEN PASS IS CALLED TO LONG
BLOCKS TA
QUARTER MUST HIT T. LOW AND HARD
Nº1 BACK GOES IN FRONT OF R.G.
QUARTER MUST
HIT TACKLE LOW
AND HARD
DELAY

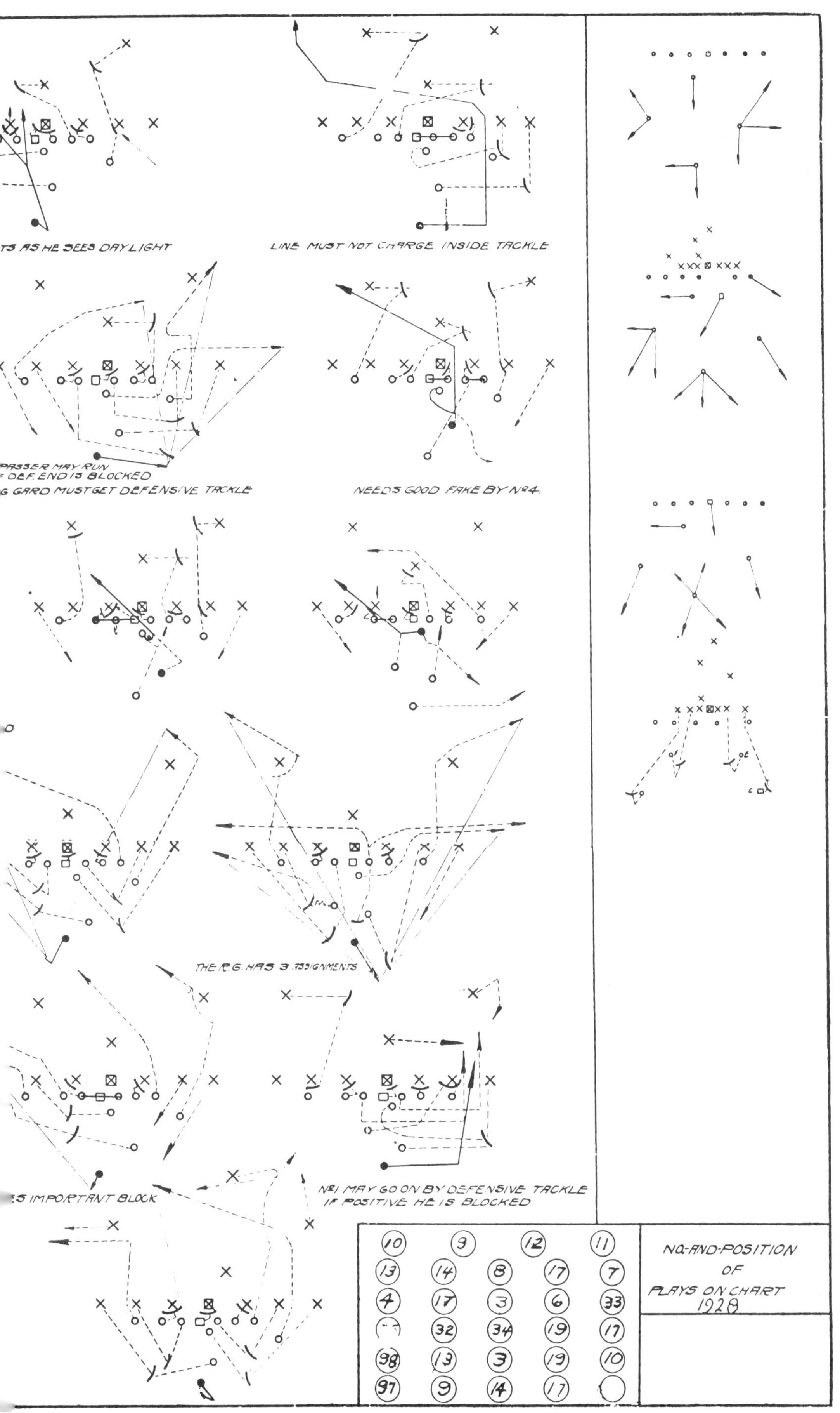
AS HE SEES DAYLIGHT
LINE MUST NOT CHARGE INSIDE TACKLE
PASSER MAY RUN
DEF. END IS BLOCKED
GARD MUST GET DEFENSIVE TACKLE
NEEDS GOOD FAKE BY Nº4.
THE R.G. HAS 3 ASSIGNMENTS
IMPORTANT BLOCK
Nº1 MAY GO ON BY DEFENSIVE TACKLE
IF POSITIVE HE IS BLOCKED
10 9 12 11
13 14 8 17 7
4 17 3 6 33
32 34 19 17
98 13 3 19 10
97 9 14 17
NO. AND POSITION OF PLAYS ON CHART
1928

NEYLAND STATISTICS

1926—Won 8, Lost 1

13	Carson-Newman	0	Knoxville	Sept. 25
34	North Carolina	0	Knoxville	Oct. 2
14	Louisiana St.	7	Baton Rouge	Oct. 9
6	Maryville	0	Knoxville	Oct. 15
30	Centre	7	Knoxville	Oct. 23
33	Miss. A&M	0	Starkville	Oct. 30
12	Sewanee	0	Knoxville	Nov. 6
3	Vanderbilt	20	Nashville	Nov. 13
6	Kentucky	0	Knoxville	Nov. 25
151		34		

1927—Won 8, Lost 0, Tied 1

33	Carson-Newman	0	Knoxville	Sept. 24
26	North Carolina	0	Chapel Hill	Oct. 1
7	Maryville	0	Knoxville	Oct. 8
21	Mississippi	7	Knoxville	Oct. 15
57	Transylvania	0	Knoxville	Oct. 22
42	Virginia	0	Knoxville	Oct. 29
32	Sewanee	12	Knoxville	Nov. 5
7	Vanderbilt	7	Knoxville	Nov. 12
20	Kentucky	0	Lexington	Nov. 24
245		26		

1928—Won 9, Lost 0, Tied 1

41	Maryville	0	Knoxville	Sept. 29
41	Centre	7	Knoxville	Oct. 6
13	Mississippi	12	Knoxville	Oct. 13
15	Alabama	13	Tuscaloosa	Oct. 20
26	Wash. & Lee	7	Knoxville	Oct. 27
57	Carson-Newman	0	Knoxville	Nov. 3
37	Sewanee	0	Knoxville	Nov. 10
6	Vanderbilt	0	Nashville	Nov. 17
0	Kentucky	0	Knoxville	Nov. 29
13	Florida	12	Knoxville	Dec. 8
249		51		

1929—Won 9, Lost 0, Tied 1

40	Centre	6	Knoxville	Sept. 28
20	Chattanooga	0	Chattanooga	Oct. 5
52	Mississippi	7	Knoxville	Oct. 12
6	Alabama	0	Knoxville	Oct. 19
30	Wash. & Lee	0	Roanoke	Oct. 26
27	Auburn	0	Knoxville	Nov. 2
73	Carson-Newman	0	Knoxville	Nov. 9
13	Vanderbilt	0	Knoxville	Nov. 16
6	Kentucky	6	Lexington	Nov. 28
54	South Carolina	0	Knoxville	Dec. 7
330		19		

1930—Won 9, Lost 1

54	Maryville	0	Knoxville	Sept. 27
18	Centre	0	Knoxville	Oct. 4
27	Mississippi	0	Knoxville	Oct. 11
6	Alabama	18	Tuscaloosa	Oct. 18
9	North Carolina	7	Knoxville	Oct. 25
27	Clemson	0	Knoxville	Nov. 1
34	Carson-Newman	0	Knoxville	Nov. 8
13	Vanderbilt	0	Nashville	Nov. 15
8	Kentucky	0	Knoxville	Nov. 27
13	Florida	6	Jacksonville	Dec. 6
209		31		

1931—Won 9, Lost 0, Tied 1

33	Maryville	0	Knoxville	Sept. 26
44	Clemson	0	Knoxville	Oct. 3
38	Mississippi	0	Knoxville	Oct. 10
25	Alabama	0	Knoxville	Oct. 17
7	North Carolina	0	Chapel Hill	Oct. 24
25	Duke	2	Knoxville	Oct. 31
31	Carson-Newman	0	Knoxville	Nov. 7
21	Vanderbilt	7	Knoxville	Nov.14
6	Kentucky	6	Lexington	Nov. 26
	New York Charity Game			
13	New York Univ.	0	New York	Dec. 5
243		15		

1932—Won 9, Lost 0, Tied 1

13	Chattanooga	0	Chattanooga	Sept. 24
33	Mississippi	0	Knoxville	Oct. 1
20	North Carolina	7	Knoxville	Oct. 8
7	Alabama	3	Birmingham	Oct. 15
60	Maryville	0	Knoxville	Oct. 22
16	Duke	13	Knoxville	Oct. 29
31	Miss. A&M	0	Knoxville	Nov. 5
0	Vanderbilt	0	Nashville	Nov. 12
26	Kentucky	0	Knoxville	Nov.24
32	Florida	13	Jacksonville	Dec. 3
238		36		

1933—Won 7, Lost 3

27	Virginia Tech	0	Knoxville	Sept. 30
20	Mississippi St.	0	Knoxville	Oct. 6
2	Duke	10	Durham	Oct. 13
6	Alabama	12	Knoxville	Oct. 21
13	Florida	6	Knoxville	Oct. 28
13	Geo. Wash.	0	Washington	Nov. 4
35	Mississippi	6	Knoxville	Nov. 11
33	Vanderbilt	6	Knoxville	Nov. 18
27	Kentucky	0	Lexington	Nov. 30
0	Louisiana St.	7	Baton Rouge	Dec. 9
176		47		

1934—Won 8, Lost 2

32	Centre	0	Knoxville	Sept. 29
19	North Carolina	7	Chapel Hill	Oct. 5
27	Mississippi	0	Knoxville	Oct. 13
6	Alabama	13	Birmingham	Oct. 20
14	Duke	6	Knoxville	Oct. 27
12	Fordham	13	New York	Nov. 3
14	Mississippi St.	0	Knoxville	Nov. 10
13	Vanderbilt	6	Nashville	Nov. 17
19	Kentucky	0	Knoxville	Nov. 29
19	Louisiana St.	13	Knoxville	Dec. 8
175		58		

1936—Won 6, Lost 2, Tied 2

13	Chattanooga	0	Knoxville	Sept. 26
6	North Carolina	14	Chapel Hill	Oct. 3

0	Auburn	6	Knoxville	Oct. 10
0	Alabama	0	Birmingham	Oct. 17
15	Duke	13	Knoxville	Oct. 24
46	Georgia	0	Athens	Oct. 31
34	Maryville	0	Knoxville	Nov. 7
26	Vanderbilt	13	Nashville	Nov. 14
7	Kentucky	6	Knoxville	Nov. 26
0	Mississippi	0	Memphis	Dec. 5
147		52		

1937—Won 6, Lost 3, Tied 1

32	Wake Forest	0	Knoxville	Sept. 25
27	Virginia Tech	0	Knoxville	Oct. 2
0	Duke	0	Durham	Oct. 9
7	Alabama	14	Knoxville	Oct. 19
32	Sewanee	0	Knoxville	Oct. 23
32	Georgia	0	Knoxville	Oct. 30
7	Auburn	20	Birmingham	Nov. 6
7	Vanderbilt	13	Knoxville	Nov. 13
13	Kentucky	0	Lexington	Nov. 25
32	Mississippi	0	Memphis	Dec. 4
189		47		

1938—Won 11, Lost 0

26	Sewanee	3	Knoxville	Sept. 24
20	Clemson	7	Knoxville	Oct. 1
7	Auburn	0	Knoxville	Oct. 8
13	Alabama	0	Birmingham	Oct. 15
44	The Citadel	0	Knoxville	Oct. 22
14	Louisiana St.	6	Knoxville	Oct. 29
45	Chattanooga	0	Knoxville	Nov. 5
14	Vanderbilt	0	Nashville	Nov. 12
46	Kentucky	0	Knoxville	Nov. 24
47	Mississippi	0	Memphis	Dec. 3
	Orange Bowl			
17	Oklahoma	0	Miami	Jan. 2, 1939
293		16		

1939—Won 10, Lost 1

13	N. Carolina St.	0	Raleigh	Sept. 29
40	Sewannee	0	Knoxville	Oct. 7
28	Chattanooga	0	Chattanooga	Oct. 14
21	Alabama	0	Knoxville	Oct. 21
17	Mercer	0	Knoxville	Oct. 28
20	Louisiana St.	0	Baton Rouge	Nov. 4
34	The Citadel	0	Knoxville	Nov. 11
13	Vanderbilt	0	Knoxville	Nov. 18
19	Kentucky	0	Lexington	Nov. 30
7	Auburn	0	Knoxville	Dec. 9
	Rose Bowl			
0	Southern Calif.	14	Pasadena	Jan.1,1940
212		14		

1940—Won 10, Lost 1

49	Mercer	0	Knoxville	Sept. 28
13	Duke	0	Knoxville	Oct. 5
53	Chattanooga	0	Knoxville	Oct. 12
27	Alabama	12	Birmingham	Oct. 19
14	Florida	0	Knoxville	Oct. 26
28	Louisiana St.	0	Knoxville	Nov. 2
41	Southwestern	0	Memphis	Nov. 9
41	Virginia	14	Knoxville	Nov. 16
33	Kentucky	0	Knoxville	Nov. 23
20	Vanderbilt	0	Nashville	Nov. 30
	Sugar Bowl			
13	Boston Col.	19	New Orleans	Jan. 1, 1941
332		45		

1946—Won 9,Lost 2

13	Georgia Tech	9	Knoxville	Sept. 28
12	Duke	7	Durham	Oct. 5
47	Chattanooga	7	Knoxville	Oct. 12
12	Alabama	0	Knoxville	Oct. 19
6	Wake Forest	19	Knoxville	Oct. 26
20	North Carolina	14	Knoxville	Nov. 2
18	Mississippi	14	Memphis	Nov. 9
33	Boston College	13	Boston	Nov. 16
7	Kentucky	0	Knoxville	Nov. 23
7	Vanderbilt	6	Nashville	Nov. 30
	Orange Bowl			
0	Rice	8	Miami	Jan. 1, 1947
175		97		

1947—Won 5, Lost 5

0	Georgia Tech	27	Atlanta	Sept. 27
7	Duke	19	Knoxville	Oct. 4
26	Chattanooga	7	Knoxville	Oct. 11
0	Alabama	10	Birmingham	Oct. 18
49	Tenn. Tech	0	Knoxville	Oct. 25
6	North Carolina	20	Chapel Hill	Nov. 1
13	Mississippi	43	Memphis	Nov. 8
38	Boston Col.	13	Knoxville	Nov. 15
13	Kentucky	6	Lexington	Nov. 22
12	Vanderbilt	7	Knoxville	Nov. 29
164		152		

1948—Won 4, Lost 4, Tied 2

6	Miss. State	21	Knoxville	Sept. 25
7	Duke	7	Durham	Oct. 2
26	Chattanooga	0	Knoxville	Oct. 9
21	Alabama	6	Knoxville	Oct. 16
41	Tennessee Tech	0	Knoxville	Oct. 23
7	North Carolina	14	Knoxville	Oct. 30
13	Georgia Tech	6	Atlanta	Nov. 6
13	Mississippi	16	Memphis	Nov. 13
0	Kentucky	0	Knoxville	Nov. 20
6	Vanderbilt	28	Nashville	Nov. 27
140		98		

1949—Won 7, Lost 2, Tied 1

10	Miss. State	0	Knoxville	Sept. 24
7	Duke	21	Knoxville	Oct. 1
39	Chattanooga	7	Knoxville	Oct. 8
7	Alabama	7	Birmingham	Oct. 15
36	Tenn. Tech	6	Knoxville	Oct. 22
35	North Carolina	6	Chapel Hill	Oct. 29
13	Georgia Tech	30	Knoxville	Nov. 5
35	Mississippi	7	Memphis	Nov. 12
6	Kentucky	0	Lexington	Nov. 19
26	Vanderbilt	20	Knoxville	Nov. 26
214		104		

1950—Won 11, Lost 1

56	Southern Miss.	0	Knoxville	Sept. 23
0	Miss. State	7	Starkville	Sept. 30
28	Duke	7	Durham	Oct. 7
41	Chattanooga	0	Knoxville	Oct. 14
14	Alabama	9	Knoxville	Oct. 21
27	Wash. & Lee	20	Knoxville	Oct. 28
16	North Carolina	0	Knoxville	Nov. 4
48	Tenn. Tech	14	Knoxville	Nov. 11
35	Mississippi	0	Knoxville	Nov. 18
7	Kentucky	0	Knoxville	Nov. 25
43	Vanderbilt	0	Nashville	Dec. 2
	Cotton Bowl			
20	Texas	14	Dallas	Jan. 1, 1951
335		71		

1951—Won 10, Lost 1

14	Miss. State	0	Knoxville	Sept. 29
26	Duke	0	Knoxville	Oct. 6
42	Chattanooga	13	Knoxville	Oct. 13
27	Alabama	13	Birmingham	Oct. 20
68	Tenn. Tech	0	Knoxville	Oct. 27
27	North Carolina	0	Chapel Hill	Nov. 3
60	Wash.-Lee	14	Knoxville	Nov. 10
46	Mississippi	21	Oxford	Nov. 17
28	Kentucky	0	Lexington	Nov. 24
35	Vanderbilt	27	Knoxville	Dec. 1
	Sugar Bowl			
13	Maryland	28	New Orleans	Jan. 1, 1952
386		116		

1952—Won 8, Lost 2, Tied 1

14	Miss. State	7	Memphis	Sept. 27
0	Duke	7	Durham	Oct. 4
26	Chattanooga	6	Knoxville	Oct. 11
20	Alabama	0	Knoxville	Oct. 18
50	Wofford	0	Knoxville	Oct. 25
41	North Carolina	14	Knoxville	Nov. 1
22	Louisiana St.	3	Baton Rouge	Nov. 8
26	Florida	12	Knoxville	Nov. 15
14	Kentucky	14	Knoxville	Nov. 22
46	Vanderbilt	0	Nashville	Nov. 29
	Cotton Bowl			
0	Texas	16	Dallas	Jan. 1, 1953
259		79		

NEYLAND'S 21-YEAR RECORD VS. ALL OPPONENTS

	WON	*LOST*	*TIED*
Alabama	12	5	2
Auburn	3	2	0
Boston College	2	1	0
Carson-Newman	6	0	0
Centre	5	0	0
Citadel	2	0	0
Clemson	3	0	0
Duke	8	4	2
Florida	6	0	0
Fordham	0	1	0
George Washington	1	0	0
Georgia	2	0	0
Georgia Tech	2	2	0
Kentucky	16	0	5
LSU	6	1	0
Maryland	0	1	0
Maryville	7	0	0
Mercer	2	0	0
Mississippi	14	2	1
Mississippi State	7	2	0
New York University	1	0	0
North Carolina	11	3	0
N. C. State	1	0	0
Oklahoma	1	0	0
Rice	0	1	0
Sewanee	6	0	0
South Carolina	1	0	0
Southern Cal	0	1	0
Southern Mississippi	1	0	0
Southwestern	1	0	0
Tennessee Tech	5	0	0
Texas	1	1	0
Transylvania	1	0	0
UT-Chattanooga	13	0	0
Vanderbilt	16	3	2
Virginia	2	0	0
Virginia Tech	2	0	0
Wake Forest	1	1	0
Washington and Lee	4	0	0
Wofford	1	0	0
Total	**173**	**31**	**12**

NEYLAND'S LETTERMEN

( ) *Denotes year when Neyland did not coach*

A
George Abernathy, 1926-27
Norbert J. Ackermann, Sr., 1939-40 [Capt.]
Ralph Adams, 1952
Malcolm Aiken, 1930-31-32 [Capt.]
Frank Alexander, 1950-51-52
John H. Allen, 1929-30-31
E. H. "Herc" Alley, 1927-28
Malcolm S. Anderson, 1932-33-34
Bob Andridge, 1938-39-40
Jack Armstrong, 1946-47-48
Doug Atkins, 1950-51-52
Alfred Austelle, 1934

B
Pryor E. Bacon, 1938-39
Howard H. Bailey, 1932-33-34
John W. "Skeeter" Bailey, 1938
Charles F. Baker, 1947-48-49
George Balitsaris, 1946-47-48
Mike Balitsaris, 1939-40-(41)
Bill "Moose" Barbish, 1951-52-(53)
Billy Barnes, 1937-38-39
John H. Barnhill, (1925)-26-27
Sam Bartholomew, 1937-38-39 [Capt.]
John D. Bayless, 1931-32-33
Hubert Becker, 1947
L. Phillip Beene, 1928-29-30
Joe Bender, [Mgr.] 1949
Ron Bergmeier, 1947-48-49
M. Bert Bibee, 1932-33
Bill Blackstock, 1951
Don Bordinger, 1951
Frank "Boomer" Boring, 1949-50-51
Harrison O. Bourkard, 1934-(35)
H. B. "Deke" Brackett, 1931-32-33
Fritz Brandt, 1928-29-30
Bobby Brengle, 1952-(53-54)
Tom Brixey, 1948-49
Albert Brooks, [Mgr.] 1932
W. Lloyd Broome, 1938, 1940
Earle W. Brown, 1939, (1945)
Herbert T. Brown, 1928-29-30
William J. Bryson, 1940
Robert E. Burgess, 1927
Elvin Butcher, (1925)-26-27
Dan Butler, 1951, (1953)
Johnny Butler, 1939-40-(41)
Joe T. Bybee, 1927
Ray Byrd, 1951-52

C
George Cafego, 1937-38-39
Chan Caldwell, (1945)-46-47
Earl Campbell, 1950-51-52
George Carter, 1950
Ralph Chancey, 1946-47-48-49 [Co-Capt.]
Ed Cifers, 1938-39-40
Jim Claxton, 1932-33-34
Boyd Clay, 1937-38-39
H. H. Clements, [Mgr.] 1930
Bob Cloninger, 1952-(53)
Leonard Coffman, 1937-38-39
Roger Coggins, 1948-49
James L. Coleman, 1938-39-40
W. C. Cooper, 1948-49-50
William G. Cox, 1929, 1931
George P. Craig, 1933-34-(35)
Denver Crawford, (1942), 1946-47 [Capt.]
Edwin S. Crawford, 1934-(35)
Frank J. Crawford, (1935)-36-37
Larry Crowson, 1951
Charles H. Cummins, 1949

D
Ted Daffer, 1949-50-51
Bob Davis, 1949-50-51
John "Tex" Davis, 1951-52
Quinn Decker, 1928-29-30
F. Woodrow Derryberry, (1935)-36
O. Merton Derryberry, 1930-31
W. Everett Derryberry, (1925), 1927
Phil Dickens, 1934-(35)-36
Theodore "Ty" Disney, 1929-30-31
Elmer Disspayne, 1939
Frank M. Ditmore, 1934-(35)
Russ Dobelstein, (1944-45)-46
Robert Lee "Bobby" Dodd, 1928-29-30
Richard Dodson, (1925)-26-27
Ken Donahue, 1949-50
Richard Dorsey, 1932-33-34
Joe Q. Dougherty, 1933, (1935)-36
Clark Dowling, [Mgr.] 1932-33
Ray Drost, (1942), 1946-47
Edwin Cheek Duncan, 1936-37-38

E
Don Edmiston, 1939-40-(41)
Ralph E. Eldred, 1936-37-38
Robert "Dink" Eldridge, [Mgr.] 1939-40
Ray Elkas, 1948-49
Frank S. Elliott, (1925), 1927
J. B. Ellis, 1931-32-33
James W. Elmore, (1925)-26-27
Harry Epperson, (1935)-36
Dick Ernsberger, 1949-50-51

F
Hugh Faust, 1930
Beattie Feathers, 1931-32-33
Gene Felty, 1949-50
Alan Fielden, 1947-48-49
James I. Finney, 1928-29
Bob Fisher, 1951-52-(53)
Hector Flenniken, [Mgr.] 1933
Charles Flora, 1949-50
Howard Ford, [Mgr.] 1931
Nate Fourman, [Mgr.] 1950
W. S. "Monk" Fowler, 1947
Bob Foxx, 1938-39-40
John Francis, (1941), 1946-47
Milton Frank, 1931-32-33
Richard Frank, [Mgr.] 1936
John Franklin, 1930-31-32
Mack Franklin, 1951-52-(53) [Capt.]
Ben F. Fuller, 1927-28-29
Robert W. Fulton, (1935)-36

G
John Galbreath, [Mgr.] 1926
Hugh Garner, 1952-(53-54)
Paul Gearing, 1946-47-48-49
Clarence E. Giddens, 1934-(35)
Ed Godzak, 1952
Bill Gold, (1941-42), 1946
Quinn B. Goodrich, 1932-33
Ray Graves, 1940-(41) [Capt.]
Louis A. Green, 1926
Bob Griesbach, 1952
Dave Griffith, 1952-(53)
John Gruble, 1947-48-49-50
Ron Gust, 1952-(53-54)

H
J.S. "Buddy" Hackman, 1928-29-30
Jimmy R. Hahn, 1949-50-51
W. S. "Billy" Harkness, (1923-24-25)-26 [Capt.]
Thomas "Red" Harp, (1935)-36-37
Jim Haslam, 1950-51-52 [Capt.]
Ralph L. Hatley, 1932-33-34 [Capt.]
Joe Black Hayes, (1935)-36-37 [Capt.]
Gerald S. Hendricks, 1936-37-38
Tom Hensley, 1952-(53)
L. Houston Herndon, 1928-29
Melvin G. Herring, 1936-37
Gary Herrmann, 1951
Paul D. Heydrick, 1929
Herman Hickman, 1929-30-31
Bob Hicks, 1947
Claude Hill, 1946-47-48
Jimmy "Cowboy" Hill, 1948-49-50
Bill Hillman, (1942), 1946
Bonnie Hodge, 1937
Francis Holohan, 1950-51-52
Laird Holt, 1929-30-31
Hobert P. "Hobe" Hooser, 1927
Amos J. Horner, 1927-28
Ermal Howard, 1946-47-48
Hal Hubbard, 1951-52-(53)
Franklin S. "Bud" Hubbell, (1941-42), 1946
Carl Hubbuck, 1937
Ben Huddleston, 1946-47
Vernon Hueser, 1946-47-48
Dick Huffman, (1942), 1946
Paul Hug, 1928-29-30
Cecil C. "Sonny" Humphreys, 1933-34-(35)
Elmo Hundley, 1927
Ralph Hunneycutt, 1947-48-49
George L. Hunter, 1936-37-38
Al Hust, 1940-(41-42) [Capt.]
Emil R. Hust, 1939, (1941)
Jerry Hyde, 1951-52-(53)

J
Bill Jasper, 1949-50-51
Harold Johnson, 1948-49-50
Howard Johnson, 1926-27-28 [Capt.]
L. B. "Farmer" Johnson, 1926-27-28
Stewart Johnson, [Mgr.] 1946
James G. Johnston, 1928-29
Frank D. Jones, 1926
Sam W. Jones, (1923-24), 1926
Dick Jordan, (1942), 1946
Tommy Jumper, 1950

K
Vince Kaseta, 1949-50-51
Wade Keever, 1934
Van W. Kelly, 1936-37
Robert Kennerly, [Mgr.] 1927
Charles E. Kohlhase, 1929-30-31
George L. Koleas, (1935)-36
Vic Kolenik, 1951-52
Andrew J. "Andy" Kozar, 1950-51-52
Henry W. Krouse, 1932, 1934-35

L
Hank Lauricella, 1949-50-51
Lamar Leachman, 1952-(53, 1955)
Willie T. Leffler, 1936-37
Sam Levine, 1936-37
William T. Lippe, 1934-(35)
Stan Lis, 1952
Joe Little, 1936-37-38
Hal Littleford, 1947-48-49 [Capt.]
R. A. Long, (1942, 1945)-46
Frank Lovingood, 1934

Theodore Lowe, 1927
Bob Lund, (1945)-46-47-48
Bill Luttrell, 1938-39-40
Vernon Lyons, 1950-51

M
Joe Maiure, 1950-51-52
Mark Major, (1944-45)-46-47
Talmadge "Sheriff" Maples, 1931-32-33 [Capt.]
Alton S. Mark, 1931-32-33
Arthur Marks, [Mgr.] 1952
Ray Martin, 1951-52
Eugene "Skeet" Mayer, 1930-31 [Capt.]
Dick Mayock, 1952
Dave E. McArthur, (1925)-26-27
William "Jeep" McCarren, 1936-37-38
Bob McClellan, [Mgr.] 1928
Robert L. McClure, [Mgr.] 1929
Darris McCord, 1952-(53-54)
Frank McCroskey, 1952-(53)
Gene McEver, 1928-29-31
Allyn McKeen, (1925)-26-27
C. L. McPherson, 1932
Bill Meek, 1940-(41-42)
Norman Meseroll, 1946-47-48-49
Charles Meyer, 1951
John Michels, 1950-51-52
Albert Middleton, 1932
Orvis Milner, 1946-47
Jim Miner, 1947-48-49
Hagen Minnick, [Mgr.] 1948
Charles T. Mitchell, (1941-42), 1946
D. K. Mitchell, 1931
Gene Moeller, 1951-52
Ed Molinski, 1938-39-40
Owen "Bud" Moore, 1926
Ed Morgan, 1950-51-52
Fred Moses, 1933-34-(35)
Richard Mulloy, 1939-40-(41)
Colin Munro, 1951, (1953)
William Murrell, 1936
Andy Myers, 1950-51-52
James A. Myers, (1941-42), 1946

N
Ray Neal, [Mgr.] 1947
Kenneth "Shorty" Needham, 1933-34-(35)
Fred Newman, 1939-40
Bob Neyland, Jr., 1952-(53)
Ed Nickla, 1951-52
Henry Noel, 1940-(41)
William E. Nowling, 1940-(41-42)

O
Pat Oleksiak, 1952, (1954)

P
Mike Paidousis, (1944-45)-46
Edwin "Toby" Palmer, 1933-34-(35) [Capt.]
Max Partin, (1941, 1945)-46
John W. Paty, 1934-(35)
Harold "Herky" Payne, 1949-50-51
Bill Pearman, 1947, 1949-50-51
Ike Peel, 1939-40-(41)
Marion Perkins, 1936-37
Leo Petruzzi, 1932-33
Jack M. Pick, 1934-(35)
Patrick "Buddy" Pike, (1944-45)-46
Gordon Polofsky, 1949-50-51
James W. Porter, 1934, 1936
Louis E. Pounders, 1932-33-34
Jim Powell, (1942), 1946-47-48 [Capt.]
John Powell, 1951-52-(53)
Tracy Prater, [Mgr.] 1938
Royal Price, (1942), 1946-47
J. B. Proctor, 1946-47-48
Kenneth Pruett, 1949-50

R
Allen Ramsey, 1936-37
Virgil H. "Van" Rayburn, 1930-31-32
Bert Rechichar, 1949-50-51 [Capt.]
Charles W. Reineke, 1928-29-30
Alvin Rice, 1937
Charles P. Rice, 1925-26
Jim Rike, 1938-39
Louis T. Roberts, 1928-29-30
Harvey L. Robinson, 1931-32
Dave Romine, 1940
Gene Rose, 1933-34-(35)
Al Rotella, (1942), 1946-47
Roger Rotroff, 1951-52-(53)
Billy Joe Rowan, 1946-47
Al Russas, 1946-47-48

S
William Sanders, 1937
Glenn Sanderson, [Mgr.] 1934
Ray Saunders, 1929-30-31
Ted Schwanger, 1952-(53)
Jim Schwartzinger, 1940-(41)
Dan Sekanovich, 1951-52-(53)
J. W. "Bud" Sherrill, 1948-49-50
Horace "Bud" Sherrod, 1947-48-49-50
Marshall "Abe" Shires, 1938-39-40
Pat Shires, 1950, 1952-(53)
Austin Shofner, 1936
F. E. "Phil" Shull, 1930-31-32
Doe Silberman, 1934-(35)
Leonard Simonetti, 1940-(41)
Jim Sivert, 1949

Bernie Sizemore, 1949-50
Tom Slack, 1948
Walter Slater, (1941-42), 1946 [Capt.]
Boyd M. Smith, 1932
Gordon E. Smith, 1931-32-33
Roy "Looney" Smith, 1947-48-49-50
Thomas Smith, 1938-39
Robert "Doc" Sneed, 1936-37-38
Herman Snipes, 1931
Clayton Stapleton, (1941), 1946-47
Lee Starr, [Mgr.] 1951
Max Steiner, 1938-39-40
Dave Stephenson, 1946
Howard Stewart, 1931-32-33
J. Ralph Still, 1930-31
Charles Stokes, 1950-51
Jack Stroud, 1947-48-49-50 [Capt.]
Francis Stupar, 1949
Bob Suffridge, 1938-39-40

T
Don Tanner, 1949
Larry Tanner, 1939
Vernon Tansil, 1934-(35)
Conrad Templeton, 1929-30
Harry "Hobo" Thayer, 1928-29-30 [Capt.]
Alfred Thomas, 1937-38-39
Van Thompson, 1939-40
Arthur Tripp, 1926-27-28
Willis Tucker, 1940
Vincent Tudor, 1927-28

U
Bob Ussery, 1952-(53)

V
Charles "Pug" Vaughan, 1932-33-34
Sam A. Venable, 1932
Roger Vest, 1951-52
Jim Vugrin, 1946-47-48-49

W
Jimmy Wade, 1951-52-(53-54)
Joe Wallen, 1936-38-39
Murray Warmath, 1932-33-34
Buist Warren, 1938-39-40
DeWitt Weaver, 1934-(35)-36 [Capt.]
Nick Weber, 1939-40
Hodges "Burr" West, 1938-39-40
James Whitaker, 1929
Charles Wildman, (1944-45)-46-47
D. B. Winston, [Mgr.] 1937
Roy Witt, 1926-27-28 [Capt.]
Walter "Babe" Wood, 1936-37-38
George R. "Bob" Woodruff, 1936-37-38
Bowden Wyatt, 1936-37-38 [Capt.]
Herman D. "Breezy" Wynn, 1931-32-33

Y
Ed Young, (1925)-26

NEYLAND'S COACHING STAFFS

1926
Bob Neyland - backs
Bill Britton - ends
Paul Parker - line
Charles Lindsay - freshmen

1927-30
Neyland - backs
Britton - ends
Parker - line
Billy Harkness - freshmen

1931-33
Neyland - backs
Britton - ends
Parker - line
John Barnhill - head freshmen
Hugh Faust - freshmen

1934
Neyland - backs
Britton - ends
Parker - line
Barnhill - head freshmen
Faust - freshmen
Deke Brackett - freshmen

1936-37
Neyland - backs
Britton - ends
Barnhill - line
Murray Warmath - line
Faust - head freshmen

1938
Neyland - backs
Britton - ends
Barnhill - line
Warmath - line
Faust - head freshmen
Bill Murrell - freshmen

1939
Neyland - backs
Britton - ends
Barnhill - line
Warmath - line
Faust - head freshmen
John Mauer - ends
Murrell - line
Bob Woodruff - line

1940
Neyland - backs
Britton - ends
Barnhill - line
Mauer - ends
Murrell - line
Faust - head freshmen

1946
Neyland
Britton - ends
Warmath - line
Ike Peel - backs
Mauer - ends
Harvey Robinson - head freshmen
Faust - freshmen

1947
Neyland
Warmath - line
Peel - backs
Al Hust - ends
Murrell - line
Robinson - head freshmen
Emmett Lowery - ends

1948
Neyland
Warmath - line
Peel - backs
Hust - ends
Burr West - line
Royal Price - line
Billy Bevis - backs
Lowery - ends
Robinson - head freshmen

1949
Neyland
Robinson - backs (Off. Coordinator)
L. B. "Farmer" Johnson - line (Def. Coordinator)
Hust - ends
Bevis - backs
West - line
Chan Caldwell - ends
Lowery - ends
Peel - head freshmen

1950
Neyland
Robinson - backs (Off. Coordinator)
Johnson - line (Def. Coordinator)
Hust - ends

Peel - head freshmen
Ralph Chancey - backs
West - line
Caldwell - ends
Bill Hildebrand - freshmen
John Idzik - freshmen

1951
Neyland
Robinson - backs (Off. Coordinator)
Johnson - line (Def. Coordinator)
Hust - ends
Peel - head freshmen
Chancey - backs
West - line
Caldwell - ends
Lowery - ends

1952
Neyland
Robinson - backs (Off. Coordinator)
Johnson - line (Def. Coorinator)
Hust - ends
Peel - backs
Chancey - backs
West - line
Caldwell - ends
Lowery - ends
Bunzy O'Neill - head freshmen

GENERAL ROBERT R. NEYLAND TROPHY

The Robert R. Neyland Trophy, honoring the late Tennessee football coach and athletics director, is awarded annually to someone who has contributed greatly to college athletics. The trophy is presented by the Knoxville Quarterback Club at the annual banquet of the East Tennessee chapter of the National Football Foundation and Hall of Fame.

Past recipients are:

1967 - Herman Hickman
1967 - Nathan W. Dougherty
1968 - Wallace Wade
1969 - Bobby Dodd
1970 - John Barnhill
1971 - Jess Neely
1972 - John Vaught
1973 - Bud Wilkinson
1974 - Fritz Crisler
1975 - Lynn Waldorf
1976 - John McKay
1977 - Darrell Royal
1978 - Ralph Jordan
1979 - Frank Broyles
1980 - Bob Devaney
1981 - Ara Parseghian
1982 - Bill Murray
1983 - Paul "Bear" Bryant
1984 - Woody Hayes
1985 - Duffy Daugherty
1986 - George R. "Bob" Woodruff
1987 - Charles McClendon
1988 - LaVell Edwards
1989 - Vince Dooley
1990 - Glenn "Bo" Schembechler

BIBLIOGRAPHY

Books and Periodicals

Argyle, Christopher. *Chronology of World War II.* London: Marshall Cavendish, 1980.

Bauer, Eddy. *World War II Encyclopedia.* Monaco: H.S. Stuttman, 1966.

Bebb, Russ. *The Big Orange.* Knoxville: Bebb, 1973.

Blackland Memories. Dallas: Hunt County Historical Commission, 1983.

Boda, Steve, and James M. Van Valkenburg. *NCAA Football Media Guides and Records.* Mission, Kansas: National Collegiate Athletic Association, annuals.

Bryant, Paul W., and John Underwood. *Bear.* Boston: Little, Brown and Company, 1974.

Churchill, Winston. *The Hinge of Fate.* New York: Houghton Mifflin Company, 1950.

Cohane, Tim. *Great College Football Coaches of the Twenties and Thirties.* New York: Arlington House, 1973.

Constable, George, ed. *WWII.* New York: Prentice Hall Press, 1989.

Dineen, Joseph E. *The Illustrated History of Sports at the U.S.* Military Academy. Norfolk, Va.: The Donning Company, 1988.

Dodd, Robert Lee, and Jack Wilkinson. *Dodd's Luck.* Savannah: Golden Coast Publishing Co., 1987.

Dougherty, Nathan W. *Educators and Athletes.* Knoxville: University of Tennessee, 1976.

Edson, James S. *The Black Knights of West Point.* New York: Bradbury, Sayles, O'Neill Co., Inc., 1954.

____________. *Bowl-Manac.* Birmingham, Ala.: Johnson Printing Company, 1956.

Fields, Bud, and Bob Bertucci. *BigOrange: A Pictoral History of University of Tennessee Football.* West Point, N.Y.: Leisure Press, 1982.

Fraser, John W., ed. *The Howitzer.* West Point, N.Y.: United States War Department, 1916.

Harris, Ed. *Bob Neyland 37 Years a Volunteer.* Knoxville: Harris, 1962.

_________. *Big Orange Country.* Knoxville: Harris, 1964.

Harrison, W. Walworth. *History of Greenville & Hunt County, Texas.* Waco, Texas: Texian Press, 1976.

Herskowitz, Mickey. *The Legend of Bear Bryant.* New York: McGraw-Hill, 1987.

Majors, Johnny, with Ben Byrd. *You Can Go Home Again.* Nashville: Rutledge Hill Press, 1986.

Manchester, William. *American Caesar.* Boston: Little, Brown and Company, 1978.

McCallum, John D. *Southeastern Conference Football.* New York: Charles Scribner's Sons, 1980.

Menke, Frank G. *Encyclopedia of Sports.* New York: A.S. Barnes and Company, 1955.

Mims, Sam. *Chennault of the Flying Tigers.* Philadelphia: Macrae-Smith Company, 1943.

Morris, Richard B., ed. *Encyclopedia of American History.* New York: Harper and Row, Publishers, Inc., 1976.

Nelson, Lindsey. *Hello Everybody, I'm Lindsey Nelson.* New York: Beech Tree Books/William Morrow, 1985.

Newman, Zipp. *The Impact of Southern Football.* Montgomery, Ala.: Morros-Bell Publishing Co., Inc., 1969.

Neyland, Robert R. "*Rat Race Football.*" PIC. (October 1948).

_______________. Unpublished papers and memoirs, 1956.

Pope, Edwin. *Football's Greatest Coaches.* Atlanta: Tupper and Love, Inc., 1955.

Prange, Gordon W. *At Dawn We Slept.* New York: McGraw-Hill, 1981.

Romanus, Charles F., and Riley Sunderland. "Time Runs Out in CBI." Official U.S. Army History. Washington, D.C.: Department of the Army, 1958.

Reichler, Joseph L., ed. *The Baseball Encyclopedia.* New York: Macmillan Publishing Co., Inc., 1979.
Russell, Fred. "Touchdown Engineer." The Saturday Evening Post. (December 30, 1939).
Russell, Fred. *Bury Me in an Old Press Box.* New York: A.S. Barnes and Company, 1957.
Russell, Fred, and George Leonard. *Big Bowl Football.* New York: The Ronald Press Company, 1963.
Schlesinger, Arthur M., Jr. *The Almanac of American History.* New York: G.P. Putnam's Sons, 1983.
Scott, Robert L. *God is My Co-Pilot.* New York: Ballantine Books, 1943.
____________. *Flying Tiger.* New York: Berkley Publishing Corporation, 1959.
____________. *The Day I Owned the Sky.* New York: Bantam Books, 1988.
Siler, Tom. *Thru the Years with the Volunteers.* Knoxville: Siler, 1950.
________. "Gridiron General." Look Magazine. (December 5, 1950).
________. *Football's Greatest Dynasty.* Knoxville: The Knoxville News-Sentinel, 1961.
Sinclair, Duncan. *Assembly.* West Point, N.Y: West Point Alumni Foundation, Inc., 1962.
Siroky, Mike, and Bob Bertucci. *Orange Lightning.* West Point, N.Y.: Leisure Press, 1983.
Skidmore, Thomas E., and Peter H. Smith. *Modern Latin America.* New York: Oxford University Press, 1989.
Slim, William. *The Northern Front in Burma.* London: Dell Publishing Co., Inc., 1961.
Spector, Ronald H. *Eagle Against the Sun.* New York: Macmillan, Inc., 1985.
Van Valkenburg, James M., and Steve Boda. *NCAA Football Legends.* Mission, Kansas: National Collegiate Athletic Association, 1989.
Wedemeyer, Albert C. *Wedemeyer Reports.* New York: Henry Holt and Company, 1958.
White, Theodore H. *In Search of History.* New York: Harper and Row, Publishers, 1978.

Newspaper Files

Atlanta Constitution, Atlanta Journal, Birmingham News, Birmingham Post-Herald, Boston Globe, Boston Post, Chattanooga News-Free Press, Chattanooga Times, Chicago Sun-Times, Chicago Tribune, Dallas Morning News, Dallas Times-Herald, Durham Herald, El Paso Herald, El Paso Morning Times, Greenville (Texas) Herald-Banner, Knoxville Journal, Knoxville News-Sentinel, Memphis Commercial Appeal, Memphis Press-Scimitar, Miami Herald, Montgomery Advertiser, Nashville Banner, Nashville Tennessean, New Orleans States-Item, New Orleans Times-Picayune, New York Herald-Tribune, New York Times, Norfolk Virginian-Pilot, Sarasota Herald-Tribune, Washington Post.